CHILD-CENTRED PRACTICE

CHILD-CENTRED PRACTICE

A HANDBOOK FOR SOCIAL WORK

TRACEY RACE AND REBECCA O'KEEFE

First published 2017 by
PALGRAVE

Palgrave in the UK is an imprint of Macmillan Publishers Limited, registered in England, company number 785998, of 4 Crinan Street, London, N1 9XW.

Palgrave® and Macmillan® are registered trademarks in the United States, the United Kingdom, Europe and other countries.

ISBN 978–1–137–59702–1 paperback

This book is printed on paper suitable for recycling and made from fully managed and sustained forest sources. Logging, pulping and manufacturing processes are expected to conform to the environmental regulations of the country of origin.

A catalogue record for this book is available from the British Library.

A catalog record for this book is available from the Library of Congress.

I would like to dedicate the book to my children (now grown up) who have taught me the really important things about childhood and parenthood
— **Tracey**

I would like to dedicate this book to my wonderful family, especially Arthur and Richard
— **Rebecca**

CONTENTS

LIST OF TABLES AND FIGURES

Tables

Figures

NOTES ON THE AUTHORS

Tracey Race is a registered social worker who was employed by Leeds City Council, Barnardo's, Family Service Units and the NSPCC in a range of social work and management roles before joining the team at Leeds Beckett University. She has been a senior lecturer in social work for the last ten years with particular interests in children's rights, safeguarding and family support.

Rebecca O'Keefe is an Advanced Practitioner with Leeds Children's Services. She provides supervision and consultation around complex child protection issues and contributes to social work education through her work as a Practice Educator and input into local social work courses.

ACKNOWLEDGEMENTS

We would like to acknowledge the children and young people we have worked with in our social work careers who have taught us so much about child-centred practice. Also the young people and young adults with experience of the care system who contribute to the course at Leeds Beckett University and enable our social work students to learn about children's rights and the importance of child-centred practice. Also we would like to thank the practitioners who have contributed to this textbook and do excellent work to promote child-centred practice in our local communities.

INTRODUCTION

The child is a person not an object of concern.
(Baroness Butler-Sloss, 1988)

This oft-quoted statement of Baroness Butler-Sloss was prompted by the Cleveland crisis, an event marked by the intervention of a range of professionals, including police, health practitioners and social workers, to remove unprecedented numbers of children into care due to concerns about child sexual abuse. Butler-Sloss chaired the inquiry and made the point forcefully that the professionals involved in Cleveland, in particular social workers, failed to recognise and respect the personhood and the rights of the children they were seeking to protect. Over recent years there has been increasing impetus to acknowledge and promote the rights, dignity and agency of children as persons in their own right. The United Nations Convention on the Rights of the Child (UNCRC), adopted in 1989 and ratified in the UK in 1991, was a significant turning point in recognising the inherent rights of all children. More recently and of particular relevance to social workers, the Munro review (2011) emphasised the value of a child-centred safeguarding process and promoted the importance of child-centred practice.

In this book, we will seek to develop the argument for the importance of child-centred practice as a key focus for social work with children, young people and families. Acknowledging and promoting the rights of the child does not make practice in the area of child welfare and safeguarding any less complex. It does, however, provide a strong and value based foundation for practice, and also the means to ensure and measure effectiveness. Placing the child at the centre of any intervention into family life, ensuring their views and perspectives are heard from the outset, is a good way to commence any assessment; reviewing how we have been able to work with, for and in the best interests of the child, and involving children in this process, is a good way to evaluate outcomes. In other words, child-centred practice is important from the opening to the closing of a professional intervention in a young person's life. Recognising that child-centred practice is developing through the hard work and commitment of frontline practitioners and through listening to the feedback of children and young people, this book will include excerpts and quotes from professionals and service users, adding authentic testimonials that will further inform our evolving understanding of what we mean by child-centredness.

The aim of this book is to provide an overview of child-centred practice that will be of particular relevance to children's social workers and social work students. It is hoped that the focus of the text will also be of interest to children's centre and voluntary sector practitioners and other professionals involved in social care and safeguarding work with children and families. Terms such as social worker and children's services practitioner will be used interchangeably. Whilst recognising the importance of precise language and that young people do not enjoy being lumped together with *all* children, nevertheless for the sake of brevity there may be times when we use the terms 'children' and 'young people' interchangeably. The focus of the book is work with persons under the age of 18.

The book is divided into two sections. Part I focuses on those areas of knowledge that provide an essential foundation for child-centred practice, exploring current discourses around children, young people and families. Part II is divided into chapters that follow the process of professional intervention into the lives of children, from early help initiatives, through targeted interventions and safeguarding processes, and finally exploring corporate parenting responsibilities. The book will place emphasis on the evidence base for child-centred practice, paying particular attention to the findings from research which give voice to the perspectives of children and young people. Whilst the legal and policy framework for practice in the UK (most particularly in England and Wales) is referred to, this is not a key focus of the text. Given the increasing differences in policy and practice of countries within the UK, all references to legislation will point out the relevant jurisdiction of the statute.

The book aims to explore the ethical and theoretical precepts and the practice skills that provide a sound basis for child-centred social work, in line with the 'knowledge and skills statement' devised by the Department for Education (2014). Recognising the importance of skills development, particularly in relation to engaging and communicating with children, the book includes suggestions for good practice. Given the breadth of the focus of the book, some analysis of relevant theory is necessarily succinct. We outline areas of knowledge that provide the framework for child-centred practice and include pointers for further study.

Throughout the book we will use various features to draw the attention of the reader to key aspects of learning that are important for child-centred practice:

- **Points for Reflection**: Questions and issues for further analysis will enable the reader to make links to their own values, beliefs or practice experiences and emphasise the importance of reflexivity for effective child-centred practice. At times, commentaries will be included, providing additional guidance to support the reflective process. In Part I, some of the commentaries provide examples of practice using fictitious but realistic case scenarios that enable the reader to consider the ways in which theory might be applied in practice.

- **Learning from Research**: Highlights various studies that provide the evidence base for child-centred approaches. Attention will be paid in particular to research that gives a voice to children and enables learning from the insights and perspectives of young people.

- **Focus on Practice**: Opportunities to learn from innovative practice or to consider creative approaches that enable the practitioner to work in a child-centred way. Various models of good practice will be presented and techniques for carrying out direct work with children and young people will be highlighted.

- **Practitioner Testimonials**: Despite the challenges of contemporary practice, many front-line practitioners are carrying out child-centred work of a high quality. These short extracts provide examples of what child-centred practice means for some social workers.

- **Case Study Analysis**: Enables the application of child-centred principles into practice, through discussion of a social work intervention in a fictional family. The case scenario is introduced at the beginning of Part II, to follow the journey of the family and the experiences of the three children through each stage of professional intervention, as explored in the ensuing chapters.

- **Recommended Reading and Resources**: Each chapter will end with pointers for further reading or recommendations of websites and other useful resources. This text aims to provide an overview of relevant knowledge and a springboard to encourage wider reading and research, to equip professionals for effective child-centred practice.

Part II of the book examines various aspects of social work practice, exploring the different stages of professional intervention. A fuller introduction to Part II will be provided on page 141.

PART I
INTRODUCTION TO PART I

Throughout Part I we pay particular attention to the contribution of psycho-social theory and ecological perspectives to our understanding of child development and children's lives in the context of contemporary society. Ethical issues are examined, with a focus on rights, participation and empowerment.

In Chapter 1 we introduce what we mean by child-centred practice, exploring why this approach to practice is important and challenging. We explore the theoretical and ethical framework underpinning child-centred social work. Chapter 2 goes on to focus on children's rights, noting the legislative foundations for practice and exploring in particular the impact of the UNCRC (1989). The child's right to participation is examined, including an analysis of what is meant by 'Gillick competence' and an exploration of concepts and mechanisms that explain and enable children's participatory rights. In Chapter 3 we focus on the child, drawing on psychological and life-span theory, and sociological discourses about the nature of childhood, in order to understand children. We examine how an understanding of the ages and stages of child development is integral to child-centred practice and the contribution of knowledge drawn from neuroscience. Chapter 4 explores the context of contemporary childhood, recognising the impact of current issues such as child poverty and the development of technology. We recognise in particular that children are best understood in the context of the family; it is within their family that children develop and mature, thrive or struggle. We acknowledge the protective factors within the family and the wider community that promote the welfare of the child, enhancing their resilience. Chapter 5 focuses on communication with children and emphasises the principles and skills that form the basis of effective child-centred practice. Whilst not claiming to provide an exhaustive or comprehensive discussion of relevant theory for the childcare professional, Part I provides an overview of key aspects of knowledge that inform social work practice and promote a child-centred approach to work with children, young people and families.

1

CHILD-CENTRED PRACTICE: PRINCIPLES AND CHALLENGES

Introduction

In this chapter we begin to explore what we mean by child-centred practice – an approach that emphasises the importance of retaining a focus on the needs, interests, wishes and feelings of the child throughout any professional intervention involving or about children. We explore why it matters and why this approach to contemporary practice is relevant and important, particularly for social workers. We also recognise that this seemingly simple concept, emphasising the need to listen to children and support their involvement in decision-making about their lives, is inherently challenging, particularly in the context of safeguarding processes. We examine the principles and values that provide the imperative for this approach to practice and recognise that a strong foundation for child-centredness can be found in the theory that underpins social work practice.

Why child-centred practice?

The 'Framework for the Assessment of Children in Need and their Families' (Department of Health, 2000a) set the agenda for social work practice with children, young people and families in the new millennium. It established a theoretical and practical approach to assessment and outlined the principles and values that should underpin professional practice. Significantly, the first key principle emphasised for effective work with children and families was child-centredness: 'This means that the child is seen and kept in focus throughout the assessment and that account is always taken of the child's perspective' (Department of Health, 2000a: 10).

Since the introduction of the assessment framework there has been increasing emphasis given to the importance of child-centred practice and a recognition that social workers cannot make an assessment or intervene to promote positive outcomes without seeking to engage with the child. This means getting to know who they are, what they need, how they feel about their life and situation and what they want for their future. Child-centred practice means giving priority to the needs and welfare of the child, promoting their right to participate in the processes of assessment and decision-making that consume professional time and energy. It involves listening to children, building relationships with them, spending time to respond to their questions and enabling them to express their views. It is about seeing the world through their eyes, understanding what their day-to-day lived experience is really like. In complex situations in which the safety of the child may be compromised due to the problems of their parents, it means supporting the family whilst never losing sight of the needs and rights of the child.

The statutory guidance to inform social work and inter-professional practice, known as *Working Together to Safeguard Children: A guide to interagency working to safeguard and promote the welfare of children* (HM Government, 2015) now supersedes *The Framework for the Assessment of Children in Need and their Families* (Department of Health, 2000a). However, the principles and approach of the assessment framework remain firmly embedded within current policy and practice. In the most recent version of *Working Together*, child-centredness remains a key principle, emphasising that in all our work with families, we should recognise that: 'the child's needs are paramount, and the needs and wishes of each child, be they a baby or infant, or an older child, should be put first, so that every child receives the support they need before a problem escalates' (HM Government, 2015: 8).

Despite this important principle being increasingly acknowledged, there is evidence to suggest that at times little more than lip service is paid to implementation. There are many reasons why professionals fail to listen to children and struggle to adopt a child-centred approach. Organisations, policies and procedures are developed and driven by adults; unwittingly they often create obstacles and barriers that hinder meaningful engagement with the child's world. Nevertheless, child-centredness must become more thoroughly integrated within practice with children and young people. As the quotes cited so far in this chapter demonstrate, a commitment to child-centred practice is embedded in UK policy and government guidance. The Children Act 1989 and significant other legislation emphasise the centrality of the welfare of the child. The UNCRC provides ethical and legal impetus to ensure children's rights are recognised and upheld internationally. The foundations for child-centred practice inherent in law and policy are explored in Chapter 2. At this point, it is important to acknowledge some fundamental reasons to advocate for the advancement of child-centred practice.

It matters to children

A study carried out by Cossar and colleagues (2011) for the Children's Commissioner in England found that for children who had experienced social work involvement due to child protection issues, their relationships with social workers were very important in helping them to feel involved and supported. They valued the involvement of practitioners who were reliable and who would listen to them before making judgements or offering advice. They realised the importance of mutual trust and honesty in their relationship with their social worker in order to be able to work together effectively. In studies carried out by Thomas and O'Kane (1998) with children who were looked after, it was found that children and young people valued the opportunity to be involved in decision-making by talking with and working alongside the adults in their lives.

Learning from Research

Research carried out by the Children's Rights Director, Roger Morgan (2006: 12) found that young people who had been in contact with social workers liked working with practitioners who:

- Were approachable and easy to talk to

- Were not 'stuck up' or too formal

- Were able to get on with children and young people

- Were able to understand the way children think

- Were good listeners

- Had a sense of humour

- Were good at calming people down

- Did not judge but tried to understand.

One young person described the kind of support that mattered to them:

> '... support, advice, friend, someone I can trust, someone I know really cares about me, not just a number or a client who they really don't care about ... not just someone who just read the textbook.' (Morgan 2006: 28)

In 2010, Ciara Davey and colleagues carried out research for the Children's Commissioner in England about children's participation in decision-making. They found that children value opportunities to be involved and have their voices heard. The following quotes from children make some very valid points:

> 'Children might know something that was very important and that the adults didn't know.'

> 'They should [ask children] because children might have good ideas, better than them.'   (Davey et al., 2010: 39)

Practitioner Testimonial

From my first placement, I have learnt that if you involve the child in your practice then the child has confidence in you, trusts you and will open up more so that you get a more holistic honest overview of what is going on. This results in better safeguarding, as the child is more likely to speak to you.

The young people I have worked with have often expressed their dislike of people not keeping them informed and up to date about what is going on. The work that professionals do on behalf of young people can result in there being time delays (waiting for other professionals to reply, and so on); however the young person may not be aware of this and even one week can be a very long time in a young person's world. Professionals need to ensure that they keep a young person informed – this can be by phone, letter or a visit – and makes a huge difference to the young person.

Jeni Timmis – First Year MA Social Work Student.

The challenges of child-centred practice

It is clear then that child-centred practice is not just about policy or even rhetoric; it really matters and makes a difference in terms of the safety and welfare of children and young people. In the section below titled 'The value base for child-centred practice' we outline more fully what is meant by child-centred practice and the principles underpinning this approach. However, it is appropriate to acknowledge that what might seem relatively straightforward in theory holds many challenges in practice. If this were not the case, the failures in practice noted above would have been less likely to occur. It is appropriate to recognise some of the challenges that contemporary social workers need to grapple with in order to adopt a child-centred approach.

Working with uncertainty

There are parallels between managing the challenges of our professional responsibilities when working with children, and carrying out the role of parents and carers. In some contexts, when children are looked after by the State, the social worker becomes the representative of the 'corporate parent'. When a baby is born, the vast majority of parents welcome their offspring and endeavour to provide the care and nurture that enable their child to reach healthy adulthood. The child is often the receptor for their parents' hopes and ambitions, but is also valued as a unique individual. Parents will usually seek to guide their child in what they deem to be 'the right paths' but have no ultimate control over the life of their child and the choices they make as they mature. Nor do parents have a crystal ball to foresee future outcomes. Similarly, childcare professionals lack powers of prediction – we are never able to know for sure whether the decisions we take in seeking to protect children from harm and promote their best interests will ultimately be effective in achieving these aims. Sometimes there are simply too many variables making it impossible to predict the outcome of any chosen path. Mnookin (1983: 8) has argued: 'what is best for any child or even children in general is often indeterminate and speculative, and requires a highly individualised choice between alternatives.' Professionals, like parents, can never really know how things will turn out for a child. Social workers in particular are constantly working with uncertainty (Parton, 1998, 2006) and the challenge of effective practice is to assess and manage the risks of harm to children whilst never losing sight of their rights and interests. Maintaining a focus on the child's welfare and promoting good outcomes for them is not an exact science. Making decisions with and about children involves professional judgement – a process of assessment, analysis and reflexivity, all of which aims to manage the risk and uncertainty inherent in the work.

Working with bureaucracy

We are also working under scrutiny. As the appointed representatives of society in ensuring an effective safety net for vulnerable children, social workers are often vilified when the safety net fails to prevent a particular child from falling. Public concerns around the efficacy of the safety net provided by the apparatus of child safeguarding has led to the proliferation of policies and procedures designed to make practice safer and more accountable. The unintended consequence, however, has been the increase in bureaucracy, professional anxiety and risk-averse practice. Alongside this has been the influence of management developments adopted from the world of business, based on the assumption that efficiency can be improved through performance management strategies, including increased inspection and regulation (Skinner, 2010).

The importance of accountable practice in an era of increasing public scrutiny has led to what has been described as the 'bureaucratisation' of social work (Howe, 1992). The focus on administrative targets and adherence to procedure has increased the pressure on social workers to be compliant with a managerial culture and to prioritise bureaucratic tasks over direct contact with children and their families. These concerns have been examined by Parton (2006: 184) who described the UK child protection system as 'overly proceduralised, defensive and conflict ridden'. He has emphasised in particular that the increase in policies and guidelines has failed to reduce the uncertainty and risk involved in managing complex childcare cases. For practitioners working within this context, the demands of the organisation to demonstrate accountability have compromised their ability to engage in meaningful relationships with children and young people. When Lord Laming reviewed the progress made by safeguarding agencies in 2009, he recognised this concern, noting the alarming finding that social workers spend 70% of their time in the office and only 30% in direct contact with families (Laming, 2009). He quoted a young person with experience of social work involvement who was consulted as part of his work: 'It seems like they have to do all this form filling, their bosses' bosses make them do it, but it makes them forget about us' (boy aged 16, quoted in Laming, 2009: 23).

Learning from Research

Thomas and O'Kane (1998) carried out a series of workshops with social workers. They presented three fictional scenarios:

1. Boy (10 years old) subject to a Care Order following physical abuse by stepfather wants to return to neglectful mother now the stepfather has left;
2. Girl (8 years old) placed in long-term foster care is asking to see her mother more often, even though carers feel it should be less often as the mother often lets her down at the last minute;
3. Girl (12 years old) placed in a children's residential home wants to stay overnight with a friend whose parents have convictions for using illegal drugs.

Participants were asked (as an initial reaction) to arrange themselves in the room along a line representing a continuum from implementing the adult view of their interests at one end to doing what the child wants at the other.

Points for Reflection

- What is your first response or 'gut instinct' as you consider these scenarios?
- On a scale of one to ten, based on the continuum above (ten being to do exactly what the child wants), where would you place your own response and why?

In the workshops, the practitioner response to the scenarios was surprisingly consistent. For scenarios 1 and 2, participants ranged along the full length of the continuum, with a bulge at the end representing doing what the child wanted. Many social workers felt that despite some concerns, their doubts were outweighed by the positive value of being able to respond to the child's wishes. In scenario 3 there was greater consensus amongst participants, with the majority positioning themselves at the other end of the line, deciding to prevent the child from doing what they wanted. The adults acknowledged their concern to avoid potential repercussions for the children's home or a scandal in this case. Therefore, although the child was older, they felt the need to limit her freedom. It was clear the professionals may have justified such action as being in the child's best interests, although organisational concerns seemed to be the primary consideration. ▶

The researchers also met with several groups of looked-after children and asked them to rank in order of importance several statements that describe the reasons why young people want to be involved in decision-making. With great consistency, at the top of the list they put 'to be listened to', 'to have a say' and 'to be supported'. At the bottom of their list they ranked 'to get what I want'. When the researchers repeated the exercise with groups of social workers and asked them to rank the statements in the order they expected the children to put them, many put 'to get what I want' firmly at the top of their list.

The research highlights that some social workers are overly preoccupied with organisational concerns or may misunderstand children's motivations to be involved in decisions about their lives (Thomas and O'Kane, 1998).

The need to develop child-centred values and skills

Munro's (2011) review of the child protection system in the UK has presented a timely challenge to these concerns. Munro recognised that undue weight has been given to activities that are easy to measure and reminds us that not everything that really counts can be easily counted. She noted that managerial targets and bureaucratic outcome measures fail to take account of the importance of the relationship between the practitioner and the service user. She emphasised that: 'Helping children is a human process. When the bureaucratic aspects of the work become too dominant, the heart of the work is lost' (Munro, 2011: 10). Munro highlighted that an overly procedural approach fosters a passive mindset, simply fulfilling administrative tasks in a technically correct manner but without the relationship with the child or the understanding of their perspective to fully make sense of their world. Such an approach to child safeguarding is blinkered in the extreme, failing to engage with children, to work with them and ultimately to promote their safety and well-being. Munro emphasised the importance of principles, rather than procedures, as the basis upon which social workers could engage with the challenges of their professional role and build effective working relationships with children and young people.

There are interesting parallels in how some practitioners perceive themselves as passive agents of a dominant and domineering bureaucratic system and how children are perceived as being passive victims on whose behalf the state intervenes (D'Cruz and Stagnitti, 2008). As well as lacking the time to engage with children due to pressing administrative demands and deadlines, many practitioners feel they lack the skills and expertise to communicate with children, particularly those who may be very young, have special needs or be difficult to engage (Handley and Doyle, 2014). They may pay lip service to the importance of listening to children and advocating on their behalf, but fear that, in an age of austerity, the resources to meet the needs may not be available. Working in environments with competing and sometimes contradictory demands means that some practitioners withdraw from even the attempt to build relationships with children or to promote their rights (Boylan and Dalrymple, 2011). The Children's Rights Director carried out a consultation event with 150 children who had experience of social work involvement, to provide evidence for the Munro Committee (Munro, 2011). They found that around half of the children felt that their social worker 'rarely or never' took notice of their wishes and feelings. Thomas and O'Kane's (1999) research noted that the attitudes held by the professionals working with children had a significant impact on whether children were engaged in a way that promoted their rights and participation. They developed Welsby's typology (1996) to identify four different approaches to professional practice with children:

- The *clinical* approach sees children as vulnerable and in need of treatment.

- The *bureaucratic* approach focuses on organisational and procedural priorities.

- The *cynical* approach is characterised by negative attitudes towards children who are regarded as difficult, manipulative and already having too much of their own way.

- Professionals who managed to work most effectively with children, despite the pressures and demands of their role, adopted a *value-based* position and promoted the rights and involvement of children as both an end in itself and as an ethical process (Thomas and O'Kane, 1999).

There are clearly many challenges for contemporary social workers and issues that need to be addressed to ensure effective child-centred practice. Despite concerns, there are grounds for optimism that a confident, child-centred professional approach to practice is possible. A professional approach that is not defeated by anxiety, bureaucracy or austerity has a strong value base and sense of capability, and is more likely to engage effectively with children and to recognise their agency and competence. Nothing can eradicate the complexities of practice and there is a place for processes and procedures that aim to offer guidance to professionals as we navigate the risks, uncertainties and pressures of a demanding workload. It is essential for professionals to implement local safeguarding procedures; flowcharts and checklists can be helpful in enabling practitioners to fulfil their role confidently and proficiently. Nevertheless, recognising child-centredness as a fundamental principle to guide and underpin practice will support childcare professionals in meeting the challenges of the role. Such an approach will be based on a strong value base, an understanding of the theoretical framework for good practice and a commitment to children's rights.

Points for Reflection

- In your view, what makes social work with children and young people particularly challenging?
- What helps you to maintain a commitment to child-centred practice?

The value base for child-centred practice

Child-centred practice is a value-based approach. Put simply, child-centred practice places central value on the child. The key principle upon which practice is founded is that children matter and that the welfare of the child is the paramount consideration for any professional involved in work with children and families. Therefore, to value children and to seek to understand their experience, their perspectives, their views, wishes and feelings, is fundamentally important. In this section we explore the professional values that underpin child-centred practice.

Social work values – traditional and contemporary

It is helpful to consider the social work value base, not because social workers have a monopoly in relation to ethical practice, but because there is much to learn from the development of understanding and discourse around the professional code of ethics for social work. It can be argued that social work is a value-based profession, having its roots in Victorian philanthropy and a strong, historical tradition of promoting the welfare and best interests of service users. As the social work profession developed in the post-war period, becoming firmly established in the 1960s, an American priest and academic, Reverend Felix Biestek (1961), articulated the values that became recognised as fundamental to social work's emerging professional identity. These values included a commitment to rights such as:

- Individualisation – the right of human beings to be treated as unique individuals and to be respected as such.

- Self-determination – the right of clients to make choices and decisions for themselves.

- Confidentiality – the right of the individual to privacy, so that confidential information is only shared when necessary to protect that person or the wider community.

These values are clearly as important for children as they are for adults. From birth, the child is a unique individual, worthy of respect and recognition of their innate dignity and rights as a human being. The meaning of self-determination is, however, more complex, as this clearly needs to be understood differently for a newborn infant and for a maturing adolescent on the cusp of adulthood. Eekelaar (1994) developed the notion of dynamic self-determinism in relation to children, recognising that decisions may need to remain open to revision as the child matures and becomes more able to make decisions about their own life. The principle of self-determination is relevant for social work with children, emphasising the importance of giving consideration to the emerging 'self' of the child, their potential and actual capacity to decide for themselves what might be in their best interests.

In contemporary social work practice, Biestek's traditional values have been overtaken by a more radical approach, challenging the narrow individualism of traditional casework and emphasising the importance of the broader social and political context of social work. This radical social work movement laid the foundations for emancipatory practice, involving an inherent commitment to human rights and including values such as:

- Equality – a recognition of structural inequalities based on social divisions such as age, class, ethnicity, gender, disability, sexuality and the right of service users to equal opportunities and fair treatment.

- Empowerment – the recognition of power imbalances in human relationships, social and political structures and the right of service users to gain greater control of their own lives.

- Participation – the right of service users to be seen as 'experts in their own lives' and to be involved in the planning, development and delivery of services and policies (Thompson, 2006).

Such values are integral to the social work profession. The definition of social work that has been revised and adopted by the International Federation of Social Workers (2014) includes the following commitment: 'Principles of social justice, human rights, collective responsibility and respect for diversities are central to social work.' This understanding of the value base for social work practice in the twenty-first century is just as relevant for children's services as for work with adults. Social workers need to understand the implications of inequality and social injustice as they impact on the lives of the children they work with. They need to recognise in particular the way in which simply being a child or young person leads to social exclusion and reduces opportunities for participation. An understanding of how power operates within society and a commitment to the rights of the child are crucial to the value base underpinning child-centred practice.

Points for Reflection

- What values do you think are fundamental to social work with children?

- How should these values influence the way social workers work with children and young people?

- Consider one of the traditional or contemporary values highlighted above: can you give an example of how you have demonstrated this value in your work with a particular child or young person?

Commentary

Social workers empower and enable children. They challenge discrimination, and recognise diversity and individuality. Social workers ensure professionalism: working in an open and honest way, maintaining boundaries, and making judgements based on 'balance and considered reasoning' (BASW, 2012: 9)

For example:

Social Worker Asim reflected on the value of 'empowerment' following his work with a 10-year-old girl, Hannah, whose father was seeking contact with her through private Court proceedings. Hannah remained with her mother after her father left the family home. Hannah was struggling to tell her mother how much she missed her father and wanted to see him on a regular basis. Asim spent quality time with Hannah and built up a positive relationship with her. Asim was able to support Hannah to be open about her wishes and feelings. Hannah expressed that she felt the need to protect and support her mother, who had suffered depression following her parents' separation. Hannah did not feel able to tell her mother that she too was upset and hurt by her father leaving the family home, but desperately wanted to see him. Asim was able to work directly with both parents separately and advocate on Hannah's behalf. On completion of his report to Court, Asim recommended that the family access mediation and that direct contact for Hannah with her father should commence immediately. Asim was commended by the Judge for giving an excellent summary of Hannah's views.

Understanding power

Access to power – the ability to be in control of one's destiny and to influence the course of events – is unequal. It is self-evident that adults hold power in many ways that are not amenable to children, due to factors as divergent as age and maturity, physical strength and life experience, and access to employment, wealth and material resources. Adults as parents, teachers, politicians and in many other social roles, hold power over children, exerting influence over almost every aspect of their daily lives. In some ways this is inevitable due to the dependent nature of childhood and most adults exercise their power responsibly and benignly. However, it is clear that the relative powerlessness of childhood is a prolonged condition in Western liberal societies, where young people remain dependent upon adult, usually parental, support for far longer than in developing nations. This relative powerlessness and prolonged dependence has also led to exclusion and marginalisation, abuse and exploitation for some children and young people.

Raven (1993) defined three main kinds of social power:

- Legitimate power: authority delegated to the individual due to their position or the way society is organised.

- Expert power: related to the skills and expertise of the person which are highly valued by others.

- Coercive power: enabling the holder to enforce action or demand compliance due to the ability to apply sanctions and to punish.

Children are generally ill-equipped and poorly placed in society, in comparison to adults, to access or employ these forms of power. They lack positional power, being unable to hold political or organisational office; they are regarded as developing beings, as learners, therefore lacking expertise; they do not have the resources to confer or withhold in order to exert control. Having said that, it is useful to consider Foucault's (1983) understanding of power. The French philosopher and social theorist recognised that power is not a static force possessed by a few in order to oppress and dominate. He saw power as diffused throughout society, existing through operation and action, a force for productivity and positivity as much as for repression. From this perspective, it is evident that children and young people can use and exert power to some extent. They have particular expertise in matters of relevance to themselves and in what it means to be a young person; they are able to influence others benignly, through positive peer and familial relationships or oppressively when they might employ bullying behaviour.

Acknowledging the relative powerlessness in society of children and young people does not mean regarding them as passive beings and victims of oppression. Children use power in many forms; they exist within a range of power relationships within their family, peer groups and social spheres, through which they exert and experience power in different ways. Children may be both oppressed and excluded due to their subordinate position in a society dominated by adults; whilst at the same time, they are social actors, able to use their agency, to have a say and to make a contribution. Furthermore, children and young people do not form a homogeneous group; individuals access power unequally. Infants remain vulnerable and dependent, whilst older young people are able to participate in and contribute to many aspects of society. Children with disabilities or complex health needs may be regarded as recipients of care, rather than recognised as capable individuals. Nevertheless, all children and young people share the same human rights, as citizens and human beings.

Commitment to rights, empowerment and participation

Recognising the rights of children is fundamental to the social work value base. Promoting the rights of young people means that social workers will recognise and challenge injustice and inequality. There are aspects of practice that are disproportionately oppressive to some young people, for example opportunities for involvement that exclude younger children or those with speech impairments. A value-based approach is about believing in the skills and abilities of all children; it is about enabling children to gain power and influence over their own lives (Braye and Preston-Shoot, 1995; Davey, 2010). Foucault (1980) recognised that the way to understand power is to consider the way it is exercised and experienced from the perspective of the subject; it is particularly valuable to listen to those who are most powerless in order to understand how power dynamics impact and reinforce inequality. It is important therefore for professionals to empower children and young people to participate in planning and decision-making processes, so that all involved are able to listen to their views and perspectives.

Child-centred practice does not mean ignoring the power imbalance that exists in relations between adults and young people, compounded by the dynamic of the professional–service user relationship. Social workers need to recognise their professional power, carry it lightly and use it wisely in their work with children and young people. They need to acknowledge the agency, capacity and competence of the children they work with and seek to strengthen and build these qualities at every opportunity. Treseder (1997) has suggested that we might consider participation as the process and empowerment as the outcome; so as practitioners seek to enable young people to be involved in decision-making processes there is a sense that power is shared and young people are empowered. In implementing these emancipatory values and valuing young people, *how* social workers work is just as important as *what* they do. Recognising that power is complex and fluid, child-centred practitioners use their power purposefully and transparently, respecting the rights of the child and promoting their empowerment. We explore the central value of participation more fully in Chapter 2.

An ethic of care

A critique of traditional understandings of ethics has been developed by feminist philosophers and academics. Feminist writers, such as Jagger (1992), have noted that traditional ethics tend to overrate traits that can be regarded as masculine, such as autonomy, independence and will, and to undervalue traits that might be seen as feminine, such as interdependence, community and connection. The feminist ethic of care emphasises that human beings are fundamentally relational: learning, developing and thriving in and through relationships with others. This philosophical understanding has made an important contribution to the social work value base (Gray, 2009) and to discussions and debates about children's rights (Cockburn, 2005).

From this perspective, the discourse around rights is criticised as being based on notions of rational individuals who claim, possess or fight for their rights; there is an emphasis on autonomy rather than relationships, on adversarial contacts rather than supportive connections. Carol Gilligan (1998) emphasises that people are not just autonomous, rational individuals with rights; they are also beings with needs and vulnerabilities, who spend their lives within networks of care and interdependence. She argues that recognition of the importance of human connection and relationships is as important to ethics and morality as rights and justice. This is especially relevant for children and young people. According to Cockburn (2005), an approach founded on the feminist ethic of care takes account of the context of children's lives, recognising the importance of the network of relationships, with parents, siblings, friends, teachers, within which children live their lives. Acknowledging the individuality of each child remains important alongside an appreciation that children's identities evolve and develop in the context of their social networks, in particular within the nurturing environment usually provided by their family (Featherstone and Morris, 2012). Barnes (2012) highlights that adopting a rights-based approach remains crucial; however, neglecting to recognise the need to provide care and support to children is not helpful. For example, the child's right to education can best be met within the context of a school that takes account of the individual needs of each child and addresses pastoral as well as educational needs. When social workers intervene to protect children and promote their *right* to safety, they work closely with those providing *care* for children, recognising the importance of family bonds and long-term relationships – as long as contacts are maintained safely and in the interests of the child. Children's rights should be promoted and attention paid to their need for care and nurturance.

Rights are rarely absolute; they are usually defined and interpreted within a particular context. Many rights are conditional and need to be considered and advanced whilst taking responsibility for any impact on the rights of others. Promoting children's rights involves negotiating with the child and significant others (usually parents and other adults connected to and caring for the child) the meaning of those rights, alongside the corresponding obligations and duties of all concerned. An example of this sensitive practice might occur in cases where a mother affected by domestic violence, who separates from her abuser, wishes to protect her child from contact with her ex-partner. It can be argued that the child has a right to maintain a relationship with both parents and that the child's interest is best served by negotiating a safe and supportive context for this to occur. Professionals involved in facilitating such an arrangement will need to work with both parents to ensure they have an appreciation of the child's rights and also of their responsibilities to maintain a safe, conflict-free space for ongoing contact. Retaining a focus on the welfare of the child during and after contact sessions, professionals will seek to ensure the child is not manipulated or distressed by negative family relationships. Promoting the rights of the child should be managed with equal priority given to their need for care and protection in a stressful and potentially risky situation. This process needs to be carried out with support for the child to make sense of the complexities and interrelationships of rights and responsibilities for all involved. For the child-centred practitioner, a commitment to children's rights within a framework provided by the ethic of care provides a strong foundation for practice.

Theoretical foundations for child-centred practice

Having explored some of the key ethics and values underpinning child-centred practice, it is useful also to recognise that this approach to practice has a strong and coherent theoretical foundation. Theories and values are often inextricably linked and it will be evident that the theories outlined below are rooted in the value base discussed above.

Person-centred theory

The traditional values outlined by Biestek can be seen as inherent in the development of person-centred practice. Originally developed by the influential humanist psychologist Carl Rogers as an approach to psycho-therapy and counselling, person-centred approaches remain widely practised in social work and social care and can be seen to form the basis of child-centred practice. Rogers (1951) emphasised that work with service users should be based upon the belief in the innate capacity of the individual to achieve personal growth and self-actualisation. He emphasised the therapeutic relationship as the key to enabling this process of healing; the three core conditions for person-centred therapy being:

- Congruence – a genuine and honest professional presence;
- Unconditional positive regard – personal warmth and acceptance;
- Empathy – understanding sensitively and accurately the experience and feelings of the service user.

Child-centred practice embodies key aspects of Rogerian theory. From a child-centred perspective, there is the recognition that as children grow and move through the stages of development from infancy to adulthood, they develop their sense of identity in order to become Roger's 'fully functioning person'. There is also a commitment to enabling self-actualisation at each age and stage of development, appreciating the authentic 'self' of every child, including the very young and the very dependent. For childcare professionals, intervention when children are experiencing difficulty should be based on respect and acceptance; such an approach is integral to engagement with young people who may be involuntary service users and feel stigmatised by what they regard as professional intrusion or interference. In order to work towards engagement and congruence, the development and accurate deployment of empathy is crucial. Empathy is a key skill at the heart of social work practice (Trevithick, 2009). In adopting a child-centred approach the adult practitioner may need to take a greater leap of the imagination to fully appreciate the perspective of the young service user. Using empathy to engage with a young person is part of genuinely valuing them as a unique individual and acknowledging the value of their perspective. Empathy involves seeking to walk in the shoes of another, whether they are the over-sized trainers of a young person or the first trainer-shoes of a toddler. In these regards then child-centred practice owes a debt to person-centred theory.

Focus on Practice

Developed by clinical psychologist Dan Hughes, (2007) the PACE model provides a value-based, child-centred approach to professional practice:

- Playfulness – Recognising the importance of a light touch, connecting with the child at their level, rather than a bureaucratic or overly professionalised approach.

- Acceptance – Valuing the child, without blame or criticism.

- Curiosity – Expressing interest in the life of the child, a genuine wish to understand their world and their perspectives.

- Empathy – Working with compassion, acknowledging the emotions of the child in their particular situation.

Reflective-relational theory

The complexities of contemporary practice with children and families have led to the development of theoretical thinking evolving outside traditional ideas based in psycho-therapy. In social work in particular, new understandings of professional practice grounded in reflective-relational theory have become influential. This approach to practice challenges reductionist understandings that perceive human behaviour as rational and logical, and complex problems as amenable to straightforward categorisation in terms of cause and effect, vulnerability and risk, treatment and cure (Parton and O'Byrne, 2000). To make sense of the complexities of service user's situations, the impact of factors such as oppression, power dynamics, family background, and patterns of relationships and behaviours, practitioners cannot rely on a favourite theory or a bureaucratic assessment tool. According to Fook and Gardner (2010), critical reflection involves identifying and unsettling assumptions, applying knowledge drawn from a range of theories to inform practice, and bringing self-awareness to relationships with service users in order to explore different perspectives and meanings.

A range of ideas have developed around relationship-based practice (Howe, 1997; Folgheraiter, 2004; Ruch et al., 2010) that recognise the centrality of the practitioner–service user relationship. Commentators emphasise the responsibility of the professional to take a reflexive approach by acknowledging how their role, conduct and the quality of their interactions with service users impact upon the effectiveness of their interventions. From this perspective, the professional relationship is: 'the medium through which the practitioner can engage with the complexity of an individual's internal and external worlds' (Ruch, 2005: 113). Relationship-based practice recognises the individuality of the service user and the uniqueness of their circumstances, drawing on an eclectic range of theories, bringing reflexivity to the process of making sense of complexity and uncertainty (Ruch et al., 2010). It is perhaps not surprising that interest in this model has developed alongside critique of the kind of managerial approach that has promoted procedurally driven administrative functions and has failed to recognise the complex nature of social problems impacting on children and young people.

Contemporary understandings of relationship-based practice are grounded in emancipatory values which take account of the power relations inherent in the wider context of service users' lives and seek to challenge them (Smith, 2008). Folgheraiter (2004) acknowledges that intervention by a helping professional tends to signify deficit and incapacity, whilst noting the opportunity for the practitioner to form a supportive relationship based on the service user's agency and self-efficacy: 'The surprise of a user when s/he feels accepted and respected as an actor – at the same time as his/her case is taken on because of his/her evident inability to be such – usually leads to the building and strengthening of a trust relationship, and therefore involvement in the helping relationship' (Folgheraiter, 2004: 154).

This emphasis on involvement and trust-building through meaningful and effective professional relationships with service users is fundamental to an understanding of child-centred practice. Folgheraiter's depiction of the surprise of a service user in being listened to, taken seriously and involved in the planning process is particularly relevant to the experience of many young people, who may be more accustomed to being asked to leave the room whilst the grown-ups have important discussions and make hard decisions.

Relationship-based approaches to work with families

Relationship-based social work recognises that relationships matter and that the relationships of significance to the child matter. In many cases, the work of children's practitioners is predominantly undertaken with adults, mainly parents and carers. A great deal of social workers' time is spent providing support to parents or working with them to address issues that may be impacting on the family and on their parenting (Frost et al., 2015). In such cases, the child-centred practitioner should acknowledge that children are influenced by issues in their family and may have questions and concerns about family members. Even where the primary working relationship is with parents, professionals should introduce themselves to the children and provide an opportunity to talk about their work with the family. Where professional time and energy is focused upon supporting parents, it is important that practitioners do not become over-whelmed by parental issues, so that they no longer notice or pay attention to the children. The child's needs and best interests should always be 'held in mind'. Reviews of the work undertaken should involve children and pay attention to outcomes that improve the welfare of the child. Even where contact with children is brief, social workers should seek to develop the basis of a positive working relationship with them, whereby children understand that they are interested in them and working on their behalf. Professional interventions with adult members of the family should address and seek to enhance the quality of their relationships with their children, as the health of those relationships is likely to be fundamental to the well-being of the child.

In this sense, child-centred practice is compatible with 'think-family' approaches (Morris et al., 2008), which aim to offer integrated support to the whole family, addressing the needs of parents as well as focusing on the welfare of children. Developing relationships of trust with parents and carers to support them and to promote their parenting capacity is an important part of child-centred practice. Effective social work practice involves acknowledging the importance of family relationships for the child and seeking to develop positive professional relation-ships with parents and carers to promote the best interests of the child. This is explored more fully in Chapter 4.

Relationship-based approaches to work with children

We have already noted from the research undertaken for the Children's Com-missioner by Cossar and colleagues (2011) that relationships with their social worker matter to children involved in child protection and the looked-after system. We have also acknowledged the importance of Munro's work in challenging the malaise of overly bureaucratic practice. Munro emphasised that: 'helping children and families involves working with them and therefore the quality of the relationship between the child and family and professionals directly impacts on the effectiveness of help given' (Munro, 2011: 23). Working with the child means retaining a focus on the child and involving them in a way that is age-appropriate and meaningful for them.

Professionals need to bring a reflective approach to their efforts to build positive relationships with children. Social workers are often intervening in the lives of children at times of trauma and vulnerability. Practitioners need to bring sophisticated skills and understanding to engage with young people who may be kicking against the adult system that has let them down, or with young children who are crying out for nurture and attention. Fook and Gardner (2010) emphasise the importance of emotional intelligence and critical reflection in order to maintain a professional response, whilst also reaching out to service users with compassion and humanity. Ferguson (2011) notes the need for consistent and supportive supervision to promote reflective practice and enable social workers to carry out their work with children and families effectively. Maintaining a commitment to the values underpinning child-centred practice is crucial for practitioners to maintain professional boundaries whilst also connecting with and building relationships of trust with children and young people.

Focus on Practice

Wilson and colleagues (2011) have emphasised several key principles that form the basis of relationship-based practice with children:

- Recognising the 'child within': This means acknowledging that our own experiences as children influence how we understand the world of the child. There are advantages of being able to recall and tune into our inner child in order to relate to children and appreciate their perspectives, their emotional and behavioural responses to the professional intervention.

- Listening to the voice of the child: The responsibility lies with the social worker to seek to communicate effectively with children to build trust, listen to them and gain an understanding of their world.

- Acknowledging power and purpose: Seeking to build relationships of partnership with children and their parents enables all involved to feel that their contribution is valued and promotes engagement in the change process. However, acting as a friend or confidante is neither helpful nor ethical. The social worker must be honest about the professional power they carry and explain their role and the purpose of the intervention in a way that makes sense to the child and family.

Points for Reflection

- How useful is person-centred theory as a basis for contemporary child-centred practice?
- Can you provide an example from your own practice where you have used a relationship-based approach?

The success of the relationship between social worker and child is often in the approach and attitude of the worker. Relationship-based approaches seek to challenge power differentials and embrace individuality. Children, and the adults in their lives, are actively listened to, respected and taken seriously.

For example:
Karen, a social worker, received a referral from the single mother of a 13-year-old boy, Jack, who had been truanting from school, smoking and coming in late at night over the last two months. Jack's mother, Louise, stated that she was unable to cope with this behaviour and wanted him to be placed in foster care. Karen met with Jack and Louise separately, and she was able to see the tensions in the relationship from both perspectives. It transpired that Louise's father had died the previous year, and he had been a huge source of support to the family. This grief was impacting immensely on both parent and child. Jack felt lonely, sad and angry, and was struggling to manage these complex feelings. Louise felt unable to talk about the death of her father at all, and had tried to carry on as normal for Jack's sake. Louise felt angry that Jack, in her view, was 'making the situation worse'. Following preliminary individual work with Jack and Louise, Karen was able to see them both together and assist in repairing their relationship. Although a very emotional meeting, Jack and Louise were supported by Karen to listen to one another, to negotiate some clear ground rules and to talk openly about their feelings. Karen, with consent from Jack, accessed support for him within school, and Louise agreed to a referral to a local counselling service.

Conclusion

In this chapter, we have explored the ethical and theoretical framework for child-centred practice. We have noted that child-centredness matters to children and makes a difference in their lives. Furthermore, we have recognised some of the challenges of contemporary social work practice, the complexities, pressures and ethical dilemmas that may lead some practitioners to adopt a bureaucratic or cynical stance. Seeing professionals as competent and children as vulnerable may seem to provide a useful way forward in fulfilling organisational priorities. However, in social work practice, we are often working with risk and uncertainty, and the need for ongoing dialogue with children and their families, for continuing to listen, engage, explain and involve, is crucial. This means taking the time to work at the pace of the child; sharing, in an age-appropriate manner, the complexities of the situation; exploring the options and their possible repercussions; and working together in the interests of the child. The aim of a child-centred practitioner taking a reflective-relational approach is to seek to work alongside key stakeholders, including the child, in the process of collaboration:

> It need not be a question of adult imposition versus child autonomy: rather a matter of acknowledging the interconnectedness of our lives, of no longer seeing the relationships that children have with significant adults as naturally and necessarily hierarchic. We, as adults, might also benefit from dialogue with children in confronting our dilemmas. (Roche, 1995: 286–287)

We go on in Chapter 2 to explore the legal mandate for practice and to recognise how a commitment to children's rights, participation rights in particular, underpin this process of dialogue and provide a framework for child-centred practice.

Recommended reading and resources

- Munro's (2011) *Review of Child Protection*. The Final Report remains the seminal and authoritative text that provides the challenge to improve organisational response and professional practice with the aim of promoting child-centred practice.

- Cossar and colleagues (2011) *Don't Make Assumptions: Children's and Young People's Views of the Child Protection System and Messages for Change*. This is a useful study of particular relevance for social workers. It was completed on behalf of the Office of the Children's Commissioner in England and this website provides regular updates about the valuable work of the commissioner, whose role is to promote the participation of children and young people and make sure adults in positions of authority take their views and interests into account. www.childrenscommissioner.gov.uk

- In the book *Social Work: An Introduction to Contemporary Practice* by Kate Wilson and colleagues (2011, 2nd edition), part three focuses on relationship-based practice with a range of user groups. Chapter 16 is about working with children and families and provides an accessible overview of many aspects of practice with an emphasis on the importance of values and relationships.

- The British Association of Social Workers (BASW) have published *The Code of Ethics for Social Work – Statement of Principles*. Published in 2012 and updated in October 2014, it provides a comprehensive overview of the value base for contemporary professional practice.

2

UNDERSTANDING CHILDREN'S RIGHTS

Introduction

> The vision of children implicit in the Convention on the Rights of the Child and in the Children Act 1989 is that they are neither the property of their parents nor are they helpless objects of charity. Children are individuals, members of a family and a community, with rights and responsibilities appropriate to their age and stage of development. (Munro, 2011: 16)

Notions of rights – human rights, citizen's rights, children's rights – have always been central to the social work value base. A full understanding of the rights of young people and a commitment to promoting those rights are crucial components of child-centred practice. In this chapter, we explore the way in which children's rights are understood and underpinned internationally by the UNCRC and, more locally, by policy and legislation in the UK. We explore in particular the case law surrounding the Gillick ruling, which, though specifically focused on the rights of young people under 16 to consent to medical treatment, has been influential in making sense, more broadly, of the child's right to self-determination. Attention will be paid to the participation rights of young people and the challenges for the child-centred practitioner of ensuring children are able to participate in decision-making processes related to their own lives.

The United Nations convention on the rights of the child

A good place to start in considering children's rights is the UNCRC, adopted in 1989 and ratified in the UK in 1991. This international agreement sets out the civil, political, economic, social and cultural rights of every child, regardless of nationality, race or religion. In signing up to the UNCRC, the most widely ratified international human rights treaty in history, nation states are acknowledging that children require special care and legal protection and that they are entitled to exercise their rights as individuals and active contributors to their communities. O'Neill (2008) highlights that the UNCRC is not just about promoting good practice; it is a legally binding treaty that nation states have an obligation to implement. She emphasises the need for organisations to ensure that the children they come into contact with are able to access, claim and use their rights. The rights outlined in the Convention are embedded in UK statute through the Children Act 1989 and the Human Rights Act 1998; in implementation of the latter it is prudent for all concerned to remember that children share the same rights as adults, being fellow citizens of the nation state and equal members of the human race.

The following articles, taken from the summary version, are particularly relevant for social workers and childcare practitioners:

Article 2 (Non-discrimination): The Convention applies to all children, whatever their race, religion or abilities; whatever they think or say, whatever type of family they come from. No child should be treated unfairly on any basis.

Article 3 (Best interests of the child): The best interests of children must be the primary concern in making decisions that may affect them. All adults should do what is best for children.

Article 12 (Respect for the views of the child): When adults are making decisions that affect children, children have the right to say what they think should happen and have their opinions taken into account.

Article 16 (Right to privacy): Children have a right to privacy. The law should protect them from attacks against their way of life, their good name, their families and their homes.

Article 19 (Protection from all forms of violence): Children have the right to be protected from being hurt and mistreated, physically or mentally. Governments should ensure that children are properly cared for and protect them from violence, abuse and neglect by their parents, or anyone else who looks after them.

The rights of all children as citizens

All the Convention rights apply equally to all children. In line with the social work value base and the importance of respecting the innate dignity of every person, it is essential that childcare practitioners promote the rights of all the children they come into contact with. Difficulties related to the age, ability or circumstance of the child do not excuse the professional from fulfilling this duty. Social structures, power dynamics and adult-centric processes often marginalise the role and contribution of children. Some children may have particular difficulties in negotiating systems designed by adults. Professionals should be proactive in recognising ways in which children are excluded from exercising their rights.

Society tends to view children as future citizens, whose rights are contingent upon their achieving responsible and mature adulthood. Fattore and Mason (2005: 20) emphasise that this is not the perspective of the UNCRC: 'The important issue is that children are entitled to be taken seriously now. They are entitled to be seen and to be responded to as important players now, in their own right as children.' This rights-based approach recognises children as citizens, able to participate in their own communities, and as stakeholders in the organisations and services that impact upon them. However, some children face additional barriers in being able to access their rights. Professionals need to recognise the ways in which children with disabilities, for example, and unaccompanied asylum seekers, may experience discrimination. No child or group of children should be treated any less favourably than others and childcare practitioners have a responsibility to challenge oppressive structures, customs and practices that claim ignorance of or run roughshod over the rights of children.

Balancing the right to privacy and the right to protection

Social workers are often concerned to balance the rights of parents and the rights of children; one of the challenges of ethical practice is how to respect the right of the family to privacy from State intrusion whilst also fulfilling the statutory duty to safeguard and protect children. It is important to recognise that both rights are equally important for children. It may be more appropriate to consider parental responsibilities rather than parents' rights (the approach taken in the Children Act 1989), acknowledging that no adult has a *right* to be a parent. Parents can be seen as the custodians of their children's rights – the primary responsibility of parents being to protect and promote the welfare of their children. The UNCRC emphasises the importance for children of their family relationships in several articles, article 16 being particularly significant; the law should protect the child's private, family and home life. Article 18 goes on to emphasise the custodial responsibility of parents to bring up children in a way that promotes their best interests and the duty of the State to provide support for families in raising their children, individuals who are also citizens of the State. It is article 19 that emphasises the limits of family privacy and ensures that the State recognizes its duty to safeguard children. In signing up to the Convention, governments are accepting their responsibility to protect children from abuse and to intervene in the lives of families, where necessary, in order to do so. In fulfilling this duty, it is clear that social workers take a central role and it can be argued that safeguarding children is the core business of the profession. Nevertheless, it is crucial to recognise that child protection is everyone's responsibility. All childcare professionals share the duty to promote the child's right to be cared for by their family, alongside their right to be protected from harm and abuse.

Practitioner Testimonial

Child-centred practice to me is just a natural way of working. I don't see it as an 'add on' or an extra thing to do – in most cases, instead of doing something 'to' or 'for' a young person – we do it 'with'. I've had numerous discussions with people who have told me that children are too young to be asked what they think about things and my response is that child-centred practice isn't about handing over all of the power to a child or young person – it's about involving them in the discussions/conversations about why a decision has been made and ensuring that they at least understand. One of the best straplines that I have seen simply said 'nothing about us, without us'. To me it sums it up – let's not make decisions about young people's lives without making sure we are involving them at an appropriate level.

Shelly Eades-Jones, Team Manager, Barnardo's Children's Rights Service.

Balancing best interests and participation

As well as balancing the tension in the child's right to a private family life and their right to protection, another key challenge for the child-centred practitioner is to seek to promote the child's best interests whilst also respecting their wishes and feelings. The UNCRC emphasises that the commitment to protect the interests of the child *and* to ascertain their wishes and feelings in any matters affecting their interests should be at the heart of professional practice. Nowhere in the Convention is it suggested that any rights have pre-eminence over others, all are given equal weight and force. However, there may be tensions in the pursuance of articles 3 and 12, which could be regarded as promoting commitments that are contradictory. For example, in situations where the child's view is contrary to professional judgement about their welfare, there may be tensions around how to balance the professional responsibility to act in the child's best interests against the need to take seriously the child's perspective about what is best for them. This is an ethical challenge at the heart of child-centred practice. It is not possible for the child-centred practitioner to seek to pursue just one of these articles, as if they are options in a pick-and-mix of children's rights. The aim is to promote both, as the fundamental rights of all children in every aspect of practice. In response to debates in this area, the UN Committee issued a statement reiterating unequivocally that in order to reach any decision about best interests, children need to be consulted and enabled to participate in the decision-making process: 'There is no tension between articles 3 and 12, only a complimentary role of the two general principles: one establishes the objective of achieving the best interests of the child and the other provides the methodology for reaching the goal of hearing … the child' (UN, 2009: 74).

An essential part of deciding what is in the interests of the child is listening to the child and seeking to understand their views, perspectives and choices. There may seem to be tensions in the values underpinning articles 3 and 12 – the promotion of a child's welfare being essentially based on paternalist notions of the need to protect the vulnerable child (an adult knows best approach), whereas advocating for the child's views recognises the capacity and capability of the child (the child knows best what is important for them). However, it is a false dichotomy to consider that the two articles are incompatible. As Archard and Skivenes (2009b: 398) argue: 'It is … impossible to make legitimate and rational decisions about a child's welfare without taking proper account of the child's view.'

Thomas and O'Kane (1998: 139) note that the UNCRC emphasises particular rights for children and contingent duties for the adults involved in their lives:

- a child's right to participation

- a child's right to protection

- an adult duty to promote the child's best interests

- an adult duty to listen and consider the child's wishes and feelings.

Taking the time and making the considerable effort necessary to enable children to express their wishes and feelings will enable professionals to gain a greater insight into what may be in the child's best interests and how to promote their safety and welfare. Childcare professionals carry the obligation to support children in laying claim to their rights – they are charged with the responsibility to create the opportunities whereby children can express their views. Practitioners also carry the responsibility to assess the weight that should be given to the views of the child dependent on their age and level of understanding. Quoting the original version of article 12, as opposed to the summary version, is helpful for this point: 'the views of the child being given due weight in accordance with the age and maturity of the child.' This is an issue that will be given further attention later in this chapter, when we analyse the meaning of 'Gillick competence' and explore good practice in relation to the child's right to participation.

Points for Reflection

The summary version of the UNCRC can be accessed at: www.unicef.org/crc/files/Rights_overview.pdf

- Read through the articles of the Convention and consider the ones that are particularly relevant to your work with children and young people.

- Can you think of an example from your own practice where you have been able to promote the rights of a child or children?

The legal and policy framework for child-centred practice

It has already been noted that UK legislation prescribing the statutory duties of childcare professionals reflects and is informed by the UNCRC. This is true of a range of legal statutes in the four nations, including in particular the Children Acts 1989 and 2004, the Children (Scotland) Act 1995 and the Children (Northern Ireland) Order 1995. The Rights of Children and Young Persons (Wales) Measure 2011 made Wales the first country in the UK to incorporate the UNCRC into its domestic law. This means that all Welsh policy and legislation has to take into account children's rights. All four countries of the UK have active Children's Commissioners who have the statutory role to promote the rights of children and to ensure the principles and recommendations of the UNCRC are implemented. We will focus in particular on the key principles outlined in the Children Act 1989 and other legislation and policy underpinning practice in England and Wales, though, as the discussion will explore issues directly relevant to child-centred practice, it will have resonance for practice throughout the UK and internationally.

The welfare principle

We have noted the importance of article 3 of the UNCRC. At this point it is useful to consider the wording of the original and legal version of the Convention: 'In all actions concerning children, whether undertaken by public or private social welfare institutions, courts of law, administrative authorities or legislative bodies, the best interests of the child shall be a primary consideration.' In some ways, it can be seen then that the 'welfare principle' enshrined in the Children Act 1989 has taken this principle further, in emphasising the welfare of the child as the *paramount* consideration. Again, it is worthwhile to pay attention to the actual wording of the legislation: 'When a court determines any question with respect to the upbringing of a child ... the child's welfare shall be the court's paramount consideration' (s 1(1)). However, the Children Act is concerned in particular with the decisions of the Court; article 3 of the Convention focused their exhortation far more widely by making it applicable to *all* work of public and private welfare providers and administrative agencies as it relates to children. In taking forward these legal precepts in order to inform a child-centred approach to practice, it is appropriate for childcare professionals to be guided by a combination of the aforementioned principles and to seek to ensure that the welfare of the child is our paramount concern in every action and decision involving or impacting upon the child.

The wishes and feelings of the child

Article 12 is embedded in the Children Act 1989, as consideration is given to the views of the child in relation to particular decisions that the Court might need to make regarding the child. The 'welfare checklist' includes a range of considerations for the court to take into account, including the child's needs, the capability of parents to meet those needs, the possible impact of change, any harm suffered and any characteristics of the child that the court considers to be relevant to their decision. However, the *first* consideration on the list is: 'the ascertainable wishes and feelings of the child concerned (considered in the light of his age and understanding)' (s 1(3(a)). This requirement is of particular relevance to social workers as it also underpins decision-making processes regarding children who are looked after by the Local Authority. Section 22 of the 1989 Act stipulates that in circumstances involving a looked-after child or a child who may come into care, the Local Authority has a duty: 'so far as is reasonably practicable, to ascertain the wishes and feelings of the child and to take those views into account.' This requirement has been extended by the Children Act 2004 (s 53) to cover a much larger group of children who come to the attention of Local Authorities: children in need (as defined by s 17 of the 1989 Act), that is, children who may require supportive services in order to develop and be healthy, including children with disabilities and children at risk of significant harm. This extension of the professional duty to take into account the views of children is welcome; nevertheless, it can be seen that the key legislation fails to fully embrace the principle of article 12 which, in the original version, is unequivocal and far-reaching: 'State Parties shall assure to the child who is capable of forming his or her own views the right to express those views freely in *all* matters affecting the child.'

Focus on Practice

Ofsted (2015) has taken an important step to promote child-centred practice in its Single Inspection Framework, setting out the expectation that children and young people should be enabled to express their views about their own case (where the Local Authority is involved with their family), as well as about service development at a strategic level.

Ofsted Grade Descriptors for good practice within a Local Authority Children's Service include:

- Children and young people are listened to, practice is focused on their needs and experiences and influenced by their wishes and feelings.
- Children and young people are helped to understand their rights and the responsibilities that accompany those rights and legal entitlements.
- Children and young people's wishes and feelings are understood and influence decisions about where they live.

Godar (2015: 13)

A child-centred approach is underpinned by a commitment to ensure that in all matters impacting upon the child, adults should enable children to express their views and should take them seriously. This is certainly in line with the approach taken by the Children's Commissioners of the UK nations. Although they may take a particular interest in children living away from home or involved with statutory services, they work to promote the rights of all children and to ensure that adults listen to and take account of the views of children whenever they work with them.

Child-centredness in other key aspects of law and policy

The Children Act 1989 recognises that for the vast majority of children their interests are safeguarded most effectively by enabling them to live with their own families. Under s17(1), Local Authorities have a duty to safeguard and promote the welfare of children who have particular needs and: 'to promote the upbringing of such children by their families by providing a range and level of services appropriate to those children's needs.' Current government policy, as expressed in the Department for Education (2016b) document *Putting Children First*, emphasises the importance of supporting and strengthening families, in order to enhance the life chances of children.

The 'Assessment Framework' (see Figure 1) is used by childcare professionals to assess and address the needs of children and this approach to practice is embedded in the statutory guidance provided by *Working Together to Safeguard Children* (2015). As noted in Chapter 1, the assessment framework can be seen as a key intervention of the UK government to institute and promote a child-centred approach to professional practice with families. The framework places the child at the centre of the assessment process, meaning that the child is the focus of the professional intervention, emphasising the importance of understanding the development of the child and their perspectives about the world. The assessment triangle introduced an ecological model for assessment, recognising the importance of the context of the child's life, that is, their immediate family relationships and the impact of the wider family, their community and environment.

It is worth acknowledging that for social work practice with children and families, the law is a blunt instrument for making sense of the nuanced attachment relationships, complex family dynamics and intricate web of community relations within which the child is embedded. Sensitive and rigorous assessment is required and the ecological and holistic approach of the assessment framework, focusing on the needs of the child, provides a way forward for the child-centred practitioner.

The Equality Act 2010 is relevant to the whole of the UK and places a responsibility on all public authorities to identify and eliminate discrimination and promote equality of opportunity. This applies to the work of childcare professionals and focuses attention on the need to ensure that young people are not excluded from processes of assessment and decision-making

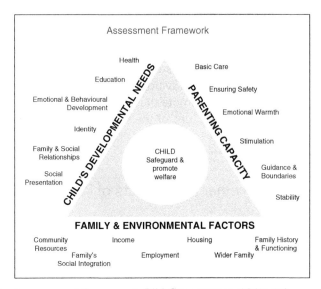

Figure 1 The Assessment Framework (HM Government, 2015: 22)

or from being able to access their rights and appropriate services on the basis of their age or ability. The statutory guidance provided in *Working Together* (2015) for all professionals in England working with children, has summed up the various legal principles relating to the paramountcy of the child's interests and the importance of ascertaining and giving due consideration to the views of all children in the following statement: 'the child's needs are paramount, and the needs and wishes of each child, be they a baby or infant, or an older child, should be put first' (HM Government 2015: 8).

Key principles underpinning child-centred practice in law and policy

It is helpful to draw together some of the key principles inherent in current law and policy that underpin best practice in work with children. Karen Winter (2011a) has made an important contribution in outlining the principles emphasised by the UN, both in the Convention and in their General Comments that support the implementation of the UNCRC. In Table 1 these have been adapted, alongside key principles drawn from the Children Act 1989 and the social work value base, summarised and applied to practice:

Table 1 Key principles of the UNCRC and the Children Act 1989, adapted from K. Winter (2011a)

Practice principles	Meaning	Translation into practice
Paramountcy	The welfare of the child is the paramount consideration in all matters that impact upon children.	Practitioners should ensure they constantly question whether the welfare principle is underpinning and informing their actions and decisions.
Participation	Children have the right to be involved and to contribute to decisions in all matters pertaining to their own lives.	Practitioners should assume the capability of children and enable children to be involved in ways that are meaningful to them.
Family privacy	Children have a right to a private family life.	Interventions in families should be made in a proportionate and supportive manner, balancing confidentiality with statutory duties.
Empowerment	Awareness of the ways in which social, cultural and organisational power dynamics impact on children.	Practitioners should recognise children as stakeholders in their work together and seek to negotiate and share power in an ethical manner.
Transparent and informative	Children must be provided with information about their rights and how their views will be taken into consideration in decision-making processes.	Practitioners to explain about their role and the intervention, ensuring information is accessible to children.
Voluntary	Children should never be forced to express their views or be involved in any work against their will.	Practitioners to explain concepts of informed consent and seek to build a trusting relationship. Where children are involuntary service users, the reasons for the intervention should be explained.
Respectful	Children should be treated with respect.	Practitioners should respect the views and perspectives of children, seek to understand them and represent them fairly and fully in decision-making contexts.
Relevant and child-friendly	Issues of relevance to children should be recognised; environments and ways of working should be adapted to children's capacities.	Practitioners to seek to build reciprocal engagement with children, recognising their interests and priorities, ensuring appropriate time and space.

Inclusive	Non-discriminatory and enabling all children to participate.	Practitioners to seek to involve all children in ways appropriate to their age and ability, responsive to issues of culture, religion and matters of importance to the child.
Competent	Adults should have training and support to work effectively with children.	Practitioners should take responsibility to develop their skills, knowledge and capability to work with children.
Protection	Children have a right to be safe.	Practitioners must take responsibility to protect children from risk. They should identify, explain and manage risk, avoiding paternalism and protectionism.
Accountable	Children must be informed about how decisions have been made and be party to evaluation of process and outcomes.	Practitioners should record practice in ways children can understand and explain about feedback and complaints processes.
Timely	Time can have different meanings for children and adults.	Delays should be avoided; processes should be managed at the pace of the child.

Points for Reflection

- In relation to a piece of work you have carried out with a child, select one of the principles of good practice (from Table 1) and evaluate how well you fulfilled that principle in your work. Use a scale of one to ten, ten being fulfilled absolutely and one being not fulfilled in any way.

- If you evaluated your work with a score of less than ten, consider one thing you could have done differently to improve your practice and move it closer to a score of ten.

- Do you think the child you worked with would share your evaluation of the work or would they give the work a different score?

Commentary
It is very useful for the child-centred practitioner to reflect on specific pieces of work they have completed in light of the above principles for good practice. This involves considering the piece of work not only from their own perspective, but also from the perspective of the child.

For example:
Student social worker Rachel, scored herself eight out of ten when considering the principle of being 'transparent and informative' in relation to having explained her role to a

10-year-old boy during their first interaction. Rachel felt she had used language the child could comprehend and asked him what he understood of the information she had provided to check his understanding. However, on reflection, Rachel had not provided any age-appropriate written information for the child to refer to after the visit. She felt this could have improved her score. On considering the child's perspective, Rachel felt he may have scored her lower, perhaps a seven. Rachel acknowledged this was the first time she had met the child and he appeared a little nervous. This was a potential barrier for the child understanding and retaining the information. Therefore, a written leaflet, for example, would have assisted him further.

Gillick competence and the Fraser guidelines

Both the UNCRC and the Children Act 1989 place central importance on the views and wishes of the child whilst also recognising the duty of the adult to judge the capability of the child to express those views freely and to make decisions for themselves. Considerations about the capacity or capability of children tend to be discussed in relation to the maturity of the child and the role of parents to offer protection and nurturance until the point of independence. Tensions around the role of parents and the rights of children have been usefully explored in the case law arising from *Gillick* v. *West Norfolk & Wisbech Area Health Authority* in 1985. Although this case very specifically concerned the role of doctors in providing contraception to young people without parental consent, the guidance outlined in the case law has had much wider influence and continues to be relevant for health and social care practitioners today. The case law is binding in England and Wales with similar provision being made in Scotland, and it has been approved in Australia, Canada and New Zealand.

In 1982, Victoria Gillick, a mother of ten children who held strong views based upon her Catholic faith, took her local health authority to Court in an attempt to prevent doctors from providing contraceptive advice or treatment to children aged under 16 without parental consent. This initially local and very specific dispute has had far-reaching implications for professional and legal decision-making in matters relevant to children and young people. It is significant to note that the issue raised such a range of ethical and legal challenges that the case took three years to resolve, the High Court first dismissing Mrs Gillick's claims, the Appeal Court overturning this decision and finally the House of Lords finding in favour of the original judgement. The latter ruling resulted in the guidance offered by Lords Scarman and Fraser that continues to be relevant to contemporary practice. In considering the influence of this case and the principles upon which the decisions turned, it is useful to look in some detail at the deliberations of the Lords.

Lord Scarman and Gillick competence

Gillick competence is related to the ability of a child to consent to contraceptive treatment without the need for parental permission or knowledge. Lord Scarman, in his judgement, noted that in the UK: 'various ages of discretion have been fixed for various purposes' (*Gillick* v. *West Norfolk* (1985)). For example, the right to vote is 18, whilst the age of criminal responsibility is ten in England and Wales. Nevertheless, the age of 18 is generally seen as the line drawn between adulthood and childhood (Children Act, 1989: s 105), so that 18 year olds have the same autonomy as adults in matters of health and other rights. To a limited extent, the UK law allows 16 and 17 year olds to take medical decisions independently of parents. It is pertaining to the rights of under 16 year olds where decision-making is more open to debate. Lord Scarman recognised that the child's age alone should not be seen as a reliable predictor of competence in making difficult decisions, nor should it be assumed that parents know best and their view should always be yielded to in questions concerning the health of their offspring. He emphasised that the notion of parental rights or the power of parents to make decisions on behalf of their child: 'exists primarily to enable the parent to discharge his duty of maintenance, protection, and education until he reaches such an age as to be able to look after himself and make his own decisions.' For Lord Scarman a key principle upon which he based his judgement was that parental rights endure only as long as they are required and are channelled in order to protect the child and ensure their best interests. He noted also the arbitrary nature of fixed age limits attributed by the law to enable access to various rights. He acknowledged the tensions inherent in the limits imposed by the law, although in reality the process of 'growing up' knows no such fixed points: 'nature knows only a continuous process.' He recognised that attitudes about the level of control or influence that parents should rightfully exert in order to fulfil their parental responsibilities are also open to change and development, responding to changes in social values. He emphasised that this point was particularly relevant to the case in hand, where social attitudes to contraception and sexual behaviour in the latter part of the twentieth century were evolving rapidly. Ultimately he argued that: 'the law must be sensitive to human development and social change.' From these deliberations Lord Scarman reached the following conclusion that has had an enduring influence upon decision-making involving children and families: 'parental right yields to the child's right to make his own decisions when he reaches a sufficient understanding and intelligence to be capable of making up his own mind on the matter requiring decision.'

Based on Lord Scarman's reasoning, 'Gillick competence' refers to the ability of a young person under the age of 16 to consent to medical treatment. Such a young person would be able to demonstrate that they understand the nature and implications of their treatment – that they have the intelligence to appreciate the risks of the proposed and alternative courses of action. This understanding of the potential autonomy of the young person has been applied to medical and social care practice beyond the confines of contraceptive treatment. It has been found to provide legitimacy to the complex work of childcare professionals who may be seeking to support a young person whose views are at odds with those of their parents. In Chapter 1, we made some comparisons between the role of parents and the work of children's services practitioners. The notion of Gillick competence is equally important and should be taken into consideration when a young person disagrees with the decisions of professionals working with them. Professionals, like parents, do not always know best.

The Fraser guidelines

It was Lord Fraser who developed the principles and guidance in order to apply the concept of Gillick competence in practice. It is worth quoting Lord Fraser at length as he explained the process the medical practitioner should go through in considering cases where a young person may require contraceptive advice and treatment. In order to proceed without parental consent, he argued that the doctor involved (referred to in the ruling as 'he') should be satisfied in all the following respects:

- that the girl (although under 16 years of age) will understand his advice;
- that he cannot persuade her to inform her parents or to allow him to inform the parents that she is seeking contraceptive advice;
- that she is very likely to begin or to continue having sexual intercourse with or without contraceptive treatment;
- that unless she receives contraceptive advice or treatment her physical or mental health or both are likely to suffer;
- that her best interests require him to give her contraceptive advice, treatment or both without parental consent. (*Gillick* v. *West Norfolk*, 1985)

Although specific to the liaison of doctor and young person in relation to contraceptive treatment, the above points provide a useful way to approach work with a child where parental involvement or consent is problematic. However, implementing the Fraser guidelines also raises some ethical challenges.

Professionals might be concerned about the meaning and nature of 'persuasion' in this context. Mindful of the unequal power dynamics already impacting upon the relationship between adult and child, service user and professional, the main aim of a child-centred practitioner is to promote the agency of the young person, to empower them to make their own decision. *Persuading* a child who may have been reluctant to approach an adult, or to seek any advice, to talk to their parents may feel counterproductive and risks alienating the young person from the support that could have been offered by that professional on an ongoing basis. Having said that, professionals recognise that most parents share with them the aim of wishing to protect the best interests of the child. Even in situations where children may fear parental disapproval, disappointment or anger, with the support of a childcare professional, they may be enabled to involve their parents in their concerns and, possibly after some negotiation pertaining to the needs and wishes of the young person, they may be able to gain the more enduring support of their family.

Ethical dilemmas

Ethical issues have been raised around whether the notion of Gillick competence and the Fraser guidelines, developed specifically in relation to consent to medical treatment, can be applied to cases where children refuse life-saving treatment. There have been a number of cases involving young people who are clearly mature and intelligent, but who nevertheless refuse treatment. For example, in the case *Re E (a minor) (Wardship: Medical Treatment)* (1993), a 15-year-old boy suffering from leukaemia, who shared the Jehovah's Witness faith of his family, refused the blood transfusion that was needed to save his life. When he was made a Ward of Court, the judge ruled that the young man lacked competence due to the seriousness of the implications of his views, that is, a death that could be avoided, and authorised the transfusion. It could be argued that such decisions make a mockery of the notion of adolescent autonomy, as no young person has the right to refuse treatment that would save their lives, treatment that would be regarded as fundamentally in their best interests. Nevertheless, Downie (1999: 818) has argued: 'Where the life of the teenage patient is in danger, it is difficult to disagree with the conclusion that he should not be allowed to bring about his own death, however strong his objections to treatment … The court will base its decision on its view of the child's welfare; and it may, therefore, be preferable to avoid the process of finding him incompetent in order to legitimise such a decision.'

The right to life, article 6 of the UNCRC, is fundamental and most childcare professionals would agree that the welfare of the child should be the paramount consideration in such complex cases. Practitioners also need to fully consider the Human Rights Act 1998, as well as the European Convention on Human Rights (ECHR), in decision-making for children. Downie's views at the end of the twentieth century about the legitimacy of judgements pertaining to competence or incompetence remain a focus for debate. More recently, Archard and Skivenes (2009a) have argued that at times the decisions the Court (or professionals) are taking concerning children are so difficult that it is not surprising they may query the competence of the child to make their own decisions. The problems may be too complex, with too many variables beyond the control of the child and too many possible outcomes. There may be one clear choice (as in the case of *Re E*) but the implications are too enormous. The notion of Gillick competence, whereby a child would be able to weigh the risks of alternative actions and make a rational, autonomous choice, is perhaps too simplistic. Many adults similarly struggle to make rational decisions in complex and emotionally fraught situations. Archard and Skivenes conclude: 'We endorse the following principle of equity: a child should not be judged against a standard of competence by which even most adults would fail' (2009a: 10).

Contemporary practice in health and social care

Focus on Practice

The guidance to social workers provided in order to implement their statutory duties under the Children Act 1989 was updated in June 2015. Although specifically focused on work with looked-after children, the guidance is relevant to all practice involving work with a child to support them in decision-making. The guidance suggests that when assessing whether a particular child, on a particular occasion, has sufficient understanding to make a decision, the following questions should be considered:

- Can the child understand the question being asked of them?

- Do they appreciate the options open to them?

- Can they weigh up the pros and cons of each option?

- Can they express a clear personal view on the matter, as distinct from repeating what someone else thinks they should do?

- Can they be reasonably consistent in their view on the matter or are they constantly changing their mind?

(Department for Education, 2015b: 93–94)

The guidance also notes the importance of discussing with the child who are the people they might want to help them in making difficult decisions. Social workers can usefully take these questions into consideration when working with children in complex and uncertain situations.

It is worthwhile to bring this discussion into the twenty-first century by noting the case of Hannah Jones, which has had a similar social impact to the Gillick case, though a very different judicial trajectory. Reported by the *Guardian* newspaper on 11 November 2008, 13-year-old Hannah won her right to refuse the medical treatment that was being advised as essential to save her life. Having had a rare form of leukaemia from the age of four, she had experienced numerous medical interventions and after serious consideration Hannah decided that the heart transplant being urged upon her was one operation too many. Her parents supported her choice to die at home with dignity rather than endure further pain. The Hereford hospital initiated Court proceedings to enforce the treatment that they considered necessary. Significantly, the social worker in this case had an important impact on the outcome. In the words of Hannah's mother (reported in the *Guardian*): 'The child protection lady came, and she was fabulous. She listened to what Hannah wanted, she went to the barrister's chambers, and that ended proceedings.' The case was withdrawn when those involved agreed that Hannah was competent in making this major decision concerning her own life. Interestingly, Hannah decided some months later to go ahead with the transplant. In July 2009, reported in the *Guardian*, she said: 'I know I decided I definitely didn't want this, but everyone's entitled to change their mind.'

This case highlights many of the issues around capacity and capability for children and young people. The concept of fluctuating capacity is relevant for many children, as they may well change their opinion as they mature and gain different insights about their present situation and what they want for their future. What is clear is the importance of the support provided for Hannah by her parents, who gave her the time and care to reach her own judgements. Also of importance was the role played by the social worker and other professionals in the case who listened to Hannah and respected her ability to reach decisions and also to change her decision when faced with a complex life-threatening dilemma. Cornock (2010: 20), reviewing the case from a legal perspective, emphasised that 'consent is not an event, but a process', and that the professionals involved should ensure that they provide the support and information to enable children and young people to reach their own decisions when they are competent and wish to do so. Ruggeri and colleagues (2014) have noted a shift in contemporary medical practice from paternalistic approaches, whereby professionals and parents hold the authoritative role, to one that increasingly recognises the perspective of the child or young person as the determining factor. This is clearly relevant for social workers, who are often involved in children's lives when life-changing decisions are being taken.

Points for Reflection

- At what age do you think children should be able to express their views about matters affecting their lives?
- At what age do you think children should be able to make decisions for themselves?

- How have the Fraser guidelines informed your practice with a young person who was seeking your professional advice?

Commentary

The Fraser guidelines are helpful to consider in relation to social work practice with young people and decision-making in general. The practitioner needs to consider the impact of the decision on the child's physical and mental health, and ensure they are upholding the child's best interests. Taking a child-centred approach to practice provides no easy answers and there are many cases in which the ethical issues being decided are extremely difficult. It is worth remembering that when Victoria Gillick turned to the judicial process for the resolution of her question about the rights and capability of children pertaining to contraceptive treatment, it took three years, nine judges and the House of Lords to decide that children could be deemed competent.

The concept of 'persuasion', in relation to informing the child's parents, does not always sit comfortably with the child-centred practitioner. However, we must consider there are times when social workers legitimately use their powers of persuasion when working with children to promote their best interests. Consider, for example, how a practitioner might seek to persuade a young person at risk of sexual exploitation about what consent really means, in order to help them to make wise decisions. This may be seen by the social worker as an effort to apply benign influence in order to protect the young person from the malign influence of a potential abuser. The art of persuasion is embedded explicitly in the Fraser guidelines, though it is often implicit in adult–child communication. It is an important aspect of child-centred practice. Professionals must be mindful of power imbalances and use persuasion sparingly, in the context of an open and transparent dialogue with the young person that explores risks, duties, rights and responsibilities.

An understanding of Gillick competence and application of the Fraser guidelines is supportive of child-centred processes. However, assessment of the maturity of the child and the weight to be given to the child's perspective remains problematic. In order to explore these issues more fully it is pertinent to move on to an analysis of ideas around participation and how these are informing the development of child-centred practice in the twenty-first century.

The child's right to participation

Over recent years, understandings of children's rights have become synonymous with the concept of participation. Although the term is not part of the original text of article 12 of the UNCRC, the meaning has evolved and is now widely used in professional practice involving children and young people. The UN Committee on the Rights of the Child (2009) General Comment No. 12 considers the meaning of participation to describe: 'ongoing processes, which include information-sharing and dialogue between children and adults based on mutual respect, and in which children can learn how their views and those of adults are taken into account and shape the outcome of such processes.'

Participation is the most common term used for the process of listening to and engaging with children, however the exact definition remains contested; there is no one fixed meaning or definition which has universal agreement (Davey et al., 2010). A report published by the Children's Commissioner adapts the definition of participation developed by Treseder (1997) and emphasises that it is important to consider both how children are treated (process) and what the end result means for children (outcome): 'Participation is a process where someone influences decisions about their lives and this leads to change' (Davey et al., 2010: 6). The right to participate is not a right to decide outcomes; children may not want this responsibility or it may not be possible or appropriate for children to have the final say in all matters, but there should be some impact achieved through the process of participation, whether this is on the nature of the decision itself, how it is taken or implemented, or upon the attitudes and behaviours of those involved.

Points for Reflection

- What are your views about the child's right to participate?
- Can you give an example of how you have facilitated a child's participation in your own work?

Commentary

Children should not be pressurised, manipulated or constrained during participation. They have the right to express their views or choose not to. There is no minimum age by which children can participate; however, we must consider a child's evolving capacity for participation and decision-making.

For example:

David, a social worker, assisted Sally (12 years) and her sister Alice (4 years), to participate in their Initial Child Protection Conference. Sally presented as a quiet yet mature and articulate child, and Alice was very chatty and confident. Sally shared with David that she heard her parents argue at night and would go to her sister's room to ensure she was alright. Sally said sometimes Alice was crying, but Sally would hug and reassure her and she would go back to sleep. Sally said she had never talked to her parents about this and they thought she and Alice did not know about the violence in their relationship. Sally also said she knew her mother drank alcohol during the day, as she could smell it in the house when she returned from school and said her mother would often fall asleep. David asked Sally why she had never said anything before and she responded: 'You're the first person to ask me.' Alice was seen alone and was able to say that she was sometimes scared and sad at night-times. Alice drew a picture of her family, all with sad faces.

David was able to explain to Sally the reason for the Initial Child Protection Conference and what this meeting would be like. Sally wanted her views to be shared at the conference, but said she would find talking in front of the adults really hard and did not want to attend in person. Sally decided to write down her wishes and feelings to be shared in a letter to her parents. David attended the conference and read out Sally's letter. He also showed them Alice's picture. Sally's parents were both visibly upset, and it was noticeable to all the professionals that they took a few minutes to reflect on what they had heard and seen. The words of Sally were immensely powerful. Following the conference, David met with Sally and Alice on the same day to inform them of the outcome of the conference. Both children were made subject to child protection plans under the categories of neglect and emotional harm.

Citizenship and the Ladder of Participation

The right of any person to participate in the society of which one is a part has been linked to notions of citizenship. Sherry Arnstein, writing about how communities can be involved in and influence planning processes, made an important contribution to discussions about citizen's rights. She analysed the ways in which individuals are able to express opinions and exert influence in political, economic, social and administrative structures. Arnstein's ladder of citizenship (1969) is based on the recognition that people can be engaged and therefore included in society as citizens in different ways and at different levels. She also recognised that the way citizenship is experienced and enjoyed is rooted in the power relations that exist within any given society. For Arnstein, participation is central to notions of inclusion and citizenship; however, without genuine empowerment people may remain excluded and disenfranchised within their own communities. 'Participation without redistribution of power is an empty and frustrating process for the powerless. It allows the power holders to claim that all sides were considered but makes it possible for only some of these sides to benefit' (Arnstein 1969: 216).

Arnstein's approach has underpinned ideas around how young people evolve as citizens – their identity being tied in some respects to how well this is achieved. It can be said that the identity of the developing young person is founded upon participation: how integrated they are within mainstream society; how included or excluded they are from aspects of society that concern them; how able they feel to exert power about issues that matter to them. Contemporary commentators, such as Fattore and Mason (2005) and Jones and Walker (2011), emphasise that children are citizens in their own right and have the right to participate as citizens. Participation is more than a means to the end of enabling the development of healthy, integrated, included adults; children, like adults, have the right to participate in decisions, processes and systems that impact upon their lives.

The Ladder of Participation

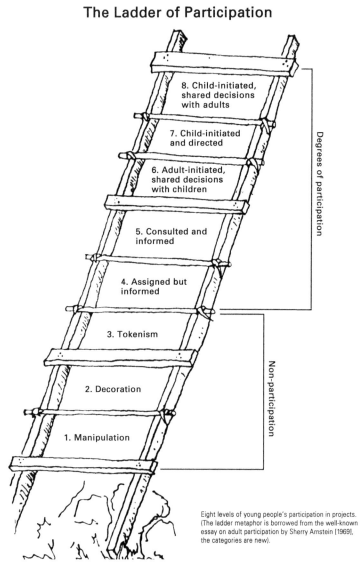

8. Child-initiated, shared decisions with adults

7. Child-initiated and directed

6. Adult-initiated, shared decisions with children

5. Consulted and informed

4. Assigned but informed

3. Tokenism

2. Decoration

1. Manipulation

Degrees of participation

Non-participation

Eight levels of young people's participation in projects. (The ladder metaphor is borrowed from the well-known essay on adult participation by Sherry Arnstein [1969], the categories are new).

Figure 2 The Ladder of Participation – R. Hart (1992: 8), reproduced with kind permission from UNICEF

The right to participation is therefore an end in itself, a fundamental right for all citizens and, therefore, for all children and young people.

Significantly, this right to participate as a citizen is not subjected to tests of competence. There is no discussion of age limits or levels of maturity. The aim is to enable the participation of the child, irrespective of age or ability, in all matters that pertain to their welfare. According to Archard and Skivenes (2009b: 393) the child should be seen as the: 'principle participant in any proceeding – administrative or judicial – which considers his or her interests.' Nevertheless, application of this principle of participation into practice is often not straightforward. Recognising the challenges of participation practice, Arnstein's model has been adapted by Roger Hart (1992) and applied to examine levels of participation in professional work with children and young people (Figure 2). Hart's model recognises that participation may be viewed as a process and that different levels may be realisable in different situations. The lower rungs of the ladder, from 1 to 3, can be seen as non-participation, whereby the involvement of children is superfluous to or overridden by the adult agenda. For the child-centred practitioner, attainment of partnership practice is the aim, whereby young people are empowered to participate as joint stakeholders with the adults involved in the decision-making process (Thomas and O'Kane, 1998).

Points for Reflection

- Consider a piece of work you have undertaken with a child or young person. How would you assess the participation of the child in this work in terms of Hart's (1992) Ladder of Participation?

- Can you give an example of social work with a child or young person that you would rate on the highest rungs of the ladder?

- How is social work with children on the lowest rungs of the ladder different to work on the highest rungs of the ladder?

Commentary

It is always useful to assess the level at which children are involved and engaged in your own work. Hart's model allows practitioners to challenge themselves and their approach, and helps to develop an awareness of and avoidance of tokenism and manipulation. It enables practitioners to be honest about the influence children they work with can have, as well as addressing issues in relation to why some children may have a lower level of engagement.

Work in which children would be placed on the highest rungs of the ladder may be where children collaborate with adults and share decision-making; they are respected as stakeholders; or are involved in designing, facilitating and running activities. Children who are looked after, for example, are able to form Youth Councils and contribute to policy or practice developments in their Local Authority. Lower-level involvement would include children being passive or excluded, with adults taking the lead; or work where adults hold most of the power.

You should not feel that work is not valuable unless children are actively sharing in every aspect of the decision-making process. What we know, however, is that when children are given the opportunity to contribute or take the lead, they gain confidence, knowledge and a sense of achievement.

Participation and decision-making processes

In a study undertaken by the Children's Commissioner in England, it was found that children were not always supported effectively to participate in decisions about their lives. The young people held reasonable expectations of being listened to and involved, but found that practice was not always based on child-centred principles. The report concluded:

> Children accepted the inherent power difference in the adult-child relationship, although they were more likely to negotiate this power difference as they grew older. What they did not accept, however, was the low status adults often accorded to children's opinions and the lack of explanation on how children's opinions had been taken into account during a decision-making process. Irrespective of the setting in which a decision was being made, the effect of not being listened to was to leave children feeling belittled, powerless and undervalued. (Davey, 2010: 42)

Child-centred practice involves taking children seriously, valuing their contribution and considering how to enable their participation.

There are times when difficult decisions are taken about the life of a child where adult opinions are likely to be determinative. For example, when a parent makes a decision about their own future that necessarily impacts upon the child, when a medical professional explains what course of treatment is necessary for the child's particular health condition or when a social worker recommends a child protection plan at a Case Conference. Parents and professionals bring knowledge that the child may not have to inform their decisions. Childcare professionals bring expertise about what interventions may be effective based on the evidence from research and from their holistic assessment of the family situation. However, in all these instances, the child's involvement will be important, should be influential and may be decisive. The parent may reconsider their options when faced with the reality of the impact of their choice upon their child and the child's concerns. Although the medical professional may be able to judge the normative issue of the best available treatment, they may not be best qualified to consider how the child feels about the kind of life they want to live and the level of medical interference (including the likelihood of pain, upheaval and disruption) they are willing to endure. For the childcare professional committed to evidence-based practice, the child's perspective is a key part of the evidence to be considered and their views about the proposed intervention are likely to impact on whether it will be effective and by whose terms effectiveness should be measured.

In some aspects of social work practice, the power of the professionals and organisations involved and the nature of the issues being addressed will mean that it is neither possible nor appropriate for children to initiate or control the decisions (rungs 7 and 8 of Hart's ladder). Statutory processes have been developed to manage complex practice issues, such as safeguarding strategy meetings and court proceedings that might involve children but cannot be led by them. However, the right to participate is about being involved in decision-making, making a contribution, expressing one's views, being listened to and influencing the process and the outcomes. The right to participate is distinct from the right to be self-determining. We have noted in Chapter 1 Eekelaar's (1994) ideas about dynamic self-determinism and how decisions pertaining to children and young people need to adapt as children mature and their understanding and ability to decide for themselves develops. This is in line with the Gillick ruling and resonates with the case of Hannah Jones, discussed in this chapter. Bell (2011: 11) makes the important point that: 'not all children wish to participate either in individual decisions or in matters of public concern. For them, respect and fairness may be more important than participation per se.'

Shier (2001) encourages practitioners to consider which of the five levels of participation (rungs 4 to 8 of the ladder) is most relevant to their work with a particular child, from listening and information-sharing through to sharing power. He suggests that workers and organisations should think about how to enable the involvement of children in all aspects of their work through promoting opportunities for participation and being aware of statutory and ethical obligations. Thomas (2002) has noted the importance of the child or young person being able to exercise choice about their participation. This includes having information about their situation and their rights, and support to speak out if they choose to do so. Some commentators have adapted Hart's model to emphasise a non-hierarchical process whereby it is acknowledged that different levels of participation are appropriate for different tasks, depending on the outcomes to be achieved, the role and duties of professionals and the wishes of the child around how much they want to be involved. Kirby and colleagues (2003) provide a useful adaptation that is circular and process-based, recognising that practice is fluid and that at different times children and social workers may work together in different ways (Figure 3).

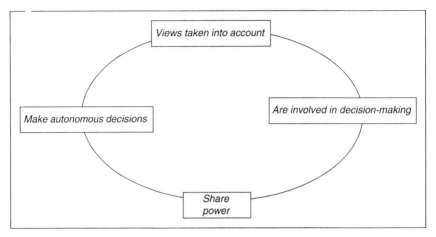

Figure 3 Kirby and colleagues' (2003) model of participation

The challenges of participatory practice

Hart's model, nevertheless, remains pertinent in recognising that, at times, professional involvement with children falls far below the standards of ethical participatory practice. Considerable research has been carried out over recent years exploring the factors that hinder participation practice, meaning that professional work is undertaken with children on the lowest three rungs of the ladder. Significantly, these factors often hinge upon the views and values of childcare professionals, some of whom are concerned about issues of capability.

When Sanders and Mace examined children's participation in child protection, they noted that 'insufficient age and understanding' (2006: 94) was often cited by social workers as the reason why children had not been consulted or included in any way in decision-making processes. Furthermore, Spyrou (2011) has recognised the concerns of practitioners about the 'authenticity' of the child's voice. Children are involved in complex power relations with the adults in their lives, in particular with parents and carers; in many cases it can be difficult, if not impossible, to disentangle the genuine wishes and feelings of the child from the influence of those adults. Similarly, for the professional to find a neutral means of ascertaining the views of the child and to pass them on within adult-centric spheres of decision-making, without undue influence or contamination, is a further challenge. Some professionals therefore question the capability of children to participate in any meaningful way. However, it can be seen that adults also struggle at times to make complex decisions and may be influenced by others in ways that might not always be benign. Such concerns are not reasons to deny individuals their rights. According to Alderson (1983: 158): 'competence is more influenced by the social context and the child's experience than by innate ability and to respect children means we must not think in sharp dichotomies of wise adult/immature child, ... but to see wisdom and uncertainty shared among people of varying ages and experiences.'

Handley and Doyle (2014) have commented on the endeavours of practitioners to promote the genuine participation of children, including the very young and those who may be seen by some to lack capability. Concerns for these child-centred practitioners is not the capability of the child, but anxieties around professional capability; about their own lack of skills and training to engage effectively with children. Commentators such as Donnelly (2010) and Winter (2011b) have emphasised the importance of the development of skills, competence and capability in professionals to enable all children to access and exercise their participation rights in ways that make sense to the child and are appropriate to their level of maturity. The knowledge and skills statement for child and family social work (Department for Education, 2014d) recognises the need for practitioners to be able to communicate effectively with young people of different ages and abilities in order to engage them purposefully in direct work. We discuss more fully in Chapter 5 the importance of professional skills in communicating with children.

Paternalism and protectionism or rights and participation

It is clear that the beliefs and values of professionals concerning children impact upon participation practice. Ideas about children's rights and participation lie at the centre of contested discourses about the nature of childhood (Sanders and Mace, 2006). Professionals are, of course, influenced by, and reflect in their practice, wider systems of belief in society about children, about how they should be viewed and treated. Mayall (1994) highlighted that the way in which adults conceptualise children and their capability directly impacts upon children's ability to participate and their level of power or powerlessness in different social settings.

Vis and colleagues (2012) discuss the differing views that professionals may hold on a continuum from child liberation (supporting children's rights to decide for themselves) to paternalism (believing that adults usually know what is best for children). Shemmings' (2000) research found that social workers tended to adopt one of two dichotomous positions: a *rights* approach, recognising the agency of children and promoting their participation, or a *rescue* position, seeing primarily the vulnerability of children and their need to be protected. Some workers hold a particular view of childhood that means they want to preserve the innocence of the child and protect them from distressing information about their family situation. Childcare practitioners steeped in the safeguarding agenda, working with children who have experienced adversity and trauma, understandably recognise the victimhood and vulnerability of children and are rightly keen to ensure that children are protected from further stress, pain or anxiety. However, concerns arise when the duty to protect the child slips into an approach that Vis and colleagues (2012: 19) have described as *protectionism,* an ideological approach that inhibits the rights of the child and tends towards risk-averse practice:

Protectionism may be used to describe the action of restricting the information that children are given, the people they are allowed to meet with or the discussions they are allowed to participate in, with the intent to protect them from possible disturbing or upsetting experiences. When what is done in the name of protection goes at the expense of children's participatory rights, and when all aspects of a case are viewed in terms of risk and danger, protection turns to protectionism.

It is evident that values based on paternalism and protectionism will lead to practice that underestimates the capability of the child and fails to promote their right to participate. To return to the UNCRC, although the Convention does not specifically use the term participation, it is clear that the right of the child to be involved in all matters and decisions pertaining to their welfare is fundamentally embedded within it. This is not dependent on the views of the adults involved or their concerns about the capabilities or vulnerabilities of the child. More recently, the UN (2009: 6) has emphasised the importance of the assumption of the capability of the child: 'State parties should presume that a child has the capacity to form her or his views and recognise that she or he has the right to express them.' The UN General Comment goes on to note the obligation placed upon professionals to create opportunities for children to freely express their views and to exercise their right to participate.

Participation and decision-making, consultation and evaluation

Legal and policy requirements to consult with children and young people about the services they receive have led to innovations in practice in order to take seriously children's participation in planning and feedback processes. Godar (2015) has highlighted how developments, such as Children in Care Councils and the increasing attention given by Ofsted to young people's involvement in evaluation of services, have led to initiatives within Local Authorities to organise meetings and feedback opportunities in order to hear the voice of children and young people and enable their contribution to service design and delivery. When we assume the capability of children and young people, it becomes clear that they should be consulted about the kinds of services being developed for them and that they should be the ones to evaluate whether those services are effective. There is much to learn from the experience of children and young people involved in these processes.

Learning from Research

The principal policy adviser for the Children's Commissioner, Jane Clifton (2014), consulted with children who had experience of receiving services as 'children in need' (s 17 of the Children Act, 1989). The aim of the project was to hear from young people about how they might feed back their views about what helped them, whether adults made things better and what could be improved.

Five key messages summarise the findings from this consultation and include some of the points made by the young people:

- *'It has to be the norm to listen to young people.'* If only adults come up with questions and ideas, they will miss what really matters to children. *'Young people see things adults don't see.'* An example of good practice young people considered important was that their views were included specifically in all written plans about them.

- *'You've really got to trust them.'* Young people wanted to build trust with their social workers so that they could feel able to give feedback to them. Building a relationship with professionals and feeling that their views mattered was of great importance to young people. How they expected feedback to be received – particularly if this was negative – would influence the likelihood of young people giving it.

- *'Not all young people are the same.'* Young people wanted to be seen as individuals and have a choice of ways to present their views according to their needs. For example, a group of young people with special needs wanted to give feedback as a group as this would make them feel stronger; they also wanted more visual and creative approaches. Young people sometimes wanted to be able to give feedback anonymously and to be supported by an independent advocate.

- *'It's about starting a conversation.'* Young people wanted to give feedback through face-to-face conversations so they could hear back from adults. Young people also wanted to understand more about the processes and roles of those working in the child protection and care systems.

- *'It's the actions afterwards that have the impact.'* It was important to the young people that their feedback had some influence, they wanted to be informed about what would happen next and to have an explanation if something could not be changed. *'We want to see the differences – that's important to us.'* Feedback to young people after they have been consulted is vital to young people.

From a child-centred perspective, it can be seen that the child's view about their own best interests is at least as legitimate and valuable as anyone else's; it should be the most important perspective that adults take into consideration in any decision-making process impacting upon the child. Children should be seen as major stakeholders and, as such, if their views are not taken forward, this must be justifiable in terms of their best interests. Children have a right not only to have a say when it comes to decisions about their life, but to be informed of the reasons for the decisions, if their voice is not the decisive one. To return to the UN General Comment (2009: 11), if children can form their own views in a 'reasonable and independent manner', it is incumbent upon the decision-maker to recognise the views of the child 'as a significant factor in the settlement of the issue'.

Involving children in decision-making forums, consultation and evaluation processes is of central importance for the adults and agencies involved, as well as for the children. If children are listened to and their views are valued, they feel more able to participate. According to Archard and Skivenes (2009b: 392):

'children's ability to participate in processes determinative of their own interests is precisely enhanced by granting them proper opportunities to do so.' The following model illustrates the ways in which the child-centred practitioner might apply these principles in practice. The circular, dynamic nature of the model (devised by the authors, responding to Kirby et al., 2003) recognises that the values and approach of the professional impacts on the process and outcome of the particular piece of work for the child. The model takes an empowerment approach, recognising that positive practice in one piece of work can have a knock-on effect for the child, in terms of their long-term well-being and their ability to participate positively in future decision-making processes (Figure 4):

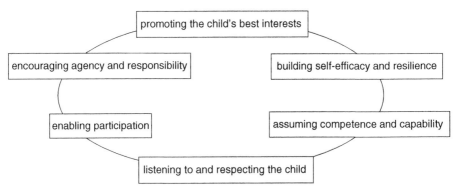

Figure 4 Circular model: promoting the child's best interests and right to participate

Conclusion

For the child-centred practitioner it is clear that there are many challenges in seeking to promote the rights of the child, to enable their participation and to ensure that their welfare remains the paramount concern. All the articles of the UNCRC are equally important and all need to be implemented to ensure children can exercise their rights. It is not possible to promote children's best interests without taking the time to listen to their views. Respecting the rights of children means working with humility, acknowledging that adults do not have the monopoly when it comes to wisdom and recognising that children have a legitimate and valuable contribution to make. Recognising the importance of participation, and that it is the responsibility of the practitioner to enable the child to fulfil their participatory rights, is central to effective social work practice. The key to managing the challenges inherent in promoting children's rights is to maintain a focus on the child, recognising the child as a person with capabilities, needs and views and enabling them to exercise their right to participate in all aspects of the work.

Recommended reading and resources

- Rebecca Godar's (2015) chapter 'The hallmarks of effective participation' (in the book *Voice of the Child*, edited by Mark Ivory for Research in Practice) provides an overview of the characteristics of good practice that support the participation of children and young people. It is a useful discussion of interest for practitioners and managers.

- The article by Karen Winter (2011a) 'The UNCRC and social workers' relationships with young children' explores the opportunities and challenges presented to social workers by the framework for children's rights provided by the UNCRC.

- Margaret Bell (2011) has written a comprehensive guide for practitioners about what participatory practice means and how to develop this approach: *Promoting Children's Rights in Social Work and Social Care.*

- Phil Jones and Gary Walker (2011) have edited a useful textbook that contributes to the debates around children's rights and shares the perspectives of a range of childcare disciplines: *Children's Rights in Practice.*

- United Nations (2009) General Comment No. 12, 'The right of the child to be heard'. Although written in a legalistic style the document provides a summary of the insightful discussion of the UN Committee about the meaning and implementation of article 12. It can be accessed at: www2.ohchr. org/english/bodies/crc/docs/AdvanceVersions/CRC-C-GC-12.pdf

- UNICEF has produced a factsheet providing a concise and helpful summary of the child's right to participation and what this means in the light of the UNCRC: www.unicef.org/crc/files/Right-to-Participation.pdf

- International children's charity Save the Children has developed a comprehensive and practical guide to children's participation. It contains a useful toolkit of activities to enable children's participation in a range of projects: www.savethechildren.org.uk/sites/default/files/docs/Putting_Children_at_ the_Centre_final_(2)_1.pdf

3

UNDERSTANDING CHILDREN

Introduction

Whilst recognising that uncertainty and risk are features of all our work, social workers nevertheless draw upon an extensive body of research and theory that informs our practice, providing evidence upon which to base decisions intended to increase the likelihood of positive outcomes for children and young people. Although we cannot know what the future holds for the children we work with, knowledge drawn from psycho-social perspectives increases our understanding of the impact of factors such as developmental stage, family background and social environment on the life chances of the children we are working with. The 'nature versus nurture' debate seems to have burned out and there is increasing recognition that human beings are formed through the unique interplay of innate and environmental factors that combine to mould the mature individual. The Department for Education statement about the knowledge and skills required by social workers emphasises the need for an understanding of child development that enables us to 'critically evaluate theory and research findings and demonstrate informed use in practice of typical age related physical, cognitive, social, emotional and behavioural development, and the influence of cultural and social factors on child development' (Department for Education, 2014). In Chapters 3 and 4, we explore some valuable contributions to our knowledge base that increase our ability to understand children, within their family and community context, in order to develop effective and sensitive child-centred practice.

In this chapter, we focus on exploring the nature of childhood and theories of child development in relation to child-centred practice. We recognise that the way in which we make sense of childhood is socially constructed, acknowledging that ideas about children have evolved historically and are culturally variable. The chapter offers an overview of theories about child development that have been particularly influential, noting the contribution of developmental psychologists such as Piaget and Erikson, and linking these to child-centred practice. Attention is given to the ages and stages of child development, recognising the importance of understanding the needs and respecting the rights of children as they mature from infancy to adulthood. We note the contribution made to contemporary thinking about childhood from developments in neuroscience. These areas of knowledge are valuable in informing our understanding of children and what it means to practice in a child-centred manner. However, each area of knowledge is vast in its own right and it is not possible to explore all these areas in depth. The reader is directed to other sources at the end of the chapter to support continued learning. A thorough understanding of child development is essential for the child-centred practitioner and wider reading in this area is recommended by the authors.

Practitioner Testimonial

I am a Children's Guardian; part of my work is ensuring that the child's voice is heard within the court arena. I work directly with children to listen to their wishes and feelings; this can sometimes involve the use of practice tools such as emotion stickers. When understanding children's circumstances and situations, I use the welfare checklist as set out within section 1 of the Children Act 1989, which allows me to think about the child, what his or her needs are and what the issues affecting them are. It is also of great importance to think about diversity issues such as race, religion, disability and so on. Diversity is about recognising uniqueness. Every child is unique; their circumstances are unique to them and them alone. There should be no blanket approach to assessing what is right for the child; every assessment has a bespoke element to it – that being the child.

Steven Anderson, Social Worker, Children and Family Court
Advisory and Support Service.

Understanding childhood

Understanding children could be seen as straightforward. Children are after all people, individuals, younger versions of adults. Many of us are involved in raising children in our own families or have strong relationships with children. We have all been children. Nevertheless, how we understand childhood is a developing field of knowledge and the focus of debate. There are complexities and contradictions in the way society understands and manages its younger citizens. To make sense of childhood, and the significance of theory to support child-centred practice, it is helpful to explore contemporary sociological perspectives.

Childhood as a social construct

Social constructionism is a theoretical approach that explores the way in which ideas are developed that form the basis of assumptions or accepted understandings about reality. It is important to recognise that ideas about children are not static; how we understand childhood varies across cultures and has changed over time. Analysis of the socially constructed nature of childhood was developed by French historian Philippe Ariès, who rejected the view of childhood as biologically specified, a universal and enduring feature of all human societies. Ariès (1961) argued that notions of childhood developed alongside social and economic changes, so that childhood as a concept, as a special and set-apart phase of human life, only came into being during the seventeenth century. From this perspective, childhood in modern Western societies is viewed as a particular set of constructs, of ideas, beliefs, values and sentiments that impact upon the way adults understand and behave towards children. How childhood is defined and what distinguishes this stage of life from adulthood raises questions that challenge the perspective that childhood is a purely natural phenomenon, universally distinct from the mature majority.

Perspectives of childhood became a focus for sociological study and debate towards the end of the twentieth century. John Holt (1975) argued that children should not be excluded from any of the rights, privileges and responsibilities of adulthood. He noted that children tend to be viewed as the property of their parents or the State, and that a society predicated upon children's dependence and incompetence would nurture those characteristics, rather than enable children to be independent and competent on their own terms. He observed that: 'being a child means being wholly subservient and dependent … being seen by older people as a mixture of expensive nuisance, slave and super-pet' (Holt, 1975: 1). In response to Holt's radical perspective, Freeman (1983) argued that we may need to change the way in which we understand childhood but it would be unwise to ignore the existence of a stage of life universally recognised as childhood. Contemporary commentators have agreed on the need to promote the rights of children, but not necessarily to do away with the notion of childhood altogether. There is recognition that the physical and psychological differences between adults and children mean that the former provide supervision, protection and support for the latter. The extreme dependence of infants upon adults for their survival and well-being cannot be ignored. In all societies there is acknowledgement that children are different from adults in some ways, and that this means adults have responsibilities to ensure the welfare of children as they grow up.

Having said that, there are cultural differences in the way children are perceived and the role they play in their communities. According to Rogoff (1990), Western liberal societies tend to segregate children, regarding them as different and special, but also isolating them from the business of the adult world. Children in the developing world are integrated more fully into the day-to-day life of the community, sharing responsibilities with adult family members for work and care. The capability of children is assumed and they are ensured a role in social life as participants or close observers. Furthermore, Western concepts of childhood difference are being eroded by recognition of the inadequacy of ideas about the superior competence of adults. The assumption that competence is developed along a linear trajectory advancing from childhood ignorance and naivety to adult capability and mastery is being increasingly challenged. Studies of adult rationality highlight how mature thought processes are riddled with cognitive biases and emotional dead ends. As expressed by researchers of judgement and decision-making, Albert and Steinberg: 'if the road of normative development leads to logically rigorous decision making, most adults fail to reach the destination' (2011: 214). We could conclude, as did Freeman (1983), that whilst children are different from adults in some ways, they are not that different.

Tensions in contemporary constructions of childhood

How children are perceived and understood in contemporary Western society is characterised by tension and contradiction. An example of this is the way in which different ages are designated by legal statute to entitle children to access particular privileges or responsibilities of adulthood. Interestingly, young people aged between 16 and 17 were invited to participate in the decision-making process to decide the nation state of their homeland in the Scottish Referendum in 2014. Those same young people and their counterparts in other parts of the UK, however, were deemed not competent to participate in local and national elections a few months later. Despite the paternalism that colours attitudes towards children and young people, when it comes to crime and deviance children are seen as responsible for their own actions at a relatively young age. The age at which children in England, Wales and Northern Ireland are seen as capable of standing trial and being convicted of a criminal offence is 10 years. In 2016, the Scottish Government initiated plans to increase the minimum age of criminal responsibility from 8 to 12 years. However, when it comes to school attendance, it is parents who are held responsible if the law is broken by their child failing to attend; the parent, rather than the child, incurs the penalty of fines or imprisonment. In much else related to education, despite the fact that children spend much of their lives in school, they have little influence over decisions about the curriculum or day-to-day school life. In an article in the *Guardian* newspaper (printed on 28 March 2015) a GCSE student wrote: 'I read education-related news articles. They often seem to be about exam reform. Conspicuously absent are the opinions of actual students. I'm not saying I have all the answers, just that occasionally it could help to listen to a teenager.' Listening to children and recognising their capability, as we have learned, are significant underpinning principles of child-centred practice.

Notions of power are inherent to understanding the status of children in contemporary society, as noted in Chapter 1. A social constructionist perspective recognises that children inhabit a social space that is not only different from that of adults but also subordinate (Qvortrup et al., 1994). A universal aspect of childhood is the way that children are disadvantaged and excluded in terms of access to resources, rights and decision-making processes. James and colleagues (1998) defined children as a minority group, emphasising that they are participants in an adult-centric culture, experiencing inequality due to their minority role and status. Nevertheless, Mayall (1994) has argued that there are variations in the levels of powerlessness children experience and this goes back to differences in the ways in which adults conceptualise children. She notes that in most families, children tend to be viewed as able to contribute towards household decisions and plans; therefore, power is negotiated more in the home setting than in the school environment or other social contexts. D'Cruz and Stagnitti (2008: 156) have argued that the child in the context of child welfare, and even more so in child safeguarding practice, tends to be seen as 'the dependent waif on whose behalf professionals representing the state intervene'. We recognised in Chapter 2 that notions of protectionism lead to approaches that aim to rescue the child, so that powerful adults speak, act and ascribe meaning to the child's experiences. From a child-centred perspective, even when intervening to safeguard the most vulnerable children, professionals should ensure that the rights of the child to participate and have a voice are also protected. Child-centred practitioners must continue to struggle to make sense of contemporary ideas of childhood, despite their inherent tensions and contradictions, seeking to understand children and promote their rights.

The new sociology of childhood

Since the 1990s there has been a fundamental shift in how childhood is understood and a new paradigm of childhood studies has emerged. Given impetus by the almost universal ratification of the UNCRC and critical of dominant perspectives characterising children as developmentally inferior in comparison to adults, the new sociology of childhood emphasises children as active social agents, whose lives and identities are regulated by social systems organised by adults. According to James and Prout (1997: 7): 'the immaturity of children is a biological fact of life but the ways in which it is understood and made meaningful is a fact of culture.' They further argue that dominant cultural views of childhood, generated by powerful adults, constrain how children see themselves, how they are able to grow up and live their lives within their own families and communities. Whether society views children as vulnerable, immature and incomplete humans, or as individuals, citizens and social agents, therefore, impacts on the scope for the child to be their own person.

The new sociology of childhood (Wyness, 2011; James and James, 2012) recognises children as active citizens in society, capable agents in decision-making and able to participate and make a valid contribution. Whilst adults may possess expert knowledge in certain areas, children are experts in their own lives. Child-centred practice would support this stance, recognising that children have a superior understanding of what it means to be a child. Both adults and children possess competence and knowledge, but they may be specialists in different fields. According to Gallacher and Gallagher (2008: 503): 'Children actively shape and organise the world around them – often independently of adults and sometimes in spite of them.'

It is important to recognise that despite having capability, capacity and expertise in many areas, children's lives are constrained and organised by social factors outside their control. Children are not autonomous beings; they develop their identity and sense of self within the cultural context of their family and community. To gain a holistic understanding of childhood, we explore these aspects of children's lives more fully in Chapter 4. In this chapter, we acknowledge that children are unique, competent individuals, as well as emergent beings. Child-centred practitioners endeavour to understand and respect the authentic self of the child, promoting their rights and agency, whilst also appreciating that children are immersed in the process of growing, developing and becoming. Paying attention to theories about the biological and cognitive development of children, developmental milestones and how environmental factors impact on social and emotional behaviour assist us in making sense of childhood and seeking to understand the particular child.

Points for Reflection

- In what ways do you think children are different from adults?

- Think back to your own childhood – how different or similar are you now in relation to yourself as a child?

Theories of child development

Psychological theory provides important knowledge to enable professionals to consider the ways in which children may be similar to and different from adults, in order to develop evidence-based and sensitive child-centred practice. There are a range of theories that enable practitioners to understand the normative developmental tasks that are the prerequisites of healthy growth towards maturity (Bee and Boyd, 2014). Although it is beyond the scope of this book to do justice to the tomes of literature relating to child development, it is useful to refer to some of the key theorists whose work continues to have relevance when applied to social work practice.

The contribution of Piaget

Piaget was a clinical psychologist who pioneered research around how children develop. He was the first psychologist to systematically study the way in which children learn to think, play and make sense of their world. Prior to Piaget, people tended to believe that children think in ways that are inferior to and less competent than adults. Piaget (1936) came to see that children think differently to adults; he argued that children are biologically induced to understand the world in different ways, at different stages of their development.

Learning from Research

From his extensive studies into the nature of childhood cognitive development, Piaget defined four stages that children experience as they mature:

- *Sensorimotor – from birth to 2 years:* The infant begins to explore their world primarily by their interaction with objects through their senses. They touch and grasp objects, put them in their mouth, drop them.

- *Preoperational – ages 2 to 6 years:* Children become able to attend to features of things beyond the sensory. They are able to use words, hold mental images and understand symbols. They use objects symbolically to represent other things in their play, a box becoming a house or a train. Children tend to be egocentric, absorbed in their own play and may struggle to recognise another person's point of view.

- *Concrete operational – ages 7 to 11 years:* Abstract cognitive abilities develop so that children are able to work out more complex problems. They are able to think logically and are less egocentric. They are better at conservation tasks, understanding that when the appearance of something changes the thing itself does not, for example they appreciate that the volume of water might remain the same even when it is poured into different sized jugs.

- *Formal operations stage – 11 years plus:* Children are able to think in more abstract, logical ways, reasoning about objects without their physical presence. They can work out complex problems, using scientific, rational processes and communicate their solutions in a sophisticated manner.

For Piaget (1936, 1957), the developing child is an active agent, biologically driven to explore and to learn, to make sense of the world through a process of adaptation. He used the term schema to refer to the basic building blocks of knowledge; he described how children are able to make sense of increasingly complex schema as they mature and that humans reach a state of equilibrium (or mental balance) when they are able to make sense of what they perceive around them. Piaget explained a process of assimilation and accommodation, whereby infants adapt to changing environments and learn new schema to make sense of changing situations. He spoke of equilibration as a force that drives children forward through the process of learning, from frustration and disequilibrium towards mastery of new challenges and the restoration of balance. The child's innate drive to learn enables them to acquire and assimilate new information and adjust their schema accordingly in order to gain new understandings as they mature (McLeod, 2015).

Piaget's model of cognitive psychology continues to be useful in contemporary practice. He emphasised the ways in which children are different from adults and sought to acknowledge the validity of the child's cognitive processes. He focused on biological and psychological development, noting how the capacity of the human brain to think and reason advances with age and maturity; he also acknowledged the importance of a nurturing environment to enable children to reach their potential. For the contemporary social worker, recognising the child's inner drive to explore, to play and to learn is essential in understanding children and supporting families to provide the care and opportunities children need to thrive. The child-centred practitioner will draw from Piaget an appreciation of the ways in which children seek to make sense of and adapt to their environment. This includes recognising how some children learn to accommodate circumstances that may be impacting negatively on their welfare. For example, if children learn that their environment is unsafe and unpredictable, they may adapt to this by developing strategies of self-reliance, being well-defended in personal relationships. Appreciation of the inner drive within the child to learn, adjust their schema and to achieve equilibrium provides hope that children are able to develop new adaptations and do well, often beyond expectations, as professionals and carers work together to enhance opportunities for healthy cognitive development.

Piaget's theory is open to criticism. He tested his theories with few participants, mainly his own children and those of friends and colleagues. Psychologists such as Donaldson (1986) have criticised Piaget for failing to recognise the logical capacities of younger children and for conducting tests that were confusing or lacked meaning for children. Thomas and O'Kane (2000: 830) have noted that: 'children's competence sometimes depends on whether it is tested in ways that make sense to them.' Studies have highlighted the failure of many adults to complete Piaget's tests for formal operational cognitive ability, emphasising that children and adults might not be so very different after all. Child-centred practitioners recognise the capabilities of children, including young children, and seek to engage with them in ways that are meaningful for them.

The importance of social context for learning and development

Piaget developed his theory of cognitive development based on studies of how children interact with objects in their environment, with emphasis on distinct phases of development. Vygotsky was a Russian psychologist working at the same time as Piaget whose work led him to rather different conclusions. Vygotsky came to see child development as more of a continuous process and placed emphasis on the importance of the child's social interactions as the key to their learning. According to Vygotsky (1978, 1986), children develop their ability to think, acquire language and learn through their interaction with more knowledgeable others. Through working together with a more able peer or adult, undertaking mutual tasks pitched just beyond the child's level of mastery, known as the 'zone of proximal development', children gain the support or 'scaffolding' they need to develop their independent skills and abilities. Like Piaget, he emphasised the importance of play and the unique role of the imagination to enable learning about the world. He noted that children absorb and apply social rules through their imaginative play, for example adopting the roles of family members and imitating observed behaviours in their make-believe worlds. From this perspective, greater emphasis is placed on the importance of the wider family and cultural context in guiding both the way children learn and the meanings they derive by which they come to understand their world.

Social learning theorist Albert Bandura (1977) took these ideas forward by emphasising the way in which children learn through attending to and imitating the behaviour of others – their own behaviour then being positively or negatively reinforced depending on the reaction of others. How children identify with and model the behaviours of those around them, thereby learning not just how to behave, but also how to think and feel, fundamentally moulding their own attitudes and values, emphasises the importance of the social and cultural context for healthy child development. These theoretical approaches enable the child-centred practitioner to recognise the importance of the child's environment both in promoting learning and positive development and in moulding how the child makes sense of their world, the social rules and cultural meanings they assimilate (Nicolson, 2014). The child-centred social worker will therefore take the time to get to know the child and their immediate family, those in close relationships with the child, to gain a full understanding of the child's world and the meanings they ascribe to their life and circumstances.

Erikson's lifespan model of development

Building on these psychological theories which had focused particularly on cognition and learning, Erikson (1963, 1968) developed a psycho-social model of development, seeking to understand and explain the human life cycle within the cultural context, with emphasis on identity formation. He was particularly interested in how children socialise and develop a sense of self through their interactions with others; he identified particular crises that humans must resolve in order to function in society and develop their own identity. He developed a lifespan model of development, with eight stages from birth to old age; we will note the five stages of childhood:

- *Trust versus mistrust – from birth to around 18 months:* For the dependent infant whether the world is a safe place or not will depend on how secure they feel in the care offered by their parents and carers. Consistent and reliable nurturance will enable a baby to feel secure and develop trust in others. Lack of safe care will lead to a sense of insecurity, anxiety in relationships and mistrust in one's own ability to influence the world.

- *Autonomy versus shame – from age 18 months to 3 years:* As the infant develops physically and becomes more aware of their own skills and separate self, parents and carers need to provide opportunities for children to practise autonomy and to realise the limits of their abilities. Children are able to develop a sense of achievement and, when they fail, are to be encouraged and supported to keep trying. Children who are criticised or overly controlled will feel doubt about their ability to survive and shame about their lack of ability.

- *Initiative versus guilt – from ages 3 to 5:* As children start school and move in wider social circles, they are able to initiate play with their peers and develop confidence in their ability to be autonomous and purposeful in their activities. Children are encouraged to assert themselves, though boundaries and appropriate limits are needed to enable self-control.

- *Industry and competence versus inferiority – from ages 5 to 12:* Children will have opportunities to develop skills and prowess. Achievement will lead to increased autonomy and competence. Nurturance of talents by family, peers and school, as well as support in failure, will enable children to be confident and also appropriately modest.

- *Identity versus role confusion – from ages 12 to 18:* Children are able to explore and test out who they are and how they cope in the wider world. Young people develop a reintegrated sense of self as an emerging adult, with increasing understanding of their sexual identity and their future occupational role. A young person who successfully negotiates this stage of development will have a positive sense of their own identity and be able to form intimate relationships, rather than experiencing identity crisis and isolation.

For the child-centred practitioner, Erikson's model enables an understanding of the stages and process of child development. There is an emphasis on the psycho-social context and the importance of positive relationships and social support to enable children to successfully work through the various crises inherent in the process of growing up. The contemporary context of fragmented families, economic austerity, increasing inequality and the challenges and opportunities created by digital technology may well impose additional crises for young people to manoeuvre on the journey to adulthood. As social workers, often intervening in the lives of children when they are experiencing crises, Erikson reminds us that the main role of the adults around the child should be to support them on their journey of developmental crisis-resolution towards healthy identity formation. Children and young people are busy with the process of growing up. Important facets of this journey are opportunities for younger children to play and learn and explore their world within a safe and supportive environment; and, for teenagers, to develop their peer relationships and form their own identity through experimentation and increasing autonomy. For some children, this may mean they prefer and need to focus their time and energy on developing their own interests, rather than engaging with professional interventions. For others, making sense of and participating in decision-making processes alongside professionals will be a crucial part of their journey to maturity. Child-centred practitioners should be mindful of ensuring that their interventions are supporting and not hindering developmental processes for the children they are working with.

Points for Reflection

- Consider a child or young person you know well personally or professionally – how do the theories of child development, outlined above, help to make sense of that child's developmental progress?

Developmental ages and stages

Theoretical understanding of child development in terms of distinct stages, during which key tasks are fulfilled, success in later stages being largely contingent upon achievement of the earliest stages, has been particularly influential. It has led, for example, to the important work of British paediatrician Mary Sheridan

(1997), who formulated a framework for age-based developmental milestones which classify the parameters of child development for most children. Knowledge of the stages and characteristics of healthy development is crucial for childcare practitioners (Walker and Crawford, 2014) as we seek to engage with children in an age-appropriate manner, enable their participation and understand their wishes and feelings.

Points for Reflection
***

- Think back to your own childhood – consider the changes you experienced physically, emotionally and psychologically as you went through the process of growing up from early infancy to adulthood.

- Why do you think it is important for social workers to have a good understanding of the ages and stages of child development?

Commentary

Social workers need to identify when the development of the child is not age appropriate. This is recognising either developmental delay or children who present as older and more mature than their chronological age. Child-centred practitioners with a good knowledge of the ages and stages of development will be naturally curious about why this may be, and consider possible hypotheses to be tested through gathering and analysing information. A child who presents as developmentally delayed may have an undiagnosed health need or disability; be experiencing a lack of stimulation at home; not be engaging consistently in educational provision; or experiencing abuse or neglect. A more mature child may have been given responsibilities beyond their years by parents who have unrealistic expectations; be caring for an adult relative or siblings at home; or again be experiencing abuse and neglect having to 'grow up quickly' to survive.

The foundation years

There is wide-ranging consensus about the crucial importance of the early years and a good deal of attention has been given to the value of early intervention to support vulnerable young children and their families (Field, 2010; Allen, 2011). Characterised by a period of rapid growth, children move through the foundation years from the total dependence of early infancy to managing the complex social and behavioural demands of the school environment. Children who receive secure, warm and consistent care as babies are able to explore their world confidently and are more likely to be contented, able to learn and able to build positive peer relationships (in Chapter 4 we discuss the importance of attachment relationships in more depth). Professionals working with families with babies should be mindful of their particular vulnerability and the need for careful handling and protective nurture (Cuthbert et al., 2011). Child-centred practitioners recognise that even the youngest children without recourse to language skills are able to communicate their needs and desires, and often do so determinedly and noisily.

The development of transductive reasoning, noted by Piaget, means that children become increasingly able to link cause and effect. However, they may also make errors at this stage, putting together two immediate events and assuming one caused the other; combined with a sense of egocentricism, this can lead children to assume blame for events beyond their control. For example, children may feel responsible for incidents of domestic violence, if they believe their boisterous play provoked a parent to lose their temper. The child-centred practitioner will seek to develop their skills to engage with young children, using play and age-appropriate language. Younger children need patient interaction and careful explanations to make sense of difficult situations and explore possible confusions. Einav and Robinson's (2012) research (using puppets to assist children in naming a range of animals, some of which they were unfamiliar with) highlighted how children as young as four and five were able to decide who would be most likely to provide reliable guidance and therefore whose advice they would be most able to trust. It is important to be honest with young children, to provide age-appropriate information, so that children can learn to trust the adults in their lives at times of difficulty.

Middle childhood

Developmental theory has sometimes characterised this period as one of relative calm in between the rapid growth of the early years and the turbulence of adolescence. Recognising child development as a continuum in which children grow and mature in different ways at varying paces, it is clear that children need support throughout childhood to reach their full potential (Jack and Donnellan, 2013). At this stage, children develop greater understanding of the social rules of interaction and the meaning of cultural identity for themselves and others. Saarni's (1984) research about how children respond to a disappointing gift is important in recognising how children learn to manage their responses in the light of social expectations. The youngest children, aged around six, were largely unable to mask their disappointment and expressed their negative reaction. Slightly older children demonstrated uncertainty about the social norms, tending to look to the gift-giver for cues about how to respond. Children aged 10 to 11 usually disguised their natural reaction and gave a positive response. Professionals working with children to explore their wishes and feelings need to be mindful that as children mature they become adept at reading social cues and presenting what they may consider socially appropriate responses. This valuable developmental adaptation, enabling children to fit into wider social situations, means that child-centred practitioners need to be careful not to impose their own perspectives when seeking to enable a child to express their views. It is important to take time to enable children to explore their own reactions and their own personal feelings, as well as acknowledging the social influences that may be impacting upon them.

The need for security and responsive care is just as important as in the foundation years. Childcare professionals have an important role in supporting parents to provide the warmth, consistency and firm boundaries that enable children to thrive. Social status and peer relationships become increasingly important. Children who have a secure base are more likely to be able to form significant friendships. Social support gained through positive peer relationships can help to compensate for deficits in family bonds; however, those children who would most benefit from such interactions may be least able to find them (Bee and Boyd, 2014). Sensitive and timely interventions, for example, in circle time within the school environment or in group work with children, can enable children who might otherwise struggle to negotiate peer relationships more positively. Negative experiences can be difficult to make sense of and impact on emotional well-being; this can lead some children to externalise their feelings through disruptive behaviour and others to internalise them, becoming anxious or withdrawn. Professionals should seek to understand how a child's behaviour or emotional presentation may be their way of adapting to difficult or intolerable circumstances. Providing opportunities for children to make sense of complex situations and develop ways of coping that promote their long-term well-being is an important aspect of child-centred practice.

Learning from Research

An international team of researchers, led by Yamamoto (1996, 1998), carried out research into the circumstances that children find stressful. They worked in Western, industrialised societies with children typically aged around 7 to 13 and from a range of social backgrounds. They found a high level of correlation about what children find stressful. Fears around personal and family security were the biggest source of anxiety, such as loss of a parent and parental arguments. Furthermore, like most adults, children fear and detest events that engender shame and impact on their dignity. Being caught breaking the rules, for example stealing, or being publicly embarrassed by wetting themselves in class, scored significantly on the scale of stressful events, almost as stressful as losing a parent. Some of the issues seen as anxiety-provoking for children would prompt the attention of adults, others would be regarded by adults as routine and insignificant. The researchers describe a culture of childhood whereby there is wide consensus amongst children about what might upset them; despite many cultural differences, they have much in common in their daily lives and arrive at similar perceptions of reality. Conversely, they found that adults did not accurately perceive the possible impact of some stresses ▶

on children: 'For two peoples who have lived side by side for such a long time, adults and children seem to misunderstand each other a lot' (1996: 139).

Yamamoto and colleagues (1998) conclude that just as the world of grown-ups is often difficult and incomprehensible to the young, so too, for adults, the world of children is often unpredictable and inexplicable and the concerns of the young may not be taken as seriously as they should be. 'All in all, it would be a mistake for adults, especially professionals, to believe that they now know children well enough to cease exploring the unique reality of the young world, especially seen from the inside' (1998: 313).

Yamamoto's research is a reminder to practitioners to take seriously the perspectives of the children they work with.

Adolescence

This period of development, marking the transition from childhood to adulthood, has long been associated with turbulence and 'raging hormones'. In reality, the vast majority of young people manage the transition to healthy and productive adult life fairly smoothly. However, the rapid development of physical and mental capabilities, the increased expectations around autonomy and responsibility, the importance of close relationships and the evolution of sexual and personal identity can accumulate to create challenges for many young people (Coleman, 2011). There is some basis for an association of adolescence with intense emotions, passionate interests and sensation-seeking behaviours (Dahl, 2004). Risk-taking is an essential aspect of healthy development, enabling young people to seek out and learn from novel experiences, to explore identities and capabilities, and gain self-knowledge and respect amongst their peers (Jack and Donnellan, 2013). Albert and Steinberg (2011) have reviewed the literature about the capability of adolescents to make rational decisions and have found that they have the maturity and intellectual capacity to evaluate risky decisions in a manner very similar to that of adults. Contrary to popular ideas about the 'invulnerability complex', young people are no less able than adults to perceive risk and assess their own vulnerability. They recognised that young people may, nevertheless, make riskier choices at times and that this may be due to the reward gained in terms of their emotional state and, perhaps more significantly, the reward of peer approval. Gardner and Steinberg (2005) carried out research with two groups of young people aged between 14 and 19 and a group of adults (mean age 37), testing their propensity to carry out risky behaviours alone or in groups with their peers (using a computer driving game). When playing the game alone, each of the three age groups made comparable risky choices. When tested in groups, adolescents took twice as many risks with their peers than they had alone; the student-aged group were approximately 50% riskier in their choices in the game. Adults showed no differences in their risk-taking when alone or in a group. The evidence points to young people's tendency to make riskier decisions than adults when amongst their peers. Albert and Steinberg (2011) note that the social and emotional reward of peer approval is particularly hard to resist for adolescents. This developmental tendency may be intensified in societies that undermine the ability of young people to gain an established, respected place in the wider community. For young people who are socially excluded, therefore, gaining the respect of peers through involvement in community groups or gangs is particularly important. Child-centred practitioners will recognise the importance of peer relationships for young people, understanding that relationships that are not in their best interests, due to their exploitative or abusive nature, may be difficult for young people to break away from. Professionals should consider how their interventions may impact upon the ability of those they are working with to build and maintain positive friendships.

Adolescents are able to demonstrate remarkable problem-solving and decision-making competence. For professionals working with young people, theory and research points to the importance of recognising their capability and their cognitive and intellectual capacity to consider the options, express their opinions and make decisions. Participation in decision-making processes will further enhance their ability to make independent choices and their sense of self-efficacy. Acknowledgement of the importance of peer relationships and making time to explore how different decisions might impact on these is time well spent. Enabling exploration of short-term consequences and long-term goals is important for young people to manage the emotional repercussions for themselves and the people they are close to. Wherever possible it is important for professionals to work alongside families and significant adults in the lives of young people to ensure they retain the emotional connectedness and support they may need to complete their journey to adulthood.

Learning from Research

Ruggeri and colleagues (2014) carried out research with 63 children (aged 8 to 11) and 76 adolescents (aged 15 to 17) to explore children's views about making difficult decisions. The research focused on medical decision-making and examined what children want in terms of involvement in making tough decisions. Previous work by Botti and colleagues (2009), looking at adults' responses to tragic choices, found that where adults make the difficult decisions directly, they experience more profound emotional reactions (personal causation intensifies the negative emotions); nevertheless, adults remain reluctant to give up the autonomy to make the choice. In this study, the participants were

▶

presented with a hypothetical decision about whether or not to have their leg amputated (in the context of a poor prognosis without amputation) and asked to discuss how the decision should be made and by whom. The clear finding from the study was that both children and adolescents want to be involved in the decision-making process, even when the outcome involves serious negative consequences; many preferred making a decision for themselves rather than having an authority figure (a parent or doctor) decide for them. Perhaps unsurprisingly the older young people were more adamant and united in their wish for autonomy. More surprising was the finding that 87% of the adolescent participants chose not to amputate; whereas only 27% of the younger children made this choice. The researchers considered that the children were more likely to believe the poor prognosis that had been presented by the adults and to see them as the experts; they may also have been influenced by a belief that the adults would make this amputation decision anyway. The adolescents, in contrast, challenged the information presented; they were more likely to take the risk of ignoring medical opinion and retained the hope of saving the leg.

The research highlights that children and young people want to be involved in making decisions, even when the choice is a difficult one; they realise that such involvement will have emotional consequences. Their age and developmental stage may impact on the choices they make and they may need support to consider how they are weighing up their options and the influences upon their views. Professionals should work with children and young people and their families in order to negotiate the decision-making process and to recognise and minimise the emotional impact of their choices.

Knowledge of the developmental characteristics of children at different ages and stages is a valuable asset in the toolkit of the child-centred practitioner. It informs professional endeavours to engage with children and young people and promote their involvement in the work. Supporting parents and carers to enable children to reach their milestones and to achieve their full potential is integral to the role of childcare professionals. Having said that, we should remain mindful of the uniqueness of every child. Children are individuals and variations occur in the timescales and sequence of the fulfilment of developmental milestones for many reasons. Each child's development is shaped by their particular experience and by the interaction of factors, including their genetic inheritance and temperament and any health conditions or impairments they may have, and their social, cultural and environmental circumstances. Children who come into contact with social workers are often vulnerable or may have special needs. Child-centred practice means applying our knowledge of child development with sensitivity and skill in order to gain a full and holistic understanding of the health and well-being of the unique child, whose welfare we are seeking to promote.

Points for Reflection

- Consider a child you have worked with – how does knowledge of developmental stages help you to understand the needs of the child?
- How would you introduce yourself and explain your professional role to a child aged 6 in comparison to a child aged 14?

Commentary

Child-centred practitioners are skilled at ensuring a flexible and adaptable approach when meeting a child for the first time. A friendly and open demeanour, as well as a genuine interest in the child's life, assists in building rapport. Explaining the role of a social worker is not always an easy task, but a necessary one, and all social workers will embark on this in their own individual way. However, when engaging a younger child, a more creative approach may be useful. This could include drawing or engaging in play.

For example:

Social worker Emily met with George (aged six) for the first time at school following a referral from his class teacher. George disclosed to his teacher that his mother had smacked him across the face that morning for making the family late and he was very upset on arrival at school. George had never met a social worker before Emily arrived to see him. Emily decided to help George understand her role by exploring a range of professionals that George was already familiar with. This included a teacher, police officer, lollypop lady and doctor. Emily and George made sculptures of each professional from playdough. George was able to describe the circumstances of when he had met each professional, and was able to see how each professional helped people in their jobs. George made a sculpture of Emily the social worker, but said he did not know what her job was. Emily explained to George that she also helps people, and especially children. She told George that other professionals, or sometimes family members, friends or neighbours, tell her when a child is sad or might not be safe at home. Emily explained that her job is to meet the child and listen to them. She is then able to help. Emily felt her approach in this case also enabled her to form a relationship with George before she asked him about his daily experiences at home.

Older children may be more able to participate in a direct conversation about the role of a social worker, but this should not be taken for granted. Some older children may feel more comfortable engaging with a social worker whilst undertaking an activity or creative task, or alongside a known and trusted adult.

For example:

Social worker Jonathon attempted to meet with 14-year-old Asif who was displaying aggressive behaviour towards his mother. Asif had recently gone missing overnight and refused to tell his mother where he had been, but had been seen by neighbours with other local young people who were associated with a gang. There were concerns by the police that some of these young associates were involved in drug use, knife crime and theft. Asif had refused to see Jonathon on two occasions at the family home, and had left the house when Jonathon visited. With parental consent, Jonathon met with Asif and his learning mentor, Mr Johnson, at school. Mr Johnson had developed a positive relationship with Asif over a two-year period, supporting him through the process of assessment and diagnosis of Attention Deficit Hyperactivity Disorder (ADHD). Mr Johnson was able to help Asif understand why Jonathon had come to visit and why people were worried about Asif's behaviour. Jonathon, on advice from Mr Johnson, ensured he explained his role in clear and concise language and allowed Asif short breaks during the visit to accommodate his learning need.

Learning from neuroscience

The findings of neuroscience have had an increasing impact on social work practice over recent years and have become the focus of considerable debate. Neurobiology tells us that much of a child's brain and central nervous system develops after birth, in particular within the first three years of life. At birth the baby's brain is 25% of the weight of an adult brain, by three months it is almost 40%, when the child is three years old the brain has reached 90% of its adult size. The science indicates that the growth of the brain is not finished at birth, maturation continuing mainly over the first three years, with a further period of significant development also occurring in adolescence. Neurons are the nerve cells that form the nervous system; they are connected by synapses that allow information to pass between them. It is the synapses that organise the brain and form connections between the parts that govern physical and psychological functions, enabling the normal processes of daily life, including eating, sleeping, thinking and feeling. By around the age of two, a child's brain has developed many more synapses than they need; those synapses which are being used are strengthened, and those that are not are gradually discarded. The key learning from the science of relevance to professional practice is that it indicates, for the developing child, negative experiences and insufficient stimulation adversely impact on the construction of neural connections and thereby on the child's long-term cognitive and social development.

Furthermore, learning from neuroscience contributes to our professional understanding when working with adolescents. There are a number of developmental psychologists who make compelling arguments for the changes in brain development in adolescence having a direct impact on general increased risk-taking behaviour and reward-seeking behaviour (Spear, 2009; Dishion, 2016). Social workers, for example, are often presented with young people who are experimenting with drugs or alcohol, exploring their sexuality or have become involved in criminal activity. Developments in neuroscience in recent years emphasise that this behaviour does not appear to be due to immorality or ignorance, but is influenced by significant changes in the developing brain. Steinberg

(2007: 55) states: '[the] temporal gap between puberty, which impels adolescents toward thrill seeking, and the slow maturation of the cognitive-control system, which regulates these impulses, makes adolescence a time of heightened vulnerability for risky behaviour.' Therefore, heightened risk-taking during adolescence is likely to be 'normative, biologically driven and to some extent inevitable' (2007: 58). Supporting young people and their parents and carers to understand these natural processes of change and development can be valuable when families are struggling to provide continued care and appropriate boundaries. There is further evidence that adolescents require more intense or more frequent stimuli to achieve the same level of pleasure as an adult (Galvan, 2010), and exhibit increased negative affect and depressed mood. Issues of mental ill health, such as depression and self-harm, should be recognised and addressed in professional interventions with young people. Social workers play an important role in working with families to enable access to specialist assessment and treatment where more serious problems develop for young people during adolescence. Child-centred practitioners need to be mindful of the impact of brain development at this vulnerable stage of a child's development.

The impact of neglect on the developing child

Research carried out by Perry in the US (2002) involved carrying out brain scans with 40 children who had been referred for specialist clinical evaluation following severe sensory deprivation during the first three years of life. The research concluded that a serious lack of opportunity for stimulation and sensory experience for these children resulted in inhibited brain growth which was predicted to impact on their long-term development. The publication of this research was particularly influential as it was illustrated with a photograph showing the cross-section of the brain of a normal 3-year-old in comparison to a 3-year-old child who had suffered extreme neglect. The second brain was considerably smaller and less developed than the first. No childcare practitioner wants a child to stay in conditions of abuse and neglect, and the reminder of the possible impact of maltreatment on the child's developing brain, emphasised in this research and illustrated by the brain scan image, was powerful. However, it must be noted that the small number of children involved in Perry's study were at the most severe end of the deprivation scale; they had experienced what has been described as global neglect, a typical example being a child who had been kept in a cage in a dark room. Such extreme cases are thankfully rare and where they occur the impact on every aspect of the child's growth and development is unsurprisingly extensive. From this preliminary example, it is clear then that lessons for the day-to-day practice of social workers in the UK, who are mainly seeking to intervene to support families who are struggling for a wide range of reasons, must be drawn with caution. These points are clearly of interest and relevance to social workers, who often intervene in the lives of children who have suboptimal care experiences that impact adversely on their development. From a child-centred perspective, it is important that practitioners undertake comprehensive assessments to evaluate how the development of the child is being promoted or hampered by the care they are receiving. Social work interventions will seek to increase opportunities for positive care, play and consistent stimulation from parents and primary caregivers towards infants and children.

Learning from Research

Lessons from neuroscience have recently gained increasing prominence. Summarised by Brown and Ward (2013), key learning from research has been used to underpin significant developments in policy and practice in the UK, in particular to speed up the processes of decision-making where statutory interventions are needed. This work, published by the Childhood Wellbeing Research Centre, has emphasised some key messages:

- There is a short window of opportunity for certain types of development; these periods are widely referred to as *sensitive periods*. If the experiences upon which they depend do not occur within a predetermined time frame, children may not be able to make healthy progress both in the short and long term.

- By the time children are 2 years old, the neural pathways essential to their ability to speak and understand language have been laid down. Lack of attention and stimulation in infancy will lead to developmental delays for some children in relation to language acquisition and the ability to play and develop positive peer relationships.

- At certain times, *critical periods*, the impact of experience on development can be irreversible. An example of this is where an infant has untreated cataracts; they may be unable to develop sight even after the cataracts are removed and the eyes are restored to health.

- The architecture of the developing brain depends on the healthy completion of each phase in a logical sequence. If there is impaired development in the early stages affecting sensory development, this can impact negatively on later stages of cognitive, emotional and social development.

Thinking critically about neuroscience

It is important for professionals to be aware that neuroscientific research has been the subject of debate (Wastell and White, 2012). It is prudent to take a critical approach to views which tend to reduce the whole person of the child to their biological or neurological essence. Philosophy professor and scholar of cognitive development John Bruer (1999) has argued vehemently against what he has termed 'the myth of the first three years'. Whilst accepting that there may be some evidence for 'critical periods' of development, particularly that associated with sight, the evidence for this is based mainly on experiments with animals (testing such theory with children being impossible and opportunities for observation rare). The concern is that such critical periods are few and that the extension of this understanding to more general 'sensitive periods' is unhelpful. The science pertaining to the infant brain, indicating the irreversibility of any early damage to development, is based on evidence that is neither robust nor conclusive. According to Bruer, the view that children's healthy development is predicated upon a series of critical windows of opportunity which, if disrupted, are slammed shut, is reductionist, unrealistic and likely to lead to inappropriate interventions. Rutter (2002) has also argued that the notion of the sensitive period is over-stated, at the expense of recognition of the resilience and plasticity of the brain and the potential for recovery and life-long learning. The human brain is more complex than those of mice or rats (the main subjects of experiments underpinning some neuroscientific evidence) and more able to recover from damage of various forms, to re-form neural connections, reshape and resume healthy development. The developing brain is not readily susceptible to irreversible damage owing to psycho-social deprivation; it is unhelpful to underestimate the innate drive towards healthy development. Smidt (2013) highlights that ideas about the cumulative nature of development can lead to the conclusion that a difficult start in life can impact detrimentally throughout the life cycle. Whilst there is some evidence underpinning this notion, it is also the case that child development has a level of plasticity that enables adaptation, so that some children are able to adjust, overcome adversity and achieve good outcomes in later childhood and adulthood. It is significant to note that the aim of academics such as Bruce Perry from the Harvard Centre was to simplify complex scientific concepts in order to influence policy. Ideas about brain architecture, synaptic pruning and toxic stress can seem concrete and attractive when faced with complex and entrenched family problems or children displaying unusual and challenging behaviours. There is no shortcut for the child-centred social worker and the need for careful and rigorous assessment in messy situations is always pertinent.

Social workers are all too aware of concerns about the impact of neglect upon children's long-term welfare and development. It is important to ensure that decisions are made in a timely manner, recognising that a few months can mean a great deal in the process of healthy development, and can feel like an eternity from the perspective of the child. Nevertheless, child-centredness does not mean allowing popular concepts or organisational targets to lead to hasty judgements based on hazy understandings of science, rather than thorough and holistic assessment that works at a pace that is meaningful for the child. For the child-centred social worker, the child is much more than the sum of the parts of their brain. The aim of any assessment will be to seek to understand how children are impacted by their circumstances and to identify if their development is being detrimentally affected. A key principle of good practice is to ensure timely intervention. In some instances, speed is essential to ensure children are safeguarded and not exposed to damage inflicted by serious stress, deprivation or abuse. More often, complex situations mean it is important for professionals to take the time to build relationships of trust with children and their families, in order to make a holistic assessment and support processes of change that may be difficult and precarious. It is useful to reflect on the views of the eminent neuroscientist Steven Rose, who reminds us that what it means for a child to develop as a healthy and contented human being goes beyond our very limited understanding of the brain: 'I would argue that any genuine increase in knowledge of brain processes … can only enrich our understanding of ourselves. Nor can such increased knowledge replace or diminish the insights into what it is to be human that come from philosophy, the social sciences or the humanities – therefore, there should only be benefits, providing one can pick one's way through the 'over-hyping' of apparent neuroscientific claims' (Rose, 2011, Royal Society policy paper, quoted by White and Wastell, 2013: 9).

Points for Reflection

● How might the knowledge from neuroscientific research influence social work practice with children?

Commentary

Neuroscience provides a fascinating insight into the complexity of the human brain. Neuroscience helps us to understand how negative life experiences can have a significant and life-changing impact on the brain's growth and functioning, as well as helping to explain a child's behaviour at specific life stages, such as in adolescence. As we have learned, the brain does have the ability to recover. Encouragingly, there is evidence that nurturing educational environments, consistent parental practices and preventative work can actively support the development of resilience in children and young people, as well as reducing mental health issues (Fosco et al., 2012; Dishion, 2016). Learning from neuroscience highlights the importance of comprehensive and timely assessments, with planning that focuses on the child's individual needs.

Conclusion

Our understanding of children and child development will undoubtedly continue to evolve, alongside discourses of childhood that variably portray young people as emergent and immature or capable and rational. How much we regard children as similar to or different from adults will be influenced by our understanding of psychological theory and scientific research, as well as by our values and cultural assumptions and our own experiences of childhood and adolescence. Gallacher and Gallagher have argued that both adults and children are emergent beings 'always unfinished subjects-in-the-making – humans cannot claim to be experts: to be fully knowing, competent and rational' (2008: 511). From this critical perspective, we recognise that every age and stage of life, from infancy and throughout adulthood, involves learning and knowing, vulnerability and capability. This understanding prompts the child-centred practitioner to acknowledge that adults and children have much to learn from each other.

Alongside this analysis of the nature of childhood and theories of child development, a key aspect of our professional practice is built upon the premise that children's identities are fundamentally connected to their family and community. We will go on, in Chapter 4, to explore how the understanding of the family and environmental context is crucial to our understanding of childhood and effective practice with children and young people.

Recommended reading and resources

This chapter has offered an overview and flavour of the theories relating to childhood and child development. As each area explored is extensive, it is highly recommended that the reader explores further. The following resources are recommended to extend knowledge in these key areas:

- Gordon Jack and Helen Donnellan's (2013) *Social Work with Children* provides an excellent overview of the knowledge base about child development that is particularly useful for social work practice. Chapters explore child development in the foundation years, middle childhood and adolescence, taking into account the importance of family and the social context of children's lives.

- Bee and Boyd's (2014) textbook *The Developing Child* has been revised as a 13th edition and provides a comprehensive discussion of a wide range of theories drawn from child psychology.

- Paula Nicolson's (2014) *A Critical Approach to Human Growth and Development* provides a comprehensive introduction for social work students to psycho-social theories of human development and examination of each stage of growth and development. Interesting case scenarios and points for reflection illuminate the theoretical discussions.

- Walker and Crawford (2014) similarly have written an accessible text to enable the student social worker to develop their knowledge base around human development, including opportunities to apply theory to practice.

- John Coleman's (2011) book *The Nature of Adolescence* draws from psychology and neuroscience, presenting the scientific evidence in a way that is relevant and highly readable. This text is a valuable resource for professionals who spend their time grappling with the developmental issues presented by and significant for young people.

- Funded by the Department for Education, Research in Practice has developed a website focused around fostering and adoption that includes interesting sections that are relevant to the themes of this chapter – in particular, child development (topic number 3) and early brain development and maltreatment (topic number 4). The web pages include fascinating links to a range of YouTube clips, including Professor Robert Winston explaining baby synapse connection and videos about Piaget and child development:
  http://fosteringandadoption.rip.org.uk/topics/child-development/
  http://fosteringandadoption.rip.org.uk/topics/early-brain-development/

- Brown and Ward's (2013) *Decision-making within a Child's Timeframe* is available online and provides an extremely useful introduction to the research about neuroscience. The document has been criticised by Sue White and David Wastell and, for those interested in reading a searing critique of neuroscience as it has been applied to work with children and families, the following is insightful:
  http://dx.doi.org/10.2139/ssrn.2325357

- Professor Robert Winston's *Child of Our Time* documentary series provides interesting and entertaining insights into the process of child development. The lives of 25 children born in the year 2000 are followed, with annual films to show the progress of their lives, told from the perspectives of the children and their families. Watch out for the annual screenings or search for a sample of the films on:
  http://www.bbc.co.uk/programmes/

4

CHILDREN IN CONTEXT

Introduction

This chapter recognises that to understand children we need to adopt a holistic perspective, to see the whole child in the context of their family, community and wider social circumstances. Just as no man (or woman) is an island, according to John Donne's famous poem (1624, reproduced 2007), even more so, this sense of human connectedness applies to children. Children are dependent upon their carers, usually their birth parents; their healthy growth and development is contingent upon the quality of care they receive within their family, which is in turn influenced by the wider environment for better or for worse. Young people form their identity, their sense of who they are, through interaction with parents and siblings, friends and significant others, within the cultural context of their daily lives. To intervene effectively in the lives of young people, child-centred practitioners need to recognise the importance of family relationships, the wider community and social context.

When the assessment framework was first introduced in 2000, it emphasised that to understand a child, the professional must see the child within the context of their family and wider environment, as noted in Chapter 2. A holistic assessment of the needs of the child recognises that their health, development and well-being depends upon: 'the complex interaction of the individual, the adults who determine the child's upbringing and the social environment and the interplay between these factors' (Seden, in Ward and Rose, 2002:195). In this chapter, then, we explore sociological perspectives, in particular understandings drawn from ecological theory, that are helpful to professionals in making sense of the complexities of children's lives and social circumstances. Knowledge of attachment theory is particularly valuable in recognising the central importance of key kin and family relationships. We also explore some aspects of contemporary society of particular relevance to children, recognising the impact of poverty, in an age of austerity, and the role of digital technology in the daily lives of young people. We note the important contribution made by research about resilience that enables social workers to negotiate the vulnerability, risk and adversity they encounter and work to strengthen protective factors in the familial and community environment. Child-centred practitioners recognise the crucial role played by family in the lives of children and young people.

It is important to understand how factors in the child's family and community interact to support or undermine the welfare of the child.

The social child

As highlighted in Chapter 3, there are many discourses about children – many ways of making sense of the nature of childhood. With reference to the model of childhood developed by James and colleagues (1998), sociological perspectives have tended to see children in one of four ways:

- The 'developing child' is seen as dependent upon adults, incomplete, lacking in social status and relatively incompetent.

- The 'tribal child' acknowledges the competence of children on their own terms, as part of a subculture distinct from mainstream, adult-centric society.

- The 'adult child' emphasises how children are socially competent in ways comparable to adults.

- The 'social child' is seen as inherently capable, though their capacity is nurtured or constrained by their social and cultural environment.

In this chapter, we focus on the social child, recognising the ways in which the lives of children are shaped by structural forces, acknowledging that children are social actors, socially competent individuals who are able to contribute to and shape their domestic and cultural environments.

Ecological theory

Theory based on human ecology recognises the importance of environment and context to development and well-being. Ecological theory brings together psychosocial perspectives in order to recognise the ways in which the family and wider society impact upon and interact with the individual child as an inherent part of the process of human development. Developmental psychologist Urie Bronfenbrenner (1979) developed this holistic approach to understanding the nature of childhood. Figure 5 demonstrates how the developing child inhabits the microsystem, their immediate environment of home and family, which extends to include school and peer relationships. The exosystem embodies the formal and informal aspects of the community that impact upon the microsystem, including wider family networks, religious institutions and local services. Some aspects of this system will affect the child directly, even though they have no involvement in or control over this feature of family or community life, such as parental patterns of employment or the quality of the local school. The macrosystem describes the

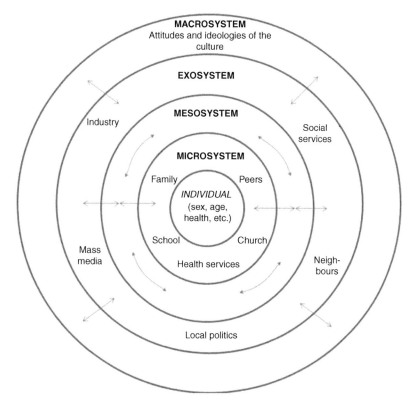

Figure 5 Bronfenbrenner's ecological model, 1979.

overarching institutional and cultural context, including economic patterns and social conditions, cultural values and political systems (Figure 5).

Bronfenbrenner defines also the mesosystem, noting the relationship between the different systems, emphasising that the spheres are not separate and independent, but connecting, overlapping and interacting in their influence upon the developing child. The assessment framework (DH, 2000) is rooted in ecological theory, recognising the importance of the micro-, exo- and macrosystems in creating the context for the child to grow and thrive. It is important to recognise that when professionals intervene in the life of a child, they become part of the child's microsystem and how they interact with the child and their family (as part of the mesosystem) will impact upon the child's development and life chances. Child-centred practitioners seek to work closely with parents and significant others in the child's community, in order to strengthen parenting capacity and enhance the network of support around the child.

Points for Reflection

- Recall a particular stage in your own childhood. Using Bronfenbrenner's model, place yourself at the centre of the concentric circles and consider what were the important elements in each of the spheres around you.
- How did the main features of each system impact upon your upbringing?

A good childhood?

Contemporary developments in sociology have brought into play an understanding of social capital, which emphasises how interactions within families and meso-level interactions between families and local communities impact upon the welfare of children and young people (Putnam, 2000). Social capital describes the formal and informal relationships within a local community, characterised by shared values that facilitate co-operation and the development of supportive networks. Social capital theory recognises the value of social networks in promoting norms of reciprocity that include neighbourliness, citizenship and civic participation. Research highlights that social capital can promote positive outcomes for a range of socio-economic measures associated with children's well-being (Ferguson, 2006). Put simply, where a child is raised in a loving family, educated in a good school and grows up in an area characterised by positive support networks, they are likely to do well. Children who have poorer access to social capital may struggle to enjoy a good childhood or to achieve positive outcomes.

Notions of social capital assist the social worker to consider the positive and negative factors in the child's circumstances and environment. However, it is important that we do not make assumptions. What matters to a particular child about their life and situation may not be what would seem of most importance to an adult. Child-centred practitioners listen to children and young people about what is important to them, what informs their sense of happiness and well-being, and what contributes to their network of support and social capital. Research from the perspective of the child helps us to make sense of the factors that make up a happy and positive experience of childhood.

Learning from Research

The Good Childhood Report (2014) summarises research carried out by the Children's Society with the University of York, involving 50,000 children over a nine-year period. The study measures the quality of children's lives, as rated by themselves, in a range of different countries. It enables analysis of children's subjective well-being and cross-cultural comparison. The study gives voice to children's views about how happy they are on a day-to-day basis and how satisfied they feel about their lives overall. Some of the key findings to date are summarised as follows:

- Most children in the UK (around 90%) have relatively good well-being; however, there is a significant minority (around half a million) who have low well-being;

- Children in England are ranked 9th out of the 11 countries studied for child well-being – behind countries including Romania, Spain and Chile.

- Children tend to be happier with some aspects of their lives than others:

  o Family, home and friendships score highly, with only 4% of children (aged 10 to 13) being unhappy with family relationships;

  o How children feel about their appearance is a concern – 13% of children feel unhappy about this aspect of their lives, girls faring worst (18%);

  o Children in England are among the most dissatisfied with school in the world (1 in 9 children being unhappy with their school life).

- 38% of 10 and 12 year olds in England report being bullied regularly and being excluded by their peer group.

- 52% of children who do not live with their family had low overall well-being, compared to 9% of those children who live with their families.

- The quality of family relationships emerges as one of the most important influences on children's subjective well-being.

- The amount of choice children feel they have in their lives consistently emerges as having a strong link with their sense of well-being.

- Children who are regularly active have higher well-being compared to children who are not. And children who use computers and the internet regularly have higher well-being than children who do not.

- Children who seek help from someone at home if they have a problem have higher well-being than those who keep problems to themselves.

- Being praised for doing well or feeling supported when upset are strongly associated with well-being.

Many of these themes are relevant to our understanding of childhood resilience and the importance of family, friends and community. We will go on to explore these themes more fully in this chapter.

The importance of families

The family is the central institution of society that provides for the care, nurturance and socialisation of children. The vast majority of children across the globe live with their parents and this bedrock of kinship usually creates the affinity and sense of responsibility upon which the domestic relations of the family are built and endure throughout life. Many aspects of social life are founded upon the premise that the family is the lynchpin of society and that people will, and should, look after their own. A fundamental human right is the right to a private family life. It is important to remember that this right is shared by children, articulated in article 16 of the UNCRC. Article 5 emphasises the duty of the State to respect and support the rights and responsibilities of families in fulfilling their important role of raising children, and article 9 affirms the importance for children of being cared for by their parents or remaining in contact with them (separation being countenanced only if the best interests of the child require this). Featherstone and colleagues (2016: 11) emphasise: 'family and relationships are central as they are fundamental to nurturance, identity, purpose, fulfilment and safekeeping. Individual rights lack meaning without social relatedness.'

From a child-centred perspective, it is important to recognise the crucial role of the family and to work with parents and carers to promote the welfare of children. Families are of central importance in the lives of most children who social workers come into contact with, including children who have experienced difficult, traumatic or abusive experiences within the family and those who live apart from their parents.

Understanding families

From a sociological perspective, families are seen as cooperative groups within the larger social sphere, built mainly around blood or kinship ties, sharing a mutual obligation to each other and overseeing the upbringing of children (Macionis and Plummer, 2012). The family is of central importance to the cohesive and efficient organisation of society, reinforcing contemporary norms and values. Families can also be seen as social constructions, their structure and function changing and evolving within and across cultures. Different family forms include small nuclear families of monogamous couples and their dependent children, involving heterosexual, gay or lesbian parents; extended families, including grandparents or other family members in the household; single-parent families; and reconstituted or blended families involving shared care of children from previous relationships. The Marriages (Same Sex Couples) Act 2013 legalised marriage for same-sex couples in England and Wales. It is likely that there will be an ongoing increase in the number of same-sex couples caring for dependent children in the UK. In the twenty-first century, the family can only be understood by recognising and celebrating its diversity and complexity. According to the Office for National Statistics in 2014, in the UK:

- There were 18.6 million families. Of these, 12.5 million were married-couple families. This remains the most common family type in the UK.

- Cohabiting-couple families grew by around 30% between 2004 and 2014. This is the fastest growing type of family.

- There were 2 million lone-parent families. Lone parents with dependent children represented 25% of all families with dependent children. Mothers accounted for 91% of single-parent families.

- Stepfamilies constitute 11% of all families with dependent children in the UK.

Frost and Dolan (2012) discuss the moral panics that regularly emerge in contemporary society, tending to focus on themes such as the decline of the traditional family and the rise of dysfunctional or single-parent families. The media at times glorifies the past, emphasising the benefits of the extended family networks of the pre-war years, rather than recognising the inevitability of change and the strengths that exist in diverse family forms. However, a new understanding of family life has been developed by contemporary sociologists. The family practices perspective emphasises that there are many ways of forming enduring emotional connections. From this standpoint, family is defined by what we do together, rather than who we are. Relationships characterised by care, nurture and responsibility are prioritised above blood ties. The family practices approach captures the complexity of modern family life; it focuses on: 'everyday interactions with close and loved ones and moves away from the fixed boundaries of co-residence, marriage, ethnicity and obligation that once defined the ... nuclear family. It registers the ways in which our networks of affection are not simply given by virtue of blood and marriage but are negotiated and shaped by us, over time and place' (Williams 2004: 17). It is important to understand the nature of the family from the perspective of family members; children are well placed to define the ties that bind and the relationships that count for them. From this perspective, family might include close family friends, pets and a range of significant others that act as key kin for the child.

The family, as a central social structure in Western liberal societies, has been criticised as a source of oppression. Sociologists such as Parsons and Bales (2002) have argued that the family is the key site for the reproduction of the prevailing social order. This is fulfilled through the socialisation of children according to the accepted moral blueprint, the reinforcement of family obligations and the maintenance of social control. Parents perform a social policing role, fostering future citizens that conform to social norms, thus perpetuating the inequality and social injustice inherent in the prevailing social order. Feminist commentators have viewed the family as the means of maintaining dominant forces of patriarchy. The role of women as mothers perpetuates the unequal division of domestic and economic labour and diminishes opportunity for women and girls. Society tolerates high levels of domestic violence towards women and children. It is important to note alongside these theoretical critiques of the family that for many children the family is a source of stress, damage and repression, instead of (or as well as) nurture and care.

Having said that, the family remains an enduring social institution and the institution of choice globally when it comes to the rearing of healthy and happy children. We have noted how theory about social capital emphasises the importance of strong and enduring networks of support. Coleman (1991) argues that the family is the central resource that functions to engender and promote the social capital of children. The Good Childhood report (2014) noted that living with their family and having positive family relationships were intrinsically linked to positive well-being for the children in this comprehensive study.

Points for Reflection

- Consider your own family background. What kind of family did you grow up in? What was the structure of and quality of relationships in your family?
- Why do you think family relationships matter for the children and young people you work with?

Child-centred practitioners respect and work with parents and key kin who provide the relationships that matter to children. A good starting point for recognising the importance of family for the healthy development of children is an understanding of attachment theory.

The importance of attachment

Attachment theory grew out of a psycho-dynamic understanding of human development and reminds us of how crucially important are the child's primary relationships, in particular with the birth mother, parents and carers. Attachment theory enables us to make sense of close relationships, how they evolve from the first contacts of infancy, how they mould every aspect of the psychosocial development of the child and why they matter throughout the lifespan. Whilst focusing fundamentally on the primary relationships of the child, according to Howe (2010), attachment theory enables the practitioner to make a holistic assessment of the developmental needs of the child, analysing the quality of parent–child interactions in the context of wider familial and environmental influences. How we develop a sense of self and an ability to relate positively to others, alongside how we learn to recognise and cope with stress in our immediate environment, is the remit of attachment theory. This understanding of attachment fits very well within the ecological approach to practice espoused by the assessment framework (DH, 2000).

John Bowlby was the first theorist to emphasise that the child's healthy development depends upon the quality of their primary relationships, in particular with their birth mother. Bowlby, a British psychologist and psychiatrist, was influenced by evolutionary biology and saw attachment behaviours as innate mechanisms enabling children to survive and thrive. Bowlby (1953) recognised that infants need to explore their environment to learn and develop, and they need to do so in the context of a secure and consistent care-giving environment. Young children demonstrate a range of attachment behaviours when they feel insecure in order to gain attention and assurance, and to restore the proximity and protection of their primary carer, usually their mother. Bowlby (1969) concluded that healthy child development is built upon a foundation of close and continuous nurture, preferably provided by one reliable carer; separation or loss of the attachment figure is detrimental to the child's development, leading to unresolved distress and possible psychological damage. Dependent upon the responsiveness of their primary carer, children form an internal working model about their own sense of worthiness and the trustworthiness of others. A cognitive and emotional framework is developed as a basis for future relationships, founded upon whether the child feels loved and valued by a dependable caregiver in early infancy, or rejected by a parent who is unavailable, unreliable or dangerous. Memories and expectations based on these earliest relationships set the pattern for future interactions; negative experiences, therefore, lead to rejection being internalised, eroding a positive sense of self.

Mary Ainsworth was a developmental psychologist who expanded and developed Bowlby's theory. Ainsworth (1970, 1978) emphasised the importance of the psychological availability and responsiveness of the primary carer, as well as their physical proximity.

Learning from Research

Ainsworth and her colleagues carried out studies in the 1970s, involving babies aged between 9 and 18 months, to analyse the strength of their bond with their primary caregiver, invariably the mother. They were interested in how children responded to the presence and absence of their parent and how attachment behaviours are demonstrated. They developed the 'strange situation' procedure in order to observe parent–child interactions and from this process identified three main attachment styles (Ainsworth et al., 1978). A fourth was added by Main and Solomon in 1990:

- Secure attachment: Children experience their caregiver as available and consistent and regard themselves as worthy of love and care. The attachment figure provides a secure base from which the child is able to explore their world, cope with stress and forge new relationships.

- Insecure-ambivalent attachment: Children experience their caregiver as inconsistently responsive and come to see themselves as not valued; they may display clingy and dependent behaviour, anticipating possible rejection.

- Insecure-avoidant attachment: Children experience their caregivers as consistently rejecting and themselves as insecure, becoming distant from others and self-reliant.

- Insecure-disorganised attachment: Children experience their caregivers as either frightening or frightened and themselves as helpless, angry and unworthy; they may display confused and contradictory behaviours in desperation and fear, unable to manage stress.

Critics of attachment theory have argued that it has been used as a means of blaming parents, particularly mothers, when things go wrong. The focus on the parent–child bond as the root of all healthy development can detract from the importance of wider socio-economic and structural factors that impact pervasively upon children and families. Nevertheless, attachment theory has continued to evolve and remains important in reinforcing the centrality for children of their primary family relationships. Rutter (1972) revised Bowlby's theory by emphasising that the quality of the primary relationship is more important than the gender of the attachment figure. This has formed the basis of wider discussions, for example, in Scourfield (2003) and Featherstone and colleagues (2007), recognising the capability of fathers as primary carers and the importance for the child of a positive relationship with their father. It is clear that children's attachment relationships may be multiple, adaptable and flexible, in that children benefit from having strong bonds with more than one carer. Children's attachment patterns may vary between different carers and across cultures and may change across the life course. Crittenden (2000) sees terms such as secure and insecure as inappropriately fixed and value-laden; she emphasises that children's attachment behaviour is an adaptive response within the context of particular relationships, a coping strategy whereby children learn to manage stress. Where children have had poor attachment bonds in the past, they can be enabled through consistent care to develop more positive relationships, new attachment styles and more effective coping mechanisms. Child-centred practitioners need a sound understanding of attachment theory in order to assess the quality of the child's attachment relationships, intervene to strengthen attachment bonds within families and support children in developing new attachments where previous bonds have been broken.

It must be remembered that social workers are not experts in attachment, and there is a risk of misdiagnosing or labelling children as having attachment difficulties. This is especially pertinent to situations where the child has suffered trauma, abuse or neglect and may display features of attachment problems. To put this into perspective, there is an established body of evidence highlighting that insecure attachments are relatively common. The attachment patterns within any given population have been estimated to be distributed in the following approximate rates:

- Secure pattern – 55%

- Ambivalent pattern – 8%

- Avoidant pattern – 23%

- Disorganised pattern – 15%.

(Shemmings, 2011)

Although only 15% of children in the general population develop a disorganised attachment, it is estimated that up to 80% of children who are maltreated develop a disorganised attachment style (Brown and Ward, 2013). These children can display unpredictable behaviour and difficulty regulating their emotions. However, not all children who have a disorganised attachment style have been maltreated. Attachment is a complex area and caution needs to be used when seeking to assess the attachment relationships of children and young people. It is important to avoid labelling families where children are demonstrating emotional or behavioural problems or where there are difficulties in their relationships. Nevertheless, developing a good understanding of attachment theory is a valuable tool for child-centred practice. It reminds us that relationships matter and prompts interventions with children and carers aimed at strengthening attachment bonds.

Points for Reflection

- What were your primary attachment relationships in infancy? How did these relationships influence your childhood and your adulthood?

- How might the attachment experiences of parents and carers influence their parenting?

Commentary

It is useful to reflect on and consider how our own attachment experiences influence our adult styles of relating to others. This might be important in understanding how we form and manage our professional relationships. Furthermore, a thorough understanding of parents' own personal parenting experience from early childhood can offer a useful insight into how they have formed relationships with their own children, and how their children's needs are met.

For example:

Annabelle, a social work student, co-works the case of George (3 months old) with a qualified social worker whilst on her final placement. George is the son of 18-year-old Sarah who is a care leaver and now lives independently. Sarah entered the care system aged 9, due to physical abuse by her mother, and moved placements three times. Sarah struggled to form a positive relationship with her foster carers and presented as self-reliant, detached and distant. Sarah's placements broke down when she began to display challenging behaviour.

George was placed on a child protection plan under the category of neglect as an unborn child following assessment, due to Sarah's lifestyle. Annabelle helped Sarah to spend her maternity grant on essential items for George before his arrival; supported Sarah with practical skills, such as feeding, changing and bathing her baby; and helped Sarah register George's birth and access benefits. They have built up a good working relationship, and Sarah has begun to make positive changes enabling her to confidently care for George. However, in the last few weeks Annabelle has noticed that Sarah has not responded to George's cries immediately, which is unusual for Sarah. Sarah seems less motivated and flat in mood. Sarah says she's 'OK' and 'nothing is wrong'. When Sarah does pick up George, Annabelle has observed Sarah does not always look at him or hold him very close to her. On speaking with the allocated social worker about her concerns, Annabelle agrees to contact the health visitor. Annabelle raises Sarah's own childhood difficulties with the health visitor, especially in relation to struggling to build relationships in the past, which may be impacting on her bond with George. The health visitor meets with Sarah the following day and talks with her about whether she may be suffering from post-natal depression. However, the crucial information obtained regarding Sarah's own early childhood history also prompts the health visitor, with Sarah's permission, to refer Sarah and George for one-to-one attachment work. This is accessed through a specialist infant mental health service, and a worker is allocated to meet with the family. Through weekly inputs, including counselling and baby massage sessions, Sarah is able to build her bond with George and respond more sensitively to his needs.

Parenting

Sociological perspectives recognise parenting as a socially constructed concept; what it means to be a good parent changes over time and is dependent upon cultural context. The very notion of parenting is a relatively modern concept, previously regarded as the domain of motherhood. The fact that the term is no longer linked to one gender acknowledges changes in social understanding of equality and learning from research that recognises that men are just as capable as women of fulfilling the role and functions of parenthood. Parenting relates to a relationship, a role, a responsibility and a range of activities undertaken to facilitate the healthy development of the child from infancy to adulthood. Professional understanding in the UK has been shaped by the focus of the assessment framework (Department of Health, 2000a: 21) on parenting capacity, which involves the effective fulfilment of the following: 'basic care; ensuring safety and providing stability; emotional warmth and stimulation; guidance and boundaries.'

There is a wealth of research exploring what it means to be a parent and the qualities that enable people to succeed in the challenging task of raising happy, healthy children who are able to fulfil their potential. Baumrind (1967) emphasised the importance of authoritative parenting. This is distinct from authoritarian or punitive parenting; authoritative parenting is a confident style of communication with children, providing clear rules and supportive guidance. High expectations are combined with warmth and responsiveness; assertiveness is coupled with nurturance and encouragement. Recent research has reinforced the crucial role parents play in raising children, particularly in the early years. Ramey and Ramey (2004) emphasise that parents provide the secure base for their child, enabling them to learn new skills. Across cultures, good parents are characterised by how they support effort and achievement, protect children from inappropriate levels of stress or disapproval, communicate with them richly and responsively and guide their behaviour through modelling emotional control and good conduct. To enable progress through adolescence, parents adjust their parenting style to be more flexible, less authority figure and more mentor, enabling the increasing independence of young people whilst maintaining family connectedness (Fergus and Zimmerman, 2005).

However, it has become increasingly recognised that parents are not necessarily naturally endowed with the range of capacities and skills to fulfil the range of roles and tasks that are required to nurture the child from early infancy through to adulthood. Donald Winnicott (1965) coined the phrase 'good enough parenting', acknowledging that for many parents their role involves negative as well as positive impacts, ambivalence as well as satisfaction. Winnicott's work has been helpful in enabling childcare policy-makers and professionals to recognise the challenges of modern parenting and the importance of providing supportive services to enable and enhance parenting.

Practitioner Testimonial

Child-centred practice is ensuring that a child is empowered to feel that their views are important and will be listened to and will not put the child at further risk or danger. Child-centred practice is ensuring that a child has a person they feel comfortable speaking to about any issues, which may not always be me as the allocated social worker.

Child-centred practice also means taking into account observations of the child's relationships within the family and wider network and how they impact on the child and their behaviour. Child-centred practice can at times mean doing things that upset children, but is for their longer-term benefit and safety. Child-centred practice is ensuring that the child's needs are paramount and that their needs are being met by their main carer, and if not, putting appropriate support in place.

Elly Giles, Senior Social Worker.

Supporting parents

Most parents have many roles. As well as caring for their children, they are busy pursuing their own personal and professional lives, seeking to maintain health, employment and relationships with varying degrees of success. The fragmented nature of modern families, coupled with social and economic stress, adds to the pressure and isolation that many parents feel. Childcare professionals are likely to work with parents who are managing additional challenges. Commentators, including Cleaver and colleagues (2011), have written extensively about factors such as parental learning difficulties, mental health problems, substance misuse and domestic violence, and how such factors impact upon parenting capacity. This is explored more fully in Chapter 7. The psychological resources of parents and their well-being, in particular the health of the co-parent relationship and their context of support or stress, directly impacts on their capability as parents and consequently on their children's well-being (Belsky, 1984). If parents are experiencing stress and distress in their own lives and relationships, this is likely to impact upon their ability to provide nurture and care for their children. Children are often aware of parental conflict and domestic strife, even if they do not fully understand what is happening in their family. Children can often be seen as barometers of family health, their well-being reflecting the atmosphere in the home. In their behaviour, children often model their caregiver's behaviour towards them, so that kindness and confidence is a reflection of positive care and attention, whereas lack of emotional responsiveness may be due to emotional neglect (Howe, 2005).

Frost and colleagues (2015) note that many parents experience a sense of stigma and shame, and may struggle to access help due to anxiety about being judged or criticised by professionals or even losing their children to the care system. Child-centred social workers have an important role to play in engaging with parents without blame, seeking to support struggling families and enabling them to access help in order to enhance parenting capacity (Featherstone et al, 2016). In Chapter 1, we noted the value of 'think family' approaches that aim to provide an integrated package of support to address the problems that parents may be grappling with, strengthen family functioning and enhance child welfare. However, Featherstone and colleagues (2014) have noted that some social workers, particularly within the context of child protection practice, adopt a stance of 'I'm only here for the child', engaging with parents in an officious, perfunctory or instrumental manner. Such an approach is unlikely to enable holistic assessment of the issues impacting upon the child or effective intervention to support the family and improve outcomes for children. Child-centred practitioners recognise the importance of engaging with parents and carers, building relationships of trust in order to work effectively to safeguard children and support families.

We have noted the importance of social capital, in particular networks of support that enable family functioning and promote the life chances of children and young people. Supporting families involves identifying key kin among extended family and friends, as well as recognising the contribution of services in the local community in order to develop effective plans to support parents. Childcare professionals mobilise and co-ordinate formal supportive services, alongside informal networks in the local community, to consolidate the support network parents can draw upon when dealing with stressful circumstances, so as to: 'enhance natural coping skills and buffer against the deleterious effects of adverse circumstances' (Ghate and Hazel, 2002: 217). As well as being a source of support for parents, it is important to recognise that factors in the wider environment and community can also increase the stress that families experience. Of particular importance for social workers, who spend most of their professional lives working with marginalised and socially excluded families, is a recognition of the impact of poverty on family functioning and the life chances of children.

Points for Reflection

- How should society support parents?
- Can you give an example of good practice in family support?

Commentary

Many children live with adults who have their own additional needs, which in turn impact on the physical and emotional needs of their children. Adult behaviour and health issues are central to understanding parenting capacity. Child-centred practitioners need to recognise the wider needs of the family and respond to these in a holistic way, ensuring the child's needs are paramount.

For example:

Maryam (12 years) arrived in the UK 18 months ago when she and her mother, Halima, sought asylum from their home country of Nigeria, West Africa. Maryam was referred by school when she was becoming increasingly withdrawn and tired. Maryam disclosed to a teacher that her mother, Halima, had become depressed and would not leave the house. Maryam was doing all the household tasks, including cooking, shopping and cleaning. Angela, a social worker, has worked with Maryam and Halima for 9 months. A child in need plan was initiated following a comprehensive assessment to support the family.

Central to Angela's work was engaging with Halima, who was initially avoidant. Halima was clearly low in mood, but she was also unfamiliar with the role of a social worker and was fearful of professional intervention. Halima had limited English and an interpreter was used on all visits, which added an additional barrier to establishing a relationship with Halima. After a series of home visits, Halima began to slowly trust Angela and share information. Halima was struggling to manage on her low income, had become very isolated and felt unable to access help regarding her own mental health. Angela, with Halima's consent, arranged an appointment for Halima with her GP, with an interpreter, for an assessment of her mental health; encouraged Halima to meet a local service supporting asylum seekers and refugees; and referred Halima for budgeting advice from a local family support service. Halima slowly began to feel better and this in turn had a positive impact on Maryam. Maryam was seen fortnightly by Angela in school. Over the months Angela saw an improvement in Maryam's presentation. She appeared happier, brighter and healthier. Maryam expressed that she was sleeping and eating better as Halima was doing more household tasks again. Maryam felt able to concentrate on her school work and see her friends.

Social and environmental factors

Parents do not raise their children in a vacuum. The social, economic and community context of family life has an impact on the health and well-being of parents and children. When the assessment framework was introduced in 2000, it reminded professionals that, in order to make an ecological and holistic assessment of the needs of the child, the impact of environmental factors needed to be considered and addressed. These include housing, employment and income of the family, and other factors, particularly those that contribute to social capital, such as extended family support and community resources, and whether the family is integrated into the local community or socially isolated. More recently, we have become aware of the impact of digital technology on social life and how the 'virtual environment' forms part of the context of children's lives.

The impact of poverty

According to the Child Poverty Action Group, in 2014–15 there were 3.9 million children living in poverty in the UK, one of the worst levels of child poverty in the industrialised world. Child poverty is becoming an entrenched and escalating feature of the British landscape. In 1979 around 14% of children lived in poverty; by 2014 this was around 28% of children. A report by Browne and colleagues (2013) for the Institute for Fiscal Studies estimates that 800,000 more children will be pushed into poverty by 2020 as a result of the government's austerity measures and welfare reforms. Research by Reed (2012) examined the impact of the economic recession and changes to the benefit system and found that the most vulnerable children were affected disproportionately and more adversely than any other social group.

Relative income is the most commonly used measure of poverty, meaning those families whose income is less than 60% of average UK incomes. Households with children are more likely to experience financial hardship than those without children, as families struggle with the additional costs for basic necessities, including childcare, alongside reduced opportunities for employment. Numerous studies have established that poverty impacts on every aspect of children's lives, meaning they grow up in cold, damp and insecure housing, leave school with lower than expected GSCE results and have fewer opportunities in further education or employment. Children from low-income families often forgo events that most of their peers take for granted. They cannot afford to go on school trips, invite friends round for tea or celebrate birthdays, and rarely manage a one-week holiday away from home. As David Utting (1995: 40) has powerfully argued: 'Living on a low income in a run-down neighbourhood does not make it impossible to be the affectionate, authoritative parent of healthy, sociable children. But it does, undeniably, make it more difficult.'

Poverty is bad for the health of children and can be a matter of life or death. The Children's Society (2013) has calculated that children born into poor families are more likely to be born prematurely, have low birth weights and die in their first year of life; throughout childhood they have a higher rate of accidents and accidental death. Furthermore, children living in low-income families are nearly three times as likely to suffer mental health problems as their more affluent peers. Poverty also has long-term effects, as children growing up in poor households are more likely to suffer poor physical and mental health in adulthood. Children who experience poverty are more likely to have problems with relationships, including an increased likelihood of being bullied, and have less supportive relationships with friends and family. These problems can affect how well children perform at school and their prospects of finding a way out of poverty as adults (Gibb et al., 2016). Some disadvantaged communities are characterised by high rates of crime and low levels of neighbourhood services, meaning the social capital resources for families are impoverished. Being alert to these impacts and seeking to mitigate them through promoting the rights of children and families affected by poverty, and seeking to improve the material conditions of their lives is an important aspect of social work practice.

Of particular relevance to social workers is how poverty impacts upon the daily lives and life chances of many of the families they work with. It has been calculated that: 'a child in Blackpool is 12 times more likely to be the subject of care and protection interventions than a child living in Richmond' (Featherstone et al., 2016: 7). This highlights the relationship between living in a deprived local authority and receiving the attention of local authority social workers. Bywaters (2015) has argued that deprivation is the most significant explanatory factor for children being on child protection plans or in care in the UK. Furthermore, a study by the Children's Society (2011) found that four in ten children with a disability are living in poverty, due to the difficulties for their parents in combining their caring roles with sustainable employment and the additional costs of raising a child with special needs. Asylum-seeking families are prohibited from working and can only claim a much lower level of welfare benefits than UK families, leaving many families at risk of destitution. Statistics collated by the Department for Work and Pensions (2013) has shown that:

- 43% of children in lone-parent households live in poverty compared to 22% in two-parent families.

- 36% of children in families with three or more children are at risk of being in poverty, in comparison to 24% of families with two children.

- 44% of children in Black or Black British households are living in poverty; this rises to 55% in Pakistani and Bangladeshi households, compared with 25% of White children.

Points for Reflection

- Are you surprised by the high level of poverty in the UK, one of the wealthiest countries in the world?

- How do you think children are affected by poverty?

Commentary
'Poverty blights children's lives and their futures', and affects many aspects of their day-to-day lives (Save the Children, 2012: 14). Families must make increasingly difficult choices about how they manage their finances and cope with financial pressures. Too often the pressure of a low income puts enormous strain on children and their families.

For example:
Graham, a children's disability social worker, is allocated the case of Jamie (14 years). His parents are Adam and Helen, and he has an 11-year-old sister called Selena. Adam works full time in a low-paid job. Jamie has a diagnosis of cerebral palsy and as a result has both physical and learning needs. He can walk with a frame in the house, but is a wheelchair user when out in the community. Jamie travels 40 minutes by taxi to and from school, as this is the nearest educational provision to meet his needs. Jamie needs constant supervision and support at home, including assistance to wash, dress and eat. Graham carries out an assessment and recognises that Adam and Helen both work very hard to meet their children's needs; however, Jamie's disability has an impact on the family's overstretched resources and as a result they are struggling with the effects of poverty. There is a lot of extra washing due to Jamie's health needs. He often has accidents and needs help to eat. The family attend regular health appointments and the hospital is 14 miles away. Adam struggles to take time off work, so Helen has to get a taxi with Jamie as she doesn't drive. The family have difficulty accessing childcare for Jamie in school holidays,

◀ due to his complex health needs. This has prevented Helen from accessing work herself. Adam and Helen generally manage bills well, but they have recently incurred bank charges due to overspending when Selena started high school and needed a new uniform and equipment. In the past, they have had to resort to high-interest pay-day loans. Graham offers support around managing finances and ensures the family are fully informed about welfare benefits. He organises short breaks once a month for Jamie; this gives Adam and Helen some quality time together and with Selena. Graham also applies for a holiday through a children's charity, recognising that the family have not had a holiday for years. He links the family to a local parent's support group that organises regional campaigns to promote disability rights and is currently working on public transport issues.

Sociological perspectives enable professionals to recognise the impact of social disadvantage, discrimination and economic hardship on children and families. Whilst acknowledging the capability of the 'social child', it is important also to note that the individualisation of agency can lead to the attribution of responsibility and blame. Personal capacity and individual agency is circumscribed by the experience of oppression and socio-economic disadvantage. Lister (2013) argues that poverty corrodes human dignity and social relations, increasing shame and stigma, and reducing opportunities for choice and participation. For some children, the constraints upon their ability to function within and contribute to society are imposed not only by their status as children, but also by the impact of social class and poverty, which may be further compounded by factors such as disability or refugee status. Recognising the structural systems that perpetuate poverty promotes practice that challenges inequality, rather than labelling families trapped in disadvantaged circumstances or blaming parents for the cycle of deprivation that may impact upon their children. Individual agency is often eclipsed by the impact of structural disadvantages that have the potential to shape a child's life chances (Llewellyn et al., 2015). Social workers have an important part to play in taking forward anti-oppressive approaches to practice in order to support children and families affected by poverty and inequality.

Learning from Research

Some studies have taken a child-centred approach to represent and understand children's perspectives of their experience of poverty. Ridge (2002, 2009) gathered children's accounts of what it meant for them to be poor. She found that children often tried to hide from their parents that they were hungry or worried about money. They particularly disliked missing out on school activities and being stigmatised and bullied due to the visible signs of poverty. Nicole, aged 13, commented: 'You can't do as much, and I don't like my ▶

clothes and that, so I don't really get to do much or do stuff like my friends are doing … I am worried about what people think of me, like they think I am sad or something.' The studies also found that children worried about their family and the pressures on them that sometimes led to stress and arguments. They assumed additional responsibilities in an effort to support their parents.

Main and Pople (2011) undertook a child-centred analysis of material deprivation and subjective well-being. In collaboration with young people they drew up a list of ten possessions and experiences regarded as being part of 'a normal kind of life' for someone their age (including having a garden or safe place to play, the right kind of clothes, satellite/cable TV, regular family trips). They surveyed 5,500 young people aged 8 to 15 across England, exploring their attitudes to these items and how they measured their happiness (using a subjective well-being scale). The researchers found that lacking two or more items meant that children were at risk of material deprivation; lacking five or more items suggested severe material deprivation. Furthermore, they found that the list was linked to children's subjective well-being in the following ways:

- Lacking each individual item was associated with higher odds of being unhappy; having the items was closely correlated to rating one's own well-being highly.

- Lacking the kind of clothes to fit in with their peers was most strongly associated with being unhappy; children lacking this item were five times more likely to be unhappy.

- Children lacking five or more items were over five times more likely to have low well-being than those who lacked none.

A focus group of 36 children and young people emphasised why these items mattered and are seen as enabling 'normal life':

- Fitting in and building relationships: Children saw some experiences as integral to developing good relationships; they felt the negative social consequences amongst their peer group of lacking certain items.

- Having fun: The items were seen as part of life's enjoyment in the present.

- Development: Participants understood that there is a relationship between their resources and experiences in the present and their future success.

Main and Pople's research highlights the link between material poverty and poor well-being for children and young people.

Child-centred practitioners need to recognise the ways in which growing up in poverty can impact on the well-being of children and young people in the present, as well as on their long-term life chances. Challenging inequality and supporting families struggling with the consequences of deprivation and disadvantage are important aspects of anti-discriminatory practice. Listening to the voices of the children we work with, and understanding what matters to them, is an integral element of anti-oppressive and child-centred social work.

Children and digital technology

An increasingly important component of the social context within which children and young people live their lives is the digital landscape. In 2001 American educationalist Marc Prensky coined the phrase 'digital native' to highlight how young people grow up immersed in a digital world which sometimes places them at odds with adults who fail to understand or relate to their world. It is clear that children's use of digital technology, particularly through the almost ubiquitous availability of smartphones, has grown exponentially over recent years. Children and young people are often experts in the digital world of the internet, social networking and online gaming, whilst many adults trail behind. The fast pace of digital development means it is difficult to gain an accurate contemporary picture from published research. In 2011, Livingstone and colleagues reported that 20% of nine year olds in the UK use social networking sites (SNSs); Lilley and Ball (2013) noted that around half of all 11 to 12 year olds use such sites, despite the fact that most popular SNSs stipulate that users must be at least 13 years old. By the time of publication of this text, all this may have changed.

Many adults, including parents and professionals, feel concern about how some aspects of digital technology impact upon the lives of children and young people. Some have argued that this amounts to a moral panic about how technology is changing childhood. There have been particular concerns around how excessive amounts of screen time among young people may affect mental and physical health, increasing risk factors ranging from social isolation, sleep deprivation and obesity to cyber-bullying and online grooming. When a ten-year study by the University of Cambridge (Corder et al., 2015) concluded that an extra hour of screen time per day was associated with a drop of two GSCE grades, a media furore ensued.

Findings from research which identify links between the use of technology and the welfare of children are often mixed. Whilst there may be concerns around excessive use of the internet leading to the inability to concentrate or develop real (rather than virtual) friendships, it may be that children are developing new and important skills, such as the ability to scan large quantities of data and identify how to access information, as well as the social acumen to develop online supportive networks with like-minded young people. Interactions with violent games may lead to increased aggressive behaviour or provide a tool to enable children to regulate their emotions and work co-operatively with other gamers. Devine and Lloyd (2012) found that heavy use of SNS and online gaming among 10- and 11-year-old children in Northern Ireland was related to poor psychological well-being, in particular because for these heavier users there was reduced opportunity for face-to-face interaction and an increased likelihood of cyber-bullying. Nevertheless, the authors note that for some socially awkward children, boys in particular, digital media can provide the means to gain acceptance and raise self-esteem.

In their review of the literature about social media and adolescent well-being, Best and colleagues (2014) emphasise that digital technology in itself is a neutral tool, acting as a value-free facilitator of human interaction. They found that the impact may be either beneficial, increasing social support and social capital, or harmful, through increased exposure to abusive and negative content, or both. Anne Longfield, Children's Commissioner for England, has recently noted:

> Childhood is being rapidly transformed by the internet in a creative but socially and legally disorganised way. Children are among the greatest users of the internet, but it was not designed with them in mind ... If children today and tomorrow are to grow up digitally we need to be sure that the rights to protection and empowerment that they enjoy in their lives are embedded in the new digital world they inhabit.

(Internet Taskforce Press Statement, August 2015)

It is evident that there is a need to develop greater understanding of how to promote and protect the interests and welfare of children online. Most commentators emphasise the importance of education about the benefits and pitfalls of online communication. Livingstone and colleagues (2011) recognise the value of encouraging the capability of children and young people, focusing on information and empowerment to enable responsible digital citizenship.

Focus on Practice

An example of positive action is the work of 'iRights', an online initiative led by the UK Safer Internet Centre, which seeks to: 'make the digital world a more transparent and empowering place for children and young people.'

Five key rights have been developed pertaining to children and digital technology:

- The Right to Remove – for young people to be able to easily edit or delete content they have previously created.

- The Right to Know – for terms and conditions to be understandable and for young people to know who is holding, using or profiting from their data.

- The Right to Safety and Support – to be protected from illegal practices and supported if confronted by troubling or upsetting scenarios online.

- The Right to Informed and Conscious Choices – to be able to engage with information and communication networks and also disengage easily.

- The Right to Digital Literacy – to access the knowledge that the Internet can deliver, be taught the skills to use, create and critique digital technologies, and given the tools to negotiate changing social norms.

(http://www.saferinternet.org.uk/blog/irights-launch)

The young people involved in developing iRights emphasised the following issues about the digital world:

'We're the generation who won't remember what life was like before the invention of the internet.'

'It's true the internet creates many positive opportunities. We can express our personality online, be creative, experiment.'

'The internet opens the door to negative things. Online bullying is a growing issue. Stumbling upon [inappropriate content] can be a daily and upsetting occurrence.'

The digital world may in some ways replicate and exacerbate patterns that exist in the real world; the evidence from research suggests that young people with high self-esteem and strong friendships gain increased social networks and other benefits from online activities, whereas the vulnerable may be more likely to be drawn into risky, addictive or isolating behaviours. For childcare professionals, it is important to recognise the importance for children and young people of their digital world and to be open to exploring with them the potential benefits and the possible risks. Some children may have limited opportunities to access digital technology, exacerbating their social exclusion and educational disadvantage. For children and families living in deprived circumstances, the internet is an important tool to access information, build social networks and thereby enhance social capital. However, there are clearly risks associated with the internet. Martellozzo and colleagues (2016), carried out online research about 'sexting' with over a thousand children aged 11–16. They found that around one in seven young people had taken a naked or semi-naked picture of themselves and over half of those children had shared the photo with someone else. Vulnerable children, including children who have experienced abuse, are in care or are disabled, may be more likely to experience cyber-bullying and online grooming.

Child-centred practitioners need to understand the significance of digital technology in the lives of children and young people, showing interest in the things that matter to them. In so doing, we might support the fulfilment of two of the iRights outlined above, enabling children to make informed choices and providing safety and support where needed. Professionals need to be alert to changes in law and policy, as society seeks to keep up with developments in digital technology, and maintain safe boundaries. For example, children are protected from online (and offline) grooming through the Sexual Offences Act 2003; and the Serious Crimes Act 2015, created the new offence of sexual communication with a child, including texts or online chat intended to elicit sexual communication. In undertaking this work, it will be important to engage with parents and carers, who are usually the main supporters of children and young people as they negotiate the virtual and the real world.

Points for Reflection

- What is your own relationship to digital technology? Would you describe yourself as a 'digital native'?
- What do you see as the positives and the risks for children and young people growing up in the digital age?

Promoting resilience and protective factors for children and young people

In recent years, social workers have gained a greater understanding of the importance of resilience and the protective factors that promote the welfare of children and young people. Knowledge drawn from research highlights that resilience is an ecological concept, related to the development of the individual child in the context of their family and the wider environment. American psychologists Masten and Coatsworth (1998) have been influential in developing this concept, explaining that:

> Successful children who do well despite adversity remind us that children grow up in multiple contexts – in families, schools, peer groups, baseball teams, religious organisations, and many other groups – and each context is a potential source of protective as well as risk factors. These children demonstrate that children are protected not only by the self-righting nature of development, but also the actions of adults, by their own actions, by the nurturing of their assets, by opportunities to succeed and by the experience of success.

(Masten and Coatsworth, 1998: 216)

The ability to develop resilience is variable and context-specific. Some children overcome experiences of extreme trauma, such as war or the death of a loved one, and develop as competent individuals; others struggle to manage what might be seen as the normal stresses of daily life, such as moving house or negotiating friendships. A young person may be confident and resilient in most aspects of life, but struggle to overcome a particular challenge. Ecological theory helps us to recognise that resilience is about factors that are intrinsic to the child, such as the strengths and vulnerabilities related to their personality, health, educational prowess, age and stage of development, ability or disability; and external factors, such as parental capacity, extended family support, community resources and experience of adversity or hardship. Rutter (2007) notes that resilience is about the ability to resist the negative impacts of environmental risks, including poverty and maltreatment, and the nurturance of personal qualities of self-efficacy and competence. The potential for a child to develop resilience seems to be contingent upon the balance of risk and protective factors in their lives (Jack and Donnellan, 2013). Ultimately a resilient child or young person is able to make positive adaptations, despite significant experiences of adversity.

The resilience matrix, developed by Brigid Daniel and colleagues (2010), has drawn on messages from research to identify those factors that might generate positive or negative outcomes for children. These can be summarised as:

- Factors intrinsic to a resilient child include secure attachments, an outgoing temperament, problem-solving skills and coping strategies.

- Factors intrinsic to a vulnerable child include early infancy, health problems, special educational needs and disabilities.

- Protective factors in the environment include positive school experiences, the consistent presence of a supportive adult, community networks of support and access to leisure activities that harness talent and promote achievement.

- Risk factors in the environment include living with poverty and deprivation, school exclusion, social isolation, experiences of racism or bullying and loss or bereavement.

(Daniel et al., 2010).

Michael Rutter's work (1979) highlighted that children are often able to do well when exposed to only one risk factor; however, the addition of risk and vulnerability factors can have a disproportionate and cumulative effect. In other words, children growing up in families coping with two risk factors may be four times more likely than their peers to experience adversity. Rutter noted that for an impoverished single parent raising four children in a dangerous neighbourhood, the likelihood of negative outcomes for the children is substantially increased. In this chapter, we have recognised the impact of poverty in exacerbating adversity and limiting the opportunities for children. We have emphasised the central role of parents and families in providing the nurture and support that children need to do well, despite challenging circumstances or difficult experiences. Current government policy, articulated in the Department for Education document *Putting Children First* (2016b), emphasises that strengthening families is integral to the aim of promoting the life chances of children who may have had a difficult start in life. It goes on to note: 'Children who grow up with safe, stable and nurturing relationships form stronger friendships, develop greater resilience, achieve more in school and are more likely to build successful careers and have positive relationships throughout their lives' (2016: 8). Professionals who intervene in the lives of children need to do so in a way that enhances

protective factors and promotes resilience, seeking to address risk and vulnerability factors and to mitigate the impact of adversity. Social workers have a key
role in supporting families and identifying and mobilising protective factors that
can act as a buffer for children against the potentially damaging consequences
of adverse circumstances.

Points for Reflection

- Considering your own childhood, what were the factors that enabled you to be resilient?
- Consider a child you have recently worked with: what are the protective factors or risk factors that have had the most impact upon the child?
- Can you think of an example of good practice that has promoted the resilience of a child or young person?

Commentary

The effects of adverse events upon children, including abuse and neglect, are not experienced in the same way for every child. Children and their families possess protective
factors and psychological resources that enable resilience, often in the face of considerable trauma. These can protect the child from longer-term harm.

For example:

Social worker Melanie has supported Justina (17 years) for the last 6 months. Justina
was the victim of human trafficking from her home country of Lithuania. This is Justina's
story:

*We lived in a poor area and there were no jobs. My father's friend had been to Eng-
land and said he could get me a job. He was a nice man. He said I was very beautiful
and he loved me. I was 16 at the time. He said I looked older and could easily work
in a bar or a factory. He got my passport and paid for my travel. When we arrived in
England he said there were no more jobs left. He said I had to pay him back. He said
I had to have sex with men. I said 'no', but I was scared. He became angry and nasty.
I had sex with men and had to give him all the money. He didn't let me out without
him or one of his friends. Then 2 other girls came from Romania and they became my
friends. The police knocked at the door one night and we were scared to tell them the
truth. But one of the girls was brave and spoke up. The police took us all for question-
ing. The girl told the police what had happened. The police and the Courts helped us.
I went to live in a housing project and Melanie became my social worker. I get on well
with Melanie. I have recently started college and am enjoying it. I am proud of my
English language skills and sometimes I interpret for other people in the housing
project. I keep in touch with my friends and have made some new friends. I still feel
scared sometimes but I'm doing okay.*

Focus on Practice

Recognising the importance of resilience, child-centred practitioners will seek to promote the following in their work with children and young people:

● Security and stability, enabling children to build positive attachments within their family, so that they feel safe to explore their wider environment and are able to learn and build healthy relationships.

● A sense of belonging, through which children can form enduring connections with family members, key kin, significant adults and siblings and peers who provide a supportive network.

● Self-esteem, whereby children will feel worthy of love and have a sense of their own individuality and competence.

● Positive experiences, including opportunities for achievement and enjoyment within school and local faith, sporting or social organisations, building skills, talents and community engagement.

● Self-efficacy, enabling children to participate and have a say, thus gaining a sense of mastery and capability.

Child-centred practitioners will recognise, in particular, that the way in which they engage with children and young people, enabling their involvement in the assessment and intervention process, will contribute to the promotion of resilience. How professionals work with children, respecting their rights and supporting their participation, engenders the sense of competence and self-efficacy, which is a fundamental building block of resilience. We go on to explore more fully in Chapter 5 effective approaches to working with children and young people to promote their capability and resilience.

Conclusion

It is clear then that effective child-centred practice involves seeking to understand the life and perspectives of the child in their particular social, environmental and familial context. For professionals to support families and maintain a child-centred approach, it is important to have a good understanding of the factors that strengthen parental functioning and promote resilience for children. Attachment theory emphasises that relationships matter, especially primary relationships within the child's family. Ecological models help us to recognise how different relationships or systems interact to provide a supportive or negative environment for the development of the child. It is evident that positive social networks, including those in the digital world, can enhance the social capital and thence the well-being of the child. Social support, both informal support within the family and community and the formal support of child care professionals, can provide a buffer for children, to mitigate the impact of harm caused by negative life experiences, poverty and disadvantage. Child-centred practitioners apply this knowledge in order to identify and strengthen the protective factors around the child and to promote the resilience, self-esteem and self-efficacy of the child.

Recommended reading and resources

- *The Good Childhood Report*, published by the Children's Society (2014), provides a fascinating overview of the lives and perspectives of children and young people across the UK, the issues impacting on their well-being and how these compare with the experiences of children in other countries.

- The chapter by David Howe (2010) on the theme of attachment in *The Child's World*, edited by Jan Horwath, provides a helpful introduction to attachment theory and why it matters in social work practice.

- Funded by the Department for Education, Research in Practice has developed a website focused around fostering and adoption that includes an excellent section on the theme of attachment theory and research (topic number 2). The web page includes fascinating links to YouTube clips that demonstrate the research on different forms of attachment, and also the 'strange situation' and the 'still face' experiments. Available at: http://fosteringandadoption.rip.org.uk/topics/attachment-theory-research/

- The chapters on 'Family and Community' and 'Children and Young People' in the textbook *Sociology for Social Workers* by Llewellyn and colleagues (2015) provide a useful overview of relevant issues from a sociological perspective.

- The author (Tracey Race) has recently contributed to a textbook, *Family Support*, alongside co-authors Frost and Abbott and Race (2015). The book explores many relevant themes about the importance of working in partnership with parents to ensure good outcomes for children and young people.

- The Social Care Institute for Excellence has developed guidance for practitioners (focusing on work around parental health) entitled *Think child, think parent, think family.* The website is useful in recognising the importance of holistic assessment and joined-up approaches to practice in complex cases. Available at: www.scie.org.uk/publications/guides/guide30/introduction/thinkchild.asp

- The NSPCC has brought together research about online risks for children and developed guidance for parents and carers. This can be useful for practitioners to be aware of and to share with children and families: www.nspcc.org.uk/preventing-abuse/keeping-children-safe/

- Documentary-maker Jezza Neumann has created a series of films about the lives of children affected by poverty in the UK, aired on television in 2011 and 2013: *Poor Kids.* The documentaries are told from the perspectives of the children featured and provide fascinating and poignant insights into the experience of childhood poverty. You can search for the films on YouTube and at: www.bbc.co.uk/programmes/

5

COMMUNICATING WITH CHILDREN AND YOUNG PEOPLE

Introduction

Child-centred practitioners see, hear and engage with children and young people. As Margaret Crompton has pointed out, this is a demanding task: 'Workers' principal skills must be really to see and to listen. This necessitates leaving all fears and assumptions behind, and endeavouring to engage with the world of the child' (Crompton, in Wilson and James, 2007: 395). Children may be anxious to know why professionals are involved in their life or working with their family, curious about their role and concerned about what might happen next. Some children may be keen to talk about their worries, ask questions and let the adults involved know what they want. Others may feel a deep distrust of adults, professionals and social workers in particular. For many children, there will be barriers to overcome, in terms of social context and power relations, level of maturity, ability or disability, language difficulties or speech impairments, in order to express themselves and communicate with a social worker. The situation may be one of crisis or trauma, whereby children are involuntary service users who have no control over the adverse circumstances they find themselves in. Some children will seek out support and advice. Some will adopt defensive strategies of fight or flight, avoiding contact or demonstrating challenging behaviour when approached by professionals. It is the job of the social worker to recognise these responses, to seek to communicate with children and make sense of their world (Tait and Wosu, 2012).

In this chapter, we explore some of the principles underpinning direct work with children. We analyse key aspects of the role of the social worker and ways in which professionals can develop their communication skills in order to carry out effective child-centred practice. We discuss the importance of play and draw on knowledge from play therapy. We recognise the value of empathy in engaging with children and the need for professionals to advocate on behalf of children. The emotional and practical challenges of working directly with children who have experienced trauma, loss or abuse are also explored.

Points for Reflection

● There is an old English proverb that says children should be seen and not heard. What do you think this means and do you believe this view continues to influence contemporary society?

● Why is it important for social workers to see and hear children and young people?

Principles underpinning effective communication with children

Throughout this book, we recognise the importance of a value-based approach in our work with children. An understanding of and commitment to principles underpinning direct work with children provide a strong foundation for child-centred practice (Jones, 2003; Dalzell and Chamberlain, 2006). Social work practice involves listening to, valuing and seeking to empower children and young people.

Ethical use of power

It is evident that power relations are inherent in all interactions between children and adults and between professionals and service users (Smith, 2008). Social workers hold power due to their statutory duties and obligations towards children. It is important to acknowledge the power embodied in the role and to recognise that this may create concerns and anxieties for children. This may be exacerbated in initial contacts with young people who might be feeling powerless and confused about their situation, uncertain about the future and lacking any control over their circumstances. A simple introduction of self and provision of information about the social work role and the purpose of the intervention, in a child-friendly manner, is therefore of crucial importance.

We have noted the value of wearing professional power lightly, which has direct implications for what to actually wear when working with children and young people. Avoiding the power dressing that may be useful for adult meetings or court hearings, and being comfortable enough to sit on the floor with a child in order to chat and play, is a good place to start. Sensitivity and informality is important in building rapport, shedding some of the baggage of officialdom and seeking to make a connection as human beings. Nevertheless, practitioners should acknowledge and pay attention to power issues, rather than denying or blurring them, or ignoring the possible concerns of the child about working with a professional (Holland et al., 2010). It is important to be open and honest about the nature of professional power, its extent and limitations, and to explain what might happen next and why. Bringing warmth and friendliness to our relationships with children is important, alongside recognition of professional role and boundaries. Most children never work with a social worker and if they do, relationships are clearly defined and delineated, and often of a relatively short-term nature. Finding a way to communicate succinctly and clearly, explaining the purpose of our involvement, is an important part of our professional role.

Respect the individuality of the child

How we construct childhood, as discussed in Chapter 3, will inform how we understand the particular child. Child-centred practitioners will respect the rights, agency and capability of the child. Social workers should seek to see the whole child, a person in their own right, and not simply a victim, or a troubled or troublesome youngster. The aim of our communication with the child will be to enable them to make their own unique contribution, to seek to understand their perspectives and to respond with honesty to their questions, acknowledging when our answers remain uncertain. Social workers will bring knowledge of child development to the interaction, recognising that children's ability to participate may vary. Winter (2011b) has noted that accepted understandings related to ages and stages of development can lead to an underestimation of what many younger children can actually understand and their ability to express their views. Respecting the child as competent and assuming their capability will mean the child-centred practitioner takes time to communicate and engage with younger children, as well as young people.

Trinder's work (1997) with children involved in divorce and contact disputes noted that sometimes children may struggle to participate in professional processes or may prefer not to participate at all; they may wish to contribute in some ways and on some occasions, but not always in response to adult expectations:

> What is remarkable and frustrating is how the adult constructions had become ensnared in ... a simple ... dichotomy, where children are classified as either subjects or objects, competent or incompetent, reliable or unreliable, harmed by decision-making or harmed by exclusion, wanting to participate or not wanting to participate ... Some children had very rational reasons for wanting to influence decisions, but others made a rational decision that they were better off acting like children by not participating in an adult decision, or choosing non-participation. (Trinder, 1997: 301–302)

Respecting the individuality of the child means we avoid assumptions about their views and do not impose our expectations about how or whether they might want to engage with us. We recognise that children are competent social actors, but they are also vulnerable and dependent (Eldén, 2012). These aspects of the child's authentic self will come to the fore at different times and in different ways. Such a respectful approach is more likely to lay the foundations for a positive professional relationship with the child and to create the conditions for effective communication.

Valuing children

In every interaction with a child, the social worker will have a clear role and purpose, a professional function to perform, their own agenda. It is essential that workers retain a focus on the task in hand and have a clear sense of their professional identity. However, this should not dominate to the extent that direct work with a child is simply a means to an end of fulfilling professional duties.

Learning from Research

Archard and Skivenes (2009b) found, in research involving child welfare workers in Norway and the UK, that professionals tend to be particularly focused on getting their job done. Whilst recognising the need to ascertain the wishes and feelings of children, as part of their statutory duty, their approach is often instrumental. In their communication with children they focus on:

- hearing the facts and any disclosures of the child;
- securing the information they need in order to complete an assessment within the prescribed timescale;
- providing information;
- encouraging the compliance of the child with ensuing decisions.

There is not always space to really value the child, to take note of their interests, to explore their views. A particular concern the researchers found was: 'a tendency to use the child's views as confirmation of their own, reasons being found to disregard the view if the child disagrees' (Archard and Skivenes, 2009b: 397).

The research also identified workers who took a principled approach, recognising the child's entitlement to contribute and acknowledging their input as equally valid to that of adults and professionals. Some social workers adopted a child-centred approach: 'The worker hears children because he thinks they deserve to be heard and is aware that it is the child's life which will have to be lived in accordance with any decision made for them' (Archard and Skivenes, 2009b: 395).

A value-based approach is informed by an exchange model of communication (Maclean and Harrison, 2015) that recognises service users as experts of their own lives, whatever their age, ability or circumstances, therefore having much to contribute to processes that may be managed by professionals. Despite the targets of the agency and the aims of the intervention, the child may have different views about what is important and the timescales they see as meaningful. Children are busy with the business of growing up and the normal concerns of daily life; decisions about where to play, hobbies, friendships, pets, food and bedtime may well matter more to them than professional concerns about managing risk and completing forms in the required timescales (Thomas and O'Kane, 2000). Valuing the child means working with flexibility to address their interests and concerns and seeking to progress at a pace that makes sense to them.

Points for Reflection

- Can you give an example of how a social worker might demonstrate that they value the child when they begin working with them?

Commentary

It is important to explain to children the purpose of our involvement in a way that makes sense to them. Valuing the contribution of the child means recognising that children are skilful communicators who have their own interests and concerns, and being willing to deviate from organisational or adult agendas in order to attend to the priorities of the child.

For example:

Social work student, Nathan, began working with Yasmin and Niall when their school made a referral in respect of their mother's alcohol misuse. She had collected the children three times within the last two weeks smelling heavily of alcohol. School is also aware that the parents have recently separated. Nathan explained to 5-year-old Yasmin that his job is to make sure that children are 'happy and safe', and 'to help mummies and daddies when they sometimes have problems'. Nathan was able to discuss his role in more depth with the older brother, Niall (aged 11). Nathan explained to Niall the process of referral and assessment in a child-friendly way. Nathan said he had been told by school that their mum had collected them a few times recently and seemed to have been drinking alcohol. The teacher was worried about how she was caring for them at home. Nathan explained his job is to visit children and find out what they are happy about and worried about. This helps him to understand what is happening in the family, and how it affects the children. Nathan said he also speaks to other people who work with children and the adults looking after them, for example mums, dads, teachers, doctors and school nurses, to make sure he has all the information. Nathan explained he can then see what the children and their family may need help with. Nathan said to both children that they are the most important people to talk to, as they know their family better than anyone else. Niall was able to talk to Nathan about his dad and the things they used to do together. He lets Nathan know that he really misses his dad and wishes he could see him more often. He also talks about his pet dog, Ted, and how he misses going home to him after school, since the dog now lives at his father's house. Nathan arranges to meet with both parents to complete the assessment. He addresses the concerns about their mother's drinking. He also advocates on behalf of Niall about how he wants to see more of his father and how important it is for him to have time with their pet dog.

Listening to children

Communication involves *being with* the child and really listening to them. One of the aims of effective communication is to silence the noise of daily life, to withdraw from the clamour for attention of personal issues and professional priorities, in order to focus one's full attention on the person and concerns of the other. The social theorist Habermas (1984) emphasised the value of noise-free dialogue, which he characterised as an authentic, mutual exchange that seeks to reduce distractions and distortions, muddle and misunderstanding. Such communication involves fully being with the person, tuning into their interests, perspectives and feelings. Children rarely receive such focused attention from adults outside their immediate family, and it can be an infrequent experience even among loved-ones, particularly for children referred for social work attention. One of the challenges for social workers who may already have gathered a good deal of information from other professionals and adults prior to meeting the child is to not make assumptions, to take the time to really listen to what a child may be trying to express.

Yamamoto and colleagues' (1998) research (as noted in Chapter 3) has shown that adults tend to inhabit a very different world to that of children and often do not perceive accurately what are the concerns of the child. Social workers need to make the effort to attune to the language and concerns of the child, which may be expressed tentatively or aggressively, or figuratively in their play. Woodcock-Ross (2011) emphasises the importance of emotional attunement, recognising the feeling-content in any conversation, much of which will be observed rather than heard, through cues manifested non-verbally. Social workers will need to draw on personal and professional resources, including reflection and supervision, to ensure that they do not 'tune out' when the going gets tough and children express strong feelings of anger or hurt which may be painful and difficult to hear. The young person who refuses to speak or responds in monosyllables is communicating a clear message to anyone who is willing to listen. The pre-verbal infant or child with a speech impairment is able to express trust and affection, fear and anger through their body language and their interaction with those caring for them. Clark and Moss (2011) emphasise that listening to children is an active process, involving hearing, interpreting and constructing meaning together. Even when contacts between workers and children are short-term or one-off conversations, it is important that professionals take a principled approach to communication with the child, and take the time to tune in to their concerns.

Enabling the involvement and participation of children

The UN (2009) General Comment 12 emphasises that it is the responsibility of the professional working with children to provide them with the opportunities and the means to freely express their views. This includes considerations about venue, a secure and appropriate environment, and materials, such as toys, games, crayons, digital tablets and other creative tools to enable expression on the child's terms. Professionals must be able and willing to adapt their adult settings and styles to the needs and preferences of children. Thomas and O'Kane (2000: 827) emphasise that children are competent social actors but note that 'competence is constructed and negotiated in specific forms of social interaction'. Therefore, through offering choice to children around methods of communication and opportunities to collaborate in order to make sense of the past and plan for the future, the professional is facilitating the competence, as well as the involvement, of the child.

Sometimes, involvement seems to be nothing more than being present in adult-led processes. As we noted in Chapter 2, participation is about more than this; it is about having a say, being able to influence process and outcomes. A commitment to participation means providing opportunities for young people to be: 'individuals with their own social and political identity ... persons with vivid imaginations, deep thoughts, ideas, skills and capacities' (Lolichen, 2009: 136). This goes back to the principle of the ethical use of professional power. To enable and empower children means that adults and professionals need to be willing to share power. How effectively children are able to communicate with their social worker and to have a genuine say in the decisions affecting their lives will depend on the extent to which adults are willing to relinquish control and enable the involvement and participation of children through child-friendly meetings and processes and the prioritisation awarded to time and training to improve the quality of direct work with children.

Learning from Research

Social workers need to listen to children and take seriously what they say. In 2006 the Children's Rights Director, Roger Morgan, consulted with children and young people who had had social work involvement and reported on their views. Young people were asked about whether their social worker takes them seriously. Those who responded said they were taken seriously by their social worker:

- All of the time: 44%

- Most of the time: 18%

- Sometimes: 18%

- Not very often or not at all: 16%

Some young people said their social workers listened to them if they agreed with what the professionals thought was best, but not so much if the child disagreed with something; one young person commented: 'social workers shouldn't have selective hearing' (Morgan, 2006: 19).

The following are other quotes from participants in this research:

'I'd rather talk to someone I feel comfortable with, who keeps in mind they are working on your behalf, rather than side with the government who they work for.'

'I would talk to them about everyday things, something I'm really worried about, someone to help, support and understand me, someone who would be there if I needed them, someone who would maybe go for a coffee, just like one of my old social workers.'

'They need to know and understand that we are human beings, we do have feelings and needs. We can come across angry, unfriendly, etc., but with time they will see a person, a nice person.'

(Morgan, 2006: 7; 10; 26)

Therapeutic support

Social workers are not therapists; nevertheless, we can, and often do, use therapeutic skills and apply therapeutic approaches in our work with children. Social workers will often refer children who are struggling or have experienced abuse and trauma for work with play therapists or child psychologists, rather than recognise that their own input can provide therapeutic support. This is not to undervalue the important work that specialist professionals undertake. For some children who have entrenched behavioural or emotional problems or are experiencing mental health problems, referral for specialist intervention is crucial. However, some referrals for specialist intervention lead to delays due to lengthy waiting lists, and missed appointments due to the difficulties for families of attending clinical settings. Social workers are often well placed to provide thera-peutic support to children, owing to the nature of the relationship they already have with the child and their family, the values they hold that are intrinsic to child-centred practice and the communication skills they have developed that can be adapted to be effective therapeutically (Lefevre, 2010; Tait and Wosu, 2012). Social workers can learn much from therapeutic approaches that can be applied to inform their day-to-day work and thereby to offer therapeutic sup-port to children.

Emotional development and the expression of feelings

Emotional development is at the core of our identity and well-being. Authen-tic expression of our thoughts and feelings is integral to growth and self-development. In their discussion of child-centred play therapy, Cochran and colleagues (2010) emphasise the importance of self-expression for children in developing confidence, autonomy, self-regulation and responsi-bility. For the children social workers come into contact with, who have often experienced upheaval, trauma and loss, opportunities to express their concerns and anxieties and to air feelings of sadness and frustration are all the more important. There is no doubt that this is a challenge for many practitioners. Many social workers feel too bogged down by bureaucracy to engage with the maelstrom of feelings a child may be experiencing. They may worry about opening the proverbial 'can of worms' and then not having the time or skills to manage or contain the emotions that spill out. Kroll's comments about the emotional demands of direct work with children are insightful:

> Working with children is painful. It is often about loss, anger, rejection, neglect and sadness; it is also often about limited options and second rate solutions. It touches private life in tender places, it is unbearable and makes us feel helpless, sad and angry. Many workers admit to keeping children at a distance in an attempt to avoid feeling these feelings, to protect themselves from the pain, and to preserve a sense of com-petence. (Kroll, 1995: 91)

Avoiding the emotional content of work with children is to do children a great disservice. Feelings that are buried in childhood do not simply go away because the adults around the child choose to ignore them. For the child, their feelings, fears and anxieties are part of who they are, a constant presence in their daily lives; failure to acknowledge this and allow space for expression of emotions is to fail to see and hear the whole child. Trusting the agency of the child and their ability to make use of therapeutic opportunities is part of the process that enables the child to move from being at the mercy of their emotions to being able to make sense of and gain mastery over them (Wilson and Ryan, 2005). For many vulnerable children, confusion and distress over past upheavals or present dilemmas are repressed and internalised, storing up mental health problems for the future. Some children externalise their feelings, acting out their anger or shame; overwhelmed and unable to articulate their sense of loss or betrayal, they demonstrate intense emotions through behaviour that challenges or distances those around them. For those children, who may be regarded by the adults around them as challenging or difficult, the opportunity to explore their feelings and come to terms with their experiences is crucial. Child-centred practitioners seek to provide children with a safe space to share their concerns, recognising that children's burdens tend to get heavier if they are carried alone.

Practitioner Testimonial

Child-centred practice means:

- *Providing reliable, uncluttered time and space*

- *Letting the child know that you are keeping them in mind when not present. For example, remembering something they have told you: 'I was thinking about what you said ...'*

- *Looking at communication in all its forms – what is the child's body language, facial expression, voice tone, eye contact, behaviour, coping strategies telling me? Is it congruent with their words?*

- *What is the feeling behind the behaviour; speak to it, even if they deny its existence; is it fear, sadness, ambivalence? For example, 'I wonder if when you did that, you were feeling frightened ...?'*

- *Be mindful and emotionally present. Be congruent and trustworthy.*

- *Sometimes work through others.*

- *Be playful, have fun, enjoy their company.*

- *Don't avoid the pain, acknowledge and empathise with it.*

- *Know their coping strategies, understanding how important they were for survival and how hard it now is to change them.*

Margaret Meade, Therapeutic Intervention Worker, Looked After and Adopted Children's Support and Therapeutic Team.

Empathic professional relationships

For the social worker, then, it is important to notice and be attuned to the emotional content that is inherent in our contacts with children – attending to and naming the feelings of the child, enquiring about and giving permission to ventilate emotions. Within the context of a positive professional relationship, the opportunity for therapeutic support thus provided should not be underestimated. In Chapter 1, we noted the importance of relationship-based approaches to social work practice and how this is based on Carl Roger's theories underpinning person-centred therapy. According to Rogers (1951), the provision of an accepting and empathetic relationship is a fundamental prerequisite for enabling a person to work through difficulties and discover the capacity for healing and self-development. When social workers bring consistency and reliability and acceptance and empathy to their relationships with young people, an opportunity for therapeutic support is engendered.

There are times when social workers are able to develop long-term relationships with children, particularly those who are looked after, and to carry out therapeutic interventions, such as life story work (discussed further in Chapter 9). These are important pieces of work that can hold lifelong significance for children. Social workers often come into contact with children at times of change and upheaval, so even short-term interventions can hold significance in the minds and memories of children (Winter, 2011). Spending time informally with a child creates opportunities for shared reflection and sense-making. Kroll (1995: 98) describes this as 'the art of "being" rather than "doing"' – those moments on a car journey when a child begins to open up and the social worker is simply receptive to what they want to share. Use of empathy is central to these exchanges. For the adult practitioner, this level of communication might take a mental leap in order to reconnect with childhood experience and imagine what life might be like for the particular child or young person. Bringing accurate empathy to the encounter, through the use of reflective responses that summarise or paraphrase what the worker is hearing and observing, is important in providing a sounding board for the child to share their thoughts and feelings. Child-centred workers can demonstrate curiosity about the child's world, tentatively exploring what might be the underlying feelings behind certain behaviours or views, giving permission for the child to confirm or correct various hypotheses. Such an approach will seek to avoid the pitfalls of making assumptions or imposing adult interpretations. The aim of empathic listening is to hold up a mirror for children to recognise for themselves matters that they wish to explore within the context of a supportive relationship.

Emotional containment

There will be times when the social worker–child relationship is not conducive to explicitly therapeutic encounters. It is important to acknowledge that, in some instances, the intervention of the social worker is a contributing factor to the strong feelings of anger, frustration or distress that a child may be feeling. In situations such as when a child is brought into care, moved to a new placement in an emergency or taken away from a difficult contact session, strong and negative feelings may be ventilated against the social worker by the family members involved, which children may witness and participate in. Nevertheless, the social worker is able to respond in a manner that can be seen as implicitly therapeutic, through application of the concept of 'emotional containment'.

Psycho-analyst Wilfred Bion (1962) developed ideas based on attachment theory (discussed in Chapter 4). He described the secure base, essential to the child's emotional development, as providing a kind of container in which the child's feelings can be projected, so that they can be returned to and processed more tolerably. According to this model of attachment, it is the child's mother who usually functions as this container, able to absorb the infant's strongest fears and anxieties and hold them consciously and unconsciously. Through the emotional availability of the parent, the child's feelings are shared, accepted and become more manageable for the child, who gradually learns to contain and regulate their own emotions. At times of stress for the child, others may also support the process of emotional containment. By coping calmly and responding with empathy to the child's strong feelings, even when directed angrily against self, the social worker can acknowledge and accept, contain and synthesise the emotional content of the encounter. This may have a therapeutic benefit, in itself, in the moment of crisis. Furthermore, it may open up the possibility of therapeutic opportunities between the child and the social worker in future, when they might be able to work together to review and make sense of what happened at the time of crisis and stress.

The importance of supportive relationships

Understanding the importance of secure relationships and emotional containment means that the child-centred practitioner is well placed to ensure that the child experiencing distress has access to a network of support or a supportive adult. Social workers cannot be that 'emotional container' for all the children they work with; it is neither possible, advisable nor appropriate. But they can take seriously the importance of identifying key kin or significant others, whether parents, siblings, family members or friends, teachers or other professionals, who can be encouraged to offer support to children during times of stress. In some cases, social workers can also offer more long-term support to enable a carer, often a parent or foster carer, to provide therapeutic support through the use of child-centred play. Filial therapy (Guerney, 2000) has been developed to enable parents and carers to apply basic play therapy skills, to enable the child in their care to express their concerns and emotions and to be supported by their main carer. The aim of filial therapy is to enable the carer to provide concentrated attention to the child, to notice and listen to their verbal and non-verbal communication, to respond to their emotions and thus reduce their anxiety. Social workers often carry out similar work in families focusing on parenting skills, or with foster carers seeking to provide a secure placement. By using positive play sessions, as in filial therapy, parents and carers, with the support of their social worker, can provide focused attention to enable the child to express and explore their feelings. This work recognises that through strengthening these key relationships, children will have the opportunity to thrive emotionally and psychologically; they will have the secure base they need in order to build resilience.

Drawing on the literature from play therapy and filial therapy can add to the confidence of the child-centred practitioner in providing support to children. It is also worth noting at this point the importance of support for the social worker. Responding to the sadness in the lives of children is emotionally demanding. Ruch (2014: 2158) has emphasised that: 'practitioners, if they are serious about being child-centred, have to be prepared to be affected, but not distracted, by the emotions involved in the work.' Professionals need to be able to draw upon support and guidance through supervision and to have positive team relationships, in order to manage the emotional challenges of the work in the long term. Ferguson (2011) has noted that the quality of attention social workers are able to offer to children is directly related to the quality of support, care and attention they themselves receive from supervision.

Points for Reflection

- In your work with children have you been able to offer support that has had a therapeutic benefit for a young person?

- Consider how social workers may be able to offer therapeutic support or facilitate supportive relationships for children.

Using play in direct work with children

Respecting and valuing children means that the child-centred practitioner will recognise the importance of play. At times, professionals need to feel free to just play with children, for example when being introduced to young children for the first time. Taking time to build rapport through play is important. Furthermore, a range of creative approaches to communication with children have been developed that provide vital tools in the practitioner's toolkit, enabling focused direct work designed to assess or address the needs of the child. Research by O'Reilly and Dolan (2016) highlights the importance of social workers developing the skills and confidence to use play techniques in order to communicate effectively with children. The participants in that study reported that using play skills with children as part of their assessments enabled them to gain a greater insight into the child's world.

The value of play

> Play is how the child tries out his world and learns about his world, and it is therefore essential to his healthy development. For the child, play is serious, purposeful business through which he develops mentally, physically and socially. Play is the child's form of self-therapy, through which confusions, anxieties and conflicts are often worked through ... Play serves as a language for the child. (Oaklander, 1988: 160)

Canadian play therapist Violet Oaklander explains how children use play as a means to communicate their inner worlds. Play is the medium through which children explore their experiences, expressing themselves in the present and experimenting with who they might become. It is a universal activity of childhood across all cultures, and is enshrined as a universal right in article 31 of the UNCRC. Through play, children build their self-awareness and self-esteem, their ability to be independent and resilient; they learn to take risks and deal with new situations, to be creative and explore their environment. The value of play can be understood in the following terms:

- Educational: Through play children learn, and in the early years the foundations are built that enable children to read, write and do mathematics. Cognitive and intellectual skills are developed as children use their imagination and problem-solve.

- Social: Through play with their peers, children learn to socialise and make friends, to understand others, to negotiate and take turns.

- Therapeutic: Children use play to express concerns or uncertainties about their daily life, to explore and make sense of situations they find themselves in. (Centre of Excellence for Early Childhood Development, 2013).

It is important for social workers to recognise the value of play in their contacts with children. This includes showing interest in the leisure activities of the children they work with, ensuring that this important aspect of the child's life is not overlooked by adult-centric planning processes. Social workers also use play as a tool for communication. This might be through simply playing a game with a child in order to provide an opportunity for relaxed conversation on the child's terms. The social worker who asks a child to draw a picture of their home or family is likely to gain greater insights into the child's world than one who fires off a stream of questions in order to fill in their assessment form. Virginia Axline was an American psychologist who adapted Roger's person-centred approach in order to develop a therapeutic method of working with children. Axline's (1947) pioneering work around play therapy has helped us to recognise that children often *play out* their feelings and concerns, rather than talk them through, as an adult might do in counselling. Learning from Axline's work, about the value of enabling children to take the lead through play activities they feel comfortable with, provides the framework for effective communication with children.

Focused approaches to direct work with children

Play therapists and social workers have developed methods of working with children which use free play to a certain extent, but also include a more directive role for the professional, who might bring various characters to the play, such as a family of dolls, or suggest games focused on particular themes, including anger management or self-esteem (Oaklander, 2006, McMahon, 2012; Wrench, 2016). Such approaches use 'third objects' to enable children to express themselves in a safer way. Complex emotions, that might be demonstrated non-verbally in the child's body language or indirectly through difficult behaviours, can be broached through sensitive communication with and through toys or artwork. Talking about a picture while it is being drawn or chatting through puppet characters can enable children to ask questions that are difficult to articulate or to uncover feelings they have not expressed before. Digital technology can be used to enable children to communicate through video games, or to explore their family histories or future selves in virtual worlds. Story-telling never goes out of fashion, and children's books can be used to share a story with relevance to the child's situation.

Focus on Practice

Stories provide safe spaces to explore events or feelings that resonate for the child, inviting exploration of similar experiences and what they might mean from the perspective of different characters (Hughes, 2007). At times, simple narratives can be composed by the worker that enable the child's story to be communicated, for example about a puppy who is bullied, a meerkat with a poorly parent or a kitten needing a new home.

Golding (2014) describes the 'three T's model' of storytelling:

- The Telling – Acknowledging the importance of the process of playful interaction to engage with a child through a story, enjoying the shared experience and affect.

- The Tale – The story itself may be from a children's book, composed by the worker or co-constructed with the child, the latter allowing exploration in new directions and of different endings.

- The Talk – The story provides a natural invitation to reflect together about meanings and connections to real life.

This model acknowledges the importance not only of the content of the story, but also of the process of sitting with a child to consider the story, its possible meanings and its significance for the child.

Social workers can harness creative tools to build relationships with children and communicate with them in ways that facilitate play and enable children to tell their stories.

Points for Reflection

- Can you call to mind memories of playing as a child? How did you play and was it important to you?

- Why do you think play is important for children?

- How can social workers use play to communicate with and build relationships with the children they work with?

Commentary
Social workers can use a range of simple and inexpensive resources to initiate play with children. These include puppets, art and craft materials, playdough, building bricks, board games and any other age-appropriate toys. It is useful to know the child's interests and preferences if possible prior to the interaction to plan accordingly. Focusing on a specific activity helps the child to relax, and allows the social worker to get to know the child better before exploring their wishes and feelings in detail.

For example:
Social worker Gurinder began working with Tommy-Lee due to sexual abuse perpetrated by his stepfather, who was currently on remand in prison for the offence. Gurinder was aware from his school teacher that 8-year-old Tommy-Lee loved superheroes. She

printed pictures of superheroes in black and white, including Batman, Superman and the Incredible Hulk. She took a range of art materials and sat on the floor with Tommy-Lee, and they coloured them in together. Whilst they were engaging in the activity, she was able to ask him simple questions, such as what he thinks about school and what he likes to do at the weekend. On a subsequent visit, Gurinder used the pictures they had created together to explore the qualities Tommy-Lee liked about each superhero. She asked him more direct questions in relation to his wishes and feelings, including 'if you were a superhero which one would you be and why?' 'What superpower would you like to have and why?' 'Which superhero would help you most at the moment?' Tommy-Lee was able to explain he liked Batman as he has a superfast car. He said he would like to be able to disappear sometimes and get away quickly. Tommy-Lee felt the Incredible Hulk would help him best as he is big, strong and scary. He shared his wish that the Incredible Hulk would make sure his stepfather did not come back, and that he would also protect his mum.

Social worker Ashleigh made a large cardboard dice with a different question on each side to get to know 10-year-old Bobby, who was referred due to behavioural problems. The questions included: What is your favourite food? What do you like best about yourself? Who do you go to for a hug? Who is your best friend? They took it in turns to throw the dice and answer a question. Ashleigh helped Bobby if he was struggling. Bobby said he did not have a best friend and was sad about this. Ashleigh then asked a supplementary question about what qualities a good friend would have, and she explored what friendship network Bobby had. Bobby was able to disclose that he was bullied at school and through social media and this was a reason for his difficulties.

Wishes and feelings work

Social workers tend to be involved in the lives of children for a particular reason, for example assessment of the needs of a child with complex health or behavioural problems, investigation of safeguarding concerns or care planning with young people who are looked after. They often need to direct the conversation, at times broaching difficult issues that the child may prefer not to discuss. They bring knowledge about the child's situation and have information that they need to share with the child. In the UK they have the specific legal duty, established by the Children Act 1989 and extended by section 53 of the Children Act 2004, to ascertain the wishes and feelings of the children they are working with about their intervention and plans. The Munro Report (2011: 30–31) describes in some detail the value of using 'the three houses tool' to explore the child's feelings about the present and their hopes for the future (see Chapter 8 for further discussion of this approach). Magic wands or Harry Potter spells can be imagined to encourage discussion about the kinds of changes children might conjure if they had magical powers. Simple pictures of faces expressing different feelings can be drawn to explore memories from the past; choosing 'emojis' or 'emoticons' on smartphones or tablets can enable discussion about different emotions.

The suggestions for further reading at the end of this chapter point to some valuable resources that assist social workers in developing their practice through play in order to engage effectively with children. The challenge for the child-centred practitioner is to find ways to carry out effective wishes and feelings work, employing creative resources with sensitivity and adapted to the needs of the child. Working according to the principles outlined at the outset of this chapter will provide the framework for child-centred practice, whether the direct work involves painting or baking, building a life story book using drawings or digital photographs, or chatting in the car or on a walk in the park.

Contracting for direct work

Whether the work being undertaken involves regular sessions over a period of some weeks or is just a single meeting, it is important for social workers to prepare for direct work with children as rigorously as for any other work. Children feel valued if their social worker is consistent and reliable (Morgan, 2006). Where the work is likely to involve a series of contacts, developing a contract or agreement with the child, involving them in discussion about the purpose and arrangements for the sessions, will provide a helpful foundation for the work.

Focus on Practice

Lefevre (2010) suggests that social workers should ask themselves a range of questions in order to prepare for an initial intervention with a child; with some adaptations they include:

- Why – why are you seeing the child; why today; what is the purpose of the intervention?
- What – what do you need to say; what might the child need to tell you or ask about; what might get in the way of this?
- Who – who is this young person; what is already known; what do you need to know in order to see the whole child?
- Who with – who might be with the child and would they want someone present to support them; is it important to see the child alone?
- How – how should you introduce yourself and your role; how should you enable the child to engage with you, paying attention to any special needs?

- What with – what tools or resources might be needed to facilitate communication with the child?

- Where – where will the child feel comfortable; where is the best place for this conversation?

- When – when is the best time to meet the child; is taking a child out of school ever appropriate?

- How long – how long should the encounter last; how many meetings might be needed?

- What support – is supervision available that will support you and enable reflection about the process of the work?

- What next – is further work needed; is a referral for specialist support appropriate; how should the child be prepared for the ending of the work?

Time and space

It is useful to develop some of these considerations further in order to recognise the need for careful preparation for direct work. Crompton (2007) emphasises the importance of time and space. Social workers need to consider what might be the implications of working with the child in their own home, visiting them at school or taking them out to some other location such as their office, a play room at the children's centre or a local café. For some children meeting a social worker at home will feel comfortable and safe; for others it may inhibit what they need to share about their worries and anxieties related to family life. Some children are happy to have time out of the classroom; for others it would impact on important learning opportunities, or be experienced as embarrassing, prompting the curiosity of peers. The practitioner will consider timings, paying attention to age and health needs that may mean the work should have a short time span or opportunities for breaks. The cultural background of the child may rule out certain times, as religious observances would need to be prioritised. Most social work involvement in family life begins with meeting parents to discuss the referral information; this may provide an opportunity to talk briefly with children alongside their parents about what might be the best time and place for the work. It must also be acknowledged that much social work practice occurs in less-than-ideal contexts or crisis situations, where the luxury of planning around time and space is not possible (Ferguson, 2011). In such cases, the professional should remain mindful of the possible impact on the child of place and circumstance, and should at the very least ensure attention is given to the child to explain what is happening, and to listen to and respond to their questions.

The child-centred social worker is responsible for setting, clarifying and maintaining appropriate professional boundaries in all work with children. This includes ensuring openness and honesty about the nature of their role, the purpose of the work and the likely end date for their contact. For some children who have experienced abuse and trauma, the kind of focused attention being offered through a planned series of direct work sessions may lead to the building of unrealistic expectations about the possibility of friendship or the deepening of an ongoing relationship. Every ending is a loss in some sense, and for children who have had painful experiences of loss, it is important to note the duration of each session and to be honest about plans for the ending of the intervention. Some form of handover that enables the child to move on from their contact with their social worker to the care of a trusted adult is of value, particularly at the end of a difficult session, when transferring the case to a new worker or when closing the case.

Professional boundaries and confidentiality

Although some forms of therapeutic work demand high thresholds of privacy to enable children to feel safe to share issues of significance with their therapist, in most of their work social workers are not able to offer this level of confidentiality. The fact that the work will be discussed in supervision, how it will be recorded and whether it will be referred to in reports for court or other meetings of professionals, will need to be shared in a way that makes sense to the child. Children also need to know how parents or carers are involved in the work being undertaken. In most cases, it will be important for the worker to share with carers the nature of their work with children and any support needs the child may have arising from the work; importantly, children must be assured that they are free to talk to their parents or carers as much as they wish to about their contact with their social worker.

Children may need help to make sense of what confidentiality means. Saying that work is confidential is saying everything and nothing, and can lead to young people feeling confused and betrayed if what they have talked to their social worker about 'in confidence' is shared with their teacher or appears in a report at their next review. The concept of privacy can be difficult for younger children to understand, as they may be unused to any sense of *separateness* from their parents or family. Older young people may be determinedly private, anxious to keep 'their stuff' in a space immune from adult interference. Conversely, in an age of reality television and social media, some young people may have lost sight of the value of keeping some aspects of their life private. Children who have been abused may have been manipulated or threatened by the perpetrator to keep their relationship secret. It is vitally important that social workers explain that their work is not secret, and explore with the young people they are working with how they understand confidentiality. It may be helpful to make connections with other aspects of the child's life that they consider private, special or important, such as a diary or journal. Breaching confidentiality can be compared to someone playing with their favourite toy without permission, or scrolling through their mobile phone messages. Explaining the need to share the work with others is important – for example, with managers to ensure the work is carried out properly, or with other professionals to enable support to be offered. Children and young people are able to grasp that confidentiality is never absolute; they recognise that sharing information may be necessary to ensure they and others are kept safe from harm. Child-centred practitioners need to find ways to communicate these key concepts succinctly and meaningfully to the children they work with.

Points for Reflection

- When you have worked with children in your professional role how have you organised your contact with the child? What attention have you paid to practical arrangements?

- What might you want to include in a contract or agreement for working with a young person?

- Write down a few sentences that explain the confidentiality of your work in a way that would make sense to a child or young person.

Commentary

It is important that sessions for direct work are organised in time slots that provide protected space for quiet, uninterrupted communication that will demonstrate respect for the child. Attention needs to be paid to managing the boundaries of confidentiality for each piece of work, depending on the nature of the work and the age, maturity and needs of the child.

For example:

Joanne, a social work student, arranged to work with 4-year-old Priya and 6-year-old Farid in the family room of their school. The children had witnessed their father's deteriorating mental health and his being compulsorily admitted to hospital. The children seemed withdrawn and Farid was having nightmares. Joanne met with the children's mother, Parmindar, and their teachers and agreed to see the children for four sessions, every Tuesday afternoon at the end of the school day. The room was booked for the sessions and Parmindar arrived at the end of each session to take the children home from school. Joanne explained to the children that she would not talk to just anyone about the work they were doing in the sessions. She explained their sessions were time that was private for the children, their time to talk about things that were important for them. She compared this privacy to having a favourite toy that they did not let just anyone play with, but they might let someone they really trust play with. She noted also that mums some-times help children look after their most special toys. Joanne explained that the sessions were not secret, and that it would be important for their mum to know about the things they were talking about, because their mum had the main job of taking care of them. They agreed to invite Parmindar into the end of each session to talk together about things that were important for mum to know about, so that she could look after them.

Advocacy

Advocacy practice has developed over recent years to provide support for vul-nerable children and adults. Advocacy is about ensuring that a person's voice is heard; this is sometimes achieved through the advocate speaking on their behalf. Ultimately, most advocacy practice aims to promote self-advocacy, sup-porting and enabling people to speak for themselves (Braye and Preston-Shoot, 1995). In recognition of the power relations that exist in society, meaning that many children are disadvantaged in accessing their fundamental human rights, there has been a growing recognition of the need for children's advocacy ser-vices (Oliver and Dalrymple, 2008). The children's rights agenda, coupled with the increasing alarm around the abuse that can be perpetrated when the voice of the child is ignored (as highlighted by David Utting in 1997, and more recently, by enquiries into child sexual exploitation, such as the Jay Report, 2014), has led to a growing recognition of the value of independent advocacy. Advocates are able to support vulnerable children when they have serious con-cerns or wish to make a complaint. An advocacy approach is very much in har-mony with child-centred practice and with the principles underpinning effective communication with children.

The role of advocacy services

In the UK, the right of children to access independent advocacy services is underpinned by legislation. The Children Act 1989 introduced the statutory right to advocacy for children who are looked after. This right was extended, by the Adoption and Children Act 2002, to care leavers and children assessed by the Local Authority as being 'in need', including children with disabilities and those involved in safeguarding processes. The recently revised *Care Planning, Placement and Case Review Guidance* (Department for Education, 2015b: 13) states explicitly: 'Where a child has difficulty in expressing his/her wishes and feelings about any decisions being made about him/her, consideration must be given to securing the support of an advocate.'

Learning from Research

Several studies have highlighted the value for young people of working with an advocate.

- In a study carried out by Barnes (2007: 147) a 15-year-old young woman commented that: *'I feel my views are heard and they involve me in decisions. They treat me like an adult.'*

- Dalrymple (2005: 8) quoted a young person living in residential care, who emphasised the difference in having an advocate from the role of their social worker: *'My social worker has more control over my life. I've not really got any control over my life. You can't influence how the home is run at all. Personally, I don't feel I can influence things. Even now everyone has closed ranks. But at the last meeting having an advocate in the room meant I felt I could influence things and I wasn't taking the whole lot on my own.'*

Advocacy services are available in every area of the UK; usually they are funded by the Local Authority and provided by independent agencies, such as Barnardo's, the Children's Society and Coram Voice. Working in accordance with the National Standards for the Provision of Children's Advocacy Services (2002), advocates or children's rights workers champion the rights of young people. Advocates work to give voice to those who are marginalised or oppressed, with the aim of ensuring they are not ignored and are able to participate in decisions about their own lives. Their intervention is young person-led, which means they act only upon the instructions of the child, representing their views and opinions. Their role is not to make a judgement about the child's welfare or best interests, but to ensure the views and perspectives of the young person are heard and taken into consideration by those in positions of authority. For example, an advocate might give voice to a child's wish to return to live at home, despite the concerns of social workers and other professionals about their safety and well-being at home. To this end, they often support children in meetings such as reviews for children who are looked after, family group conferences or child protection case conferences. They work with individual cases, for example supporting a young person through the formal complaints process. At times, Children's Rights Services are able to become a force to promote change and improve practice in a local area, by working with groups of young people to enable their participation in policy or service development, or to campaign around a particular issue.

The aim of the child-centred social worker is to ensure that the interests of the child are paramount and to seek to listen to and negotiate with children around the best way to achieve this in complex situations. It is important to acknowledge that there are times when children struggle to participate in formal, adult-centric processes or fundamentally disagree with decisions taken by professionals who are working in their best interests. There are also times when children are poorly and unfairly treated. The employment of independent advocates and complaints processes provides a means of promoting the rights of young people and holding to account the adults involved in decision-making processes. Child-centred practitioners enable children to access independent advocacy services when needed and provide information about how to make a complaint.

Social work and advocacy

Some social workers are employed in a specialist advocacy role; however, the majority working within the Local Authority are not specialist advocates. Nevertheless, social workers have advocacy skills and their role means they are often well placed to advocate on behalf of the children they are working with. For most children, their natural advocate is their parent, speaking out for them, ensuring their needs are met and encouraging them to voice their own views with increasing confidence as they mature; however, for many of the children who come into contact with social workers, parents may not be able to provide the advocacy and support their children need. In some cases, social workers play an important role in advocating on behalf of children to their own parents, seeking to enable the wider family to recognise the needs of the child. For example, in cases of domestic violence, social workers might represent to the parents the views and concerns of the children, or the way in which ongoing parental disputes may be impacting upon the child. Social workers at times represent the corporate parent and advocate on behalf of children who are looked after, to ensure all agencies are playing their part and fulfilling their responsibilities to promote the welfare of the child. This might include advocacy for the child with their own employer to ensure that the needs of the child are met and the Local Authority is meeting its statutory duties.

Points for Reflection

- What does advocacy mean – can you write a definition in one sentence?
- Can you think of a time when someone has advocated on your behalf or when you have acted as an advocate for someone?
- Why might some children and young people need the support of an advocate?

Barnes (2012) has carried out research comparing the role of the social worker to that of a specialist advocacy worker, with results to the detriment of the former and the credit of the latter. She found that advocacy workers adopted a rights position and tended to emphasise the capability and autonomy of the young people they worked with. They were experienced by their clients as reliable and caring professionals who treated them as equals. Although social work is seen as a caring profession, the work of social workers tends to be dominated by protection, risk-aversion and bureaucracy, to the extent that they are sometimes seen by young people as uncaring professionals who are 'just doing a job'. In her study Barnes (2012) notes the paradox that the rights-based organisation was providing workers who were more caring than those trained within a caring ethos. She highlights the importance of *caring advocacy* as an approach to working with children that is relevant to all professionals and underpinned by the ethic of care and a commitment to rights (as discussed in Chapter 1). Similarly, Dalrymple (2005) emphasises the importance of a *culture of advocacy* to gain greater prominence in both the organisation and the practice of social work. An organisational ethos that creates such a culture of advocacy, within which social workers are able to demonstrate caring advocacy, would uphold children's rights and promote child-centred practice.

Conclusion

In this chapter we have recognised the importance of listening to children and taking responsibility, as child-centred practitioners, to develop effective means of communication with young people. Social workers use a range of creative approaches to engage with children and carry out direct work in challenging circumstances. Based upon the ethical principles of valuing the child and respecting their individuality, social workers take time to prepare for direct work, providing a safe space and maintaining appropriate professional boundaries. At times, we work closely with specialist therapeutic workers and with independent advocates, to ensure the needs of children are addressed and the voice of the child is heard. Child-centred social workers also employ therapeutic skills and adopt an approach of caring advocacy in their day-to-day practice with children and young people.

Recommended reading and resources

- Michelle Lefevre (2010) has written a valuable textbook for social workers and other child-centred practitioners, providing a practical guide and many useful resources about how to engage and communicate with children: *Communicating with Children and Young People.*

- Katie Wrench's (2016) textbook *Helping Vulnerable Children and Adolescents to Stay Safe: Creative Ideas and Activities for Building Protective Behaviours* focuses on creative methods that can be used by social workers to work with children to promote self-esteem and protective behaviours.

- Audrey Tait and Helen Wosu's (2012) *Direct Work with Vulnerable Children: Playful Activities and Strategies for Communication* similarly provides a range of games and activities designed to enable effective engagement with children who have experienced abuse and neglect.

- Margaret Crompton's chapter 'Individual work with children' provides an excellent and concise discussion of how to plan and carry out work with children, and includes a range of methods, approaches and case examples. The chapter can be found in *The Child Protection Handbook* (2007) by Kate Wilson and Adrian James.

- Alison Clark and Peter Moss have developed an approach for working with younger children and their book explores creative methods and tools that can also be adapted for working with children with speech or language difficulties: *Listening to Young Children: The Mosaic Approach* (2nd edition, 2011).

- *Using Play and the Creative Arts to Communicate with Children and Young People* is an online learning resource that has been developed by the Social Care Institute for Excellence in collaboration with Michelle Lefevre, Sally Richards and Pamela Trevithick. This is a freely available e-learning tool that provides valuable guidance about direct work with children. It can be accessed at: www.scie.org.uk/assets/elearning/communicationskills/cs08/resource/index.html

- Talking Mats have been developed by a social enterprise involving speech and language therapists. They are indeed textured mats with a range of symbol cards that enable children, particularly those with speech difficulties, to communicate their feelings, preferences and the things that matter to them. The resource also includes a digital range of communication tools. There is a free Talking Mats taster app. Further information is available at: www.talkingmats.com/

- *In My Shoes* is a computer package designed to help children to communicate about their experiences, including potentially distressing experiences. It is particularly valuable for work with young people with learning disabilities. Information about the package and the training offered by Child and Family Training required to access the resource, is available at: www.inmyshoes.org.uk/

- Jessica Kingsley Publishers have developed a range of therapeutic books that can be used by professionals, parents and carers to read with children, to begin to sensitively explore difficult issues and emotions. The books include

Alex and the Scary Things – a story by Melissa Moses to help children who have experienced something frightening – and *The Boy Who Built a Wall around Himself* by Ali Redford.

● Similarly, Margot Sunderland, Director at the Centre for Child Mental Health, London, has written a range of children's books on the theme of 'helping children with feelings'. Published by Speechmark, titles include *Ruby and the Rubbish Bin* and *How Hattie Hated Kindness*; there is also a guidebook for carers and professionals titled *Helping Children Who Bottle Up Their Feelings*.

● Kim Golding's (2014) imaginative and practical textbook *Using Stories to Build Bridges with Traumatized Children* provides guidance for parents, carers and professionals about developing stories that can help children to understand and overcome difficult experiences. It includes sample stories and advice about how to adapt them and invaluable tips for planning direct work with children.

● Coram Voice is a charitable organisation that aims to promote children's rights and to enable children and young people to hold to account the services that are responsible for their care. They provide a range of advocacy services for children and advice for professionals, including a free national helpline. Full information is available at: http://www.coramvoice.org.uk/

CONCLUSION TO PART I

In Part I we have introduced the theoretical and ethical foundations for child-centred practice. Chapters 1 and 2 set the parameters for our discussion, focusing on key aspects of social work theory and values, emphasising a children's rights approach, based on the UNCRC, and promoting participation. Chapters 3 and 4 explored the nature of childhood and child development in the context of the family, acknowledging wider social and environmental impacts. In Chapter 5 we explored the importance of working directly with children and young people; this will be built upon by providing practice examples throughout Part II. Before moving on to Part II, it is worthwhile pulling together some of our key themes, in order to acknowledge the conceptual framework for child-centred practice developed through Part I, based, in particular, upon ecological theory and reflective-relational approaches to practice.

Primarily, we have recognised the importance of a value-based approach that promotes the rights and participation of the child. In acknowledging the individuality and agency of the child, the child-centred practitioner seeks to address and manage the power dynamics inherent in their relationship with the child, to develop trust and a safe space for dialogue and decision-making. Ecological theory is helpful in considering a multilayered conceptual approach to child-centred practice (Figure 6):

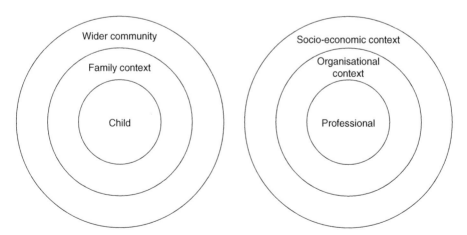

Figure 6 An ecological model of the child and the professional

For the professional, the central sphere incorporates their personal values and professional ethics. Social workers need to reflect on how their attitudes and values about children and their rights might impact on their ability to engage with the child. The core of the work will be the relationship they develop with the child to engage them, empathise with them and listen to them, as they seek to understand what the child's world means for them. They will assume the child's capability to express their views, taking into account their stage of development, and find ways to enable them to exercise their participatory rights. This approach is equally relevant in the context of a one-off home visit as it is to long-term casework. Ruch (2014) has emphasised the importance of making a human connection with children, despite organisational and bureaucratic demands and the emotional challenges of the work. Child-centred practitioners seek to manage and contain the emotional content of the work, offering support to the child. They will also work to advocate on behalf of the child within the organisational sphere, enabling the participation of the child at this level. Reflective practitioners will consider how the changing social, economic and political agenda might impact upon their work, recognising that the welfare of the child is paramount and seeking to promote their rights in all aspects of their work.

Points for Reflection

- Applying this ecological model to a case you have worked with, put yourself in the 'professional' position and consider the key influences upon your practice taking account of:

  O your own professional values;

  O the organisational context;

  O the wider socio-economic issues.

- How did you manage these influences in order to build an effective, professional relationship with the child and their family?

This ecological approach is in harmony with the ethic of care. The model takes account of the child's significant relationships and connections, and the importance of care and support, rather than focusing only on rights and autonomy. Therefore, the child-centred practitioner will recognise the importance for the child of their immediate context, engaging with their family and key kin – those who matter for the child – and ensuring that the voice of the child is heard within their wider work with family members. Good practice involves working in partnership with parents and carers, recognising that children are more likely to do well when they have the support of a family network around them.

At the level of the community and social sphere, the practitioner will seek to make sense of the way in which the child is understood within their local community and the influence of prevailing socio-economic, environmental and political factors that might impact upon the child and their situation. They will work with other professionals, coordinating the team around the child, to ensure effective support, and maintaining a focus on the wishes and feelings of the child. The aim will be to strengthen protective factors and build the social capital of the child in order to promote their resilience.

Applying an ecological perspective enables the practitioner to gain a holistic understanding of the child within the context of their family and community, as well as recognising the way in which organisational and social context informs their role and professional obligations. A child-centred, ecological approach takes account of the child's rights and their interdependence, seeking to acknowledge the whole child, their agency and their vulnerability. This ecological approach to child-centredness underpins the relationship the professional seeks to build with the child (Figure 7):

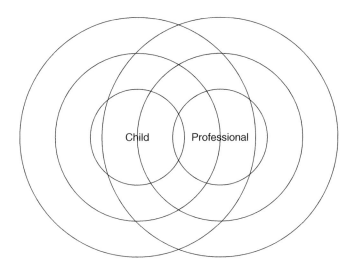

Figure 7 An ecological-relational approach to child-centred practice

The worker takes responsibility for forging the relationship with the child, recognising that the child may be an involuntary service user and may have many questions about the role of professionals in their life. The model recognises the agency of the child and the ethical use of professional power in order to negotiate a connection that is boundaried, purposeful and beneficial, enabling effective work together in the interests of the child. This conceptual approach brings together many of the ideas we have explored in Part I in order to inform child-centred practice.

Recommended Reading

- The article by Gillian Ruch (2014) '"Helping children is a human process": Researching the challenges social workers face in communicating with children' reinforces some of the ideas discussed in this concluding section and throughout Part I, recognising the importance of psycho-social approaches to practice and exploring the challenges for child-centred social workers.

PART II

INTRODUCTION TO PART II

In Part I, we explored key aspects of the ethical and theoretical foundations for child-centred practice. In our discussion of the knowledge and skills that underpin social work with children, young people and families, we developed a framework for effective practice.

In Part II we go on to explore more directly social work with children and young people, by examining aspects of practice at each stage of intervention into family life. In Chapter 6, we focus on early intervention, recognising the importance of holistic assessment that engages with parents, carers and families and pays attention to the needs and voice of the child. We recognise that some children may be vulnerable or in need (as defined by legislation in the UK) and require support and early help in order to reach their full potential. In Chapter 7, we focus on children at risk of abuse and neglect, recognising that social workers are most often involved in targeted interventions to safeguard those who might otherwise slip through the net. We explore the challenges of practice with the most vulnerable children in families affected by complex problems. Chapter 8 focuses on child protection processes, acknowledging that this is the core business of many social work professionals. We examine the challenges of child-centred practice in the context of safeguarding interventions that are undertaken at times of trauma, stress and anxiety for children and families. Chapter 9 explores social work practice with children who are looked after, emphasising the importance of a child-centred approach that promotes the rights and well-being, self-efficacy and resilience of young people who have experienced difficulty and upheaval.

Throughout Part II, we continue to employ the learning features developed in Part I, including the following:

● **Points for Reflection**: Questions to prompt analysis of relevant issues and to emphasise the value of reflective child-centred practice. At times, we include commentaries to provide further information and guidance for the reader, to enable further reflection around key issues. We do not include case examples in these sections in Part II, as the case study at the end of each chapter enables further reflection and analysis of the key issues applied to practice.

- **Learning from Research**: We continue to draw out the key messages from relevant research. We pay particular attention to studies that give voice to children and young people.

- **Focus on Practice**: Highlights creative approaches that enable the practitioner to work in a child-centred way.

- **Recommended Reading and Resources**: Points to useful resources for further learning around key themes.

A particular development in Part II will be the integration of the **case study**. This enables readers to apply the learning from research and from the discussions in each chapter to practice in a particular case. Use of a case study provides focus for the chapters. It is not possible to explore all aspects of social work practice, but each chapter addresses some of the key aspects of practice relevant to the case scenario as it develops throughout Part II. The case study tells the story of a fictional family, as difficulties develop into crises that precipitate at least one of the children entering the care system. This enables analysis of practice at each stage of social work intervention. The story unfolds through brief updates at the end of each chapter, followed by opportunities for readers to consider particular questions and ethical dilemmas and reflect upon practice issues. To highlight the importance of a child-centred approach and to enable a particular focus upon the perspective of the child, we aim to give voice to the children in the family. Each chapter, therefore, includes a short example of what might be the words or thoughts, views, wishes and feelings of each of the children in the case. These short extracts pay attention to the different developmental stages of the children in the case study, highlighting how each child might have different responses and concerns, despite sharing the same family situation. It is hoped that this creative technique will enable the reader to 'get to know' the children in this fictional, but familiar, family. This approach also emphasises the importance of recognising the individuality of each child.

The case study is introduced below with some key information about the background and social circumstances of the family. There is also a genogram that provides a visual depiction of family structure. The reader may wish to place a marker in this page to be reminded of this contextual information at the end of each of the ensuing chapters.

Case Study: The Smith–Jones–Khan family

MARK THIS PAGE!

Members of the Household:

Jade Smith – 13 years – White British – daughter of Mick and Jackie
Hanif Khan – 7 years – Mixed ethnic background – son of Fiona and Nadir
Charlotte Smith – 3 years – White British – daughter of Fiona and Mick
Fiona Jones – 27 years – White British – mother of Hanif and Charlotte
Mick Smith – 36 years – White British – father of Jade and Charlotte

Significant Family Members:

Carol Jones – 50 years– White British – mother of Fiona
Nadir Khan – 28 years – Asian British – father of Hanif
Jackie Smith – deceased – White British – mother of Jade

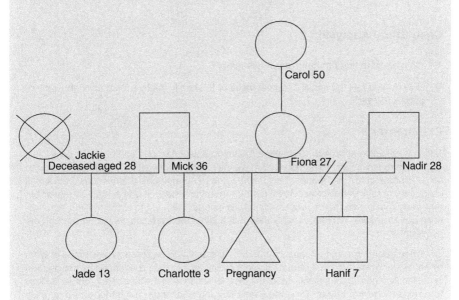

Figure 8 Genogram of the Smith–Jones–Khan family

Fiona is divorced from Nadir and has been living with Mick for the last five years. Nadir has Hanif to stay at his home on alternate weekends. Fiona works at the local superstore. Her mum, Carol, helps with the care of Charlotte and provides support to Fiona. Fiona suffers from depression.

Mick was married to Jackie for 12 years. Jackie experienced ill health for many years and died of cancer six years ago. Mick lost his job last year and is drinking excessively.

Charlotte attends the nursery at the local Children's Centre. She is making good progress in her development but has ongoing learning difficulties due to Down's Syndrome. The family are worried about what support Charlotte might need in the future.

Hanif gets on well with Charlotte and sometimes takes her to nursery, which is next door to his school. Hanif has recently complained of being bullied at school. Nadir wants to increase his contact with his son to enable him to take Hanif to Mosque every Friday.

Jade was close to her mum and does not get on with Fiona. She is increasingly pushing parental boundaries by staying out late with her friends. She regularly truants from school. Her teacher is concerned about her having an older boyfriend and thinks she may be vulnerable to sexual exploitation.

Fiona and Mick are finding it difficult to be consistent about managing their children and this is causing conflict. They have been invited to attend the Parenting Group at the Children's Centre. Fiona has recently discovered she is pregnant – she is worried about whether she will experience post-natal depression.

Case Study Analysis:

- What are your first thoughts about this family?
- How do you feel the social circumstances of the family might impact upon the welfare of the children?

Commentary:

Taking a reflective approach to practice means it is useful to be mindful of our own initial responses to a case and to recognise that we may have a 'gut instinct' or strong reaction to some aspects of the information. This may be due to our personal experiences, perhaps in childhood, or to previous professional practice in a similar case. It is important to remember that every family, and member of that family, is unique. We need to avoid making assumptions and to ensure we test our initial thoughts against the evidence we gather through the assessment process.

When adopting a child-centred approach, it is useful to begin each new piece of work by considering how the family situation might be perceived and experienced by the children in the family. For example, in this case, the early experience of the loss of her mother is likely to have a long-term impact for Jade. Hanif is living apart from his father and may miss members of his paternal extended family. Charlotte's parents may need specialist advice to ensure they can provide the care and stimulation she needs to reach her full potential. Mick's unemployment may be creating financial pressures that have repercussions for the whole family. We explore these issues more fully as we go through the chapters in Part II.

6

WORKING WITH VULNERABLE CHILDREN

Introduction

Children and young people thrive in a diverse range of families; however, family life can at times be complex and pressurised. When parents experience difficulties in their own lives, it can have a profound effect on the child, both in the present and in the future. Families sometimes need additional support to ensure their children can achieve their full potential. Child-centred practitioners seek to identify vulnerabilities and needs, providing support for children and families before problems escalate. They take a strengths-based approach, seeking to build on protective factors in the family situation, in order to promote the resilience of the child. This chapter will examine child-centred practice when working with children and young people in need, highlighting specific groups of vulnerable children. We make links to relevant policy, legislation and research. The concept of early intervention is explored as well as how children and young people can be fully involved in the assessment process.

It is not possible to examine every aspect of practice, therefore we will pay attention to some of the key themes in the case study, introduced on page 143. The case study provides the focus for our exploration of important aspects of child-centred practice, including social work with children with disabilities and supporting young carers.

Early assessment and intervention

There are numerous definitions of early intervention which continue to evolve and develop (Institute of Public Care, 2012). It is therefore helpful to differentiate between prevention, namely predicting and averting the problem before it has occurred, and early intervention, which means intervening at the first signs of trouble in family life (Little and Sodha, 2012). There is a wealth of local, national and international evidence which clearly shows that early intervention works, when appropriate interventions are 'applied well following timely identification of a problem' (C4EO, 2010: 4). For the purposes of this chapter early intervention is defined as:

Intervening early and as soon as possible to tackle problems emerging for children, young people and their families or with a population most at risk of developing problems. Early intervention may occur at any point in a child or young person's life. (C4EO, 2010: 16)

Who is a child in need or a vulnerable child?

A child in need is defined under section 17 of the Children Act 1989 as: 'a child who is unlikely to achieve or maintain a reasonable level of health or development; or whose health and development is likely to be significantly or further impaired, without the provision of services; or a child who is disabled.' Local Authorities have a duty to identify and assess the needs of these children and to work with a wide range of children and their families in order to provide supportive services.

The 'Every Child Matters' policy was launched in 2003 by the Labour Government, as a public response to the Victoria Climbie inquiry. Lord Laming's report (2003) had expressed the concern that although Victoria had been known to many professionals and organisations, the child had not really been *seen* and her vulnerability had not been recognised. The aim of the New Labour policy was to ensure that universal services were able to support all children and that targeted services were developed to reach and improve the life chances of vulnerable children (Frost et al., 2015). Children, young people and families were directly consulted and, in response, the policy set out a positive universal vision of five key outcomes that *mattered most* for children, namely:

- stay safe: *being protected from harm and neglect;*
- be healthy: *enjoying good physical and mental health and a healthy lifestyle;*
- enjoy and achieve: *getting the most out of life and developing the skills for adulthood;*
- make a positive contribution: *being involved with the community and society and not engaging in anti-social or offending behaviour;*
- achieve economic well-being: *not being prevented by economic disadvantage from achieving their full potential in life.*

(Department for Education and Skills, 2003: 6, italics added)

Although the 'Every Child Matters' policy has been largely shelved by ensuing governments, the five key outcomes remain central to many aspects of childcare practice and are embedded in the Children Act 2004, which provides the legislative framework promoting early intervention. Children and young people who are not achieving the five outcomes or whose progress is being severely hampered should be viewed as vulnerable children.

The statutory guidance (HM Government, 2015) requires all agencies to work together at an early stage when concerns are identified for vulnerable children and their families. This guidance supports the recommendations of the Munro report (2011) aiming to prevent abuse and neglect through improved, integrated early help. *Working Together* (2015) makes clear all professionals should be alert to the need to carry out an assessment and provide supportive services for a child who:

- is disabled and has specific additional needs;

- has special educational needs;

- is a young carer;

- is showing signs of engaging in anti-social or criminal behaviour;

- is in a family circumstance presenting challenges for the child, such as substance abuse, adult mental health problems and domestic violence;

- has returned home to their family from care; and/or

- is showing early signs of abuse and/or neglect.

(HM Government, 2015: 13)

It is clear, then, that many children may experience vulnerability or particular needs at different stages of their lives for a wide range of reasons. Many of these children may not be known to Local Authority Children's Services or have a social worker involved in their lives. It is the responsibility of every professional to take a child-centred approach by paying attention to the children they come into contact with and identifying if they might be vulnerable or in need of additional help.

Points for Reflection

- Why do you think early intervention is important?

- How would you define 'vulnerable children' and 'children in need'?

- What difference do you think early intervention can make for these children and their families?

Early help assessment

For early intervention to be effective, it is essential that there is a clear and agreed understanding of what the problems are, what the needs of the child are, how protective factors in the family and community can be strengthened and how supportive services might be efficiently mobilised. Early help should always start with an assessment of need (Local Government Association, 2013). The Common Assessment Framework (CAF) is a tool used to offer multi-agency intervention for vulnerable children with additional needs, with a lead professional co-ordinating the plan alongside the family. The lead professional at this stage is likely to be a health professional, learning mentor or family support worker from a children's centre or community organisation; social workers may take on this role in some cases, particularly those who work in voluntary sector organisations, or they may be involved to offer advice and consultation. Early help assessments, sometimes known as CAFs, are conducted using 'the Assessment Triangle' (HM Government, 2015), with holistic assessment focused around the three domains, namely the child's developmental needs; parenting capacity; and family and environmental factors (see Figure 1 in Chapter 2). Where there are further concerns and a child is defined as 'in need', in line with section 17 of the 1989 Children Act, a social worker is likely to be the key worker, carrying out the assessment and co-ordinating the plan for support. An assessment can focus on one child in the family, if they are identified to be particularly vulnerable. However, there is value in addressing the needs of all the children and recognising that support for parents is likely is have beneficial consequences for the whole family (Morris et al, 2008).

Milner, Myers and O'Byrne (2015: 2) have identified five stages to the assessment process. They are outlined here, with an emphasis on the importance of child-centred practice at each stage:

- Preparation – Including consideration of how to engage with parents and children in order to explain the assessment process and to enable participation.

- Collating data – Including meeting with parents, carers and children, listening to their views and observing their interactions; gaining consent of parents and children to seek information from significant others (such as extended family members, teachers, health visitors and other key professionals).

- Applying professional knowledge – Considering theory and research that is relevant to the situation in order to analyse and make sense of family dynamics. Understanding theory about child development will assist in considering the particular needs of the children.

- Making judgements – Weighing the risks and protective factors, considering parenting capacity and motivation to engage with supportive services.

Paying attention to the perspectives of children about their circumstances, including what factors may be important or influential for them, will be helpful in analysing the needs and setting the priorities.

- Decision-making – Clarifying who will do what and how progress will be evaluated and reviewed. Enabling the participation of children, young people and their parents, in order to agree the plan for the intervention will be important in enabling effective work together.

Learning from Research

To evaluate the impact of the introduction of the assessment framework, Cleaver and Walker (2004) carried out research to ascertain the views of children and young people who had been the subject of an assessment as a child in need. Only two of the eight children who participated in this research remembered the social worker explaining the assessment process to them. Here are some of the views of the children involved:

- *'A bit difficult; there were lots of questions, difficult ones.'* (10-year-old boy)

- *'I felt strange; I was not sure who I was talking to. I did not really trust them. I could not tell them about being a Jehovah's Witness. I did not know them.'* (15-year-old girl)

- *'I wanted to talk to someone, but there was no-one to do that.'* (17-year-old asylum seeker)

- *'They supported me. I got to know them a bit. I got to trust them a bit. It was better later on. She was nice.'* (15-year-old young person).

Overall, the researchers concluded that talking with children was viewed as a lesser priority than interviews with parents and carers. Many young people did not understand the assessment process and felt that what they said was frequently discounted or disbelieved.

Gilligan and Manby (2008) carried out research in response to the introduction of the Common Assessment process in the Children Act 2004. They explored the experience of vulnerable children and their families. They found that: 'for most children and young people … the process of the CAF assessment was one in which adults talked about them rather than one in which they were full participants' (2008: 183).

These research studies highlight that, as the assessment processes were introduced, professionals tended to adopt an adult-centric focus, rather than recognise the importance of child-centred practice and the participation of children and young people.

Turney and colleagues (2011) reviewed the research about the assessment of children in need, carried out since the introduction of the assessment framework in 2000. They noted also that children are not always seen or consulted and emphasised that 'keeping the child in view is fundamental to good assessment' (2011: 5).

We have noted that bureaucratic and organisational factors create challenges for practitioners seeking to undertake assessments. Strict timescales around the completion of assessments used to measure efficiency have had the unintended consequence of incentivising expedient and officious practice, rather than promoting comprehensive assessment and child-centred work. Broadhurst and colleagues (2010b) have commented on worrying short-cuts taken by some practitioners, who report that they have 'seen the child', without actually engaging them in in any meaningful contact. Thomas and Holland (2010) reviewed assessment reports written by social workers and found that children's identities tended to be 'standardised', with a lack of authentic description of the child, their personality, temperament and interests. Some sections of the reports were 'cut and pasted' from siblings' reports or textbooks, and the assessments portrayed predominantly negative, one-dimensional views of the children's identities.

Having said that, tools for good practice have been developed that enable professionals to pay attention to children and to involve them in the assessment process (Dalzell and Sawyer, 2016). From a child-centred perspective, the purpose and focus of the assessment is the child; considering what the assessment and intervention process might mean for the child is therefore crucial. The following Scottish model usefully reframes the three domains of the assessment triangle from a child's perspective, using child-centred language to enable the practitioner to take a different approach to the assessment process from the outset (Figure 9).

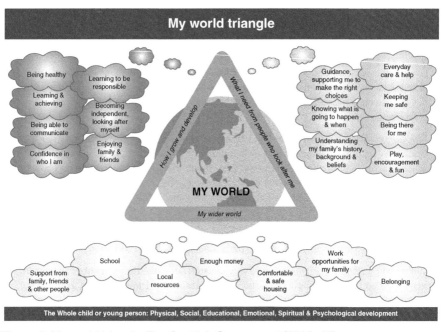

Figure 9 My world triangle. The Scottish Government (2012: 18)

Focus on Practice

The Scottish model, entitled the 'My world triangle', is useful in allowing practitioners to consider the world of the child or young person. It focuses on three key areas, namely how the child is growing and developing; what the child needs from the people caring for him or her; and the impact of their wider environment. In carrying out an early help assessment, it is not always necessary to explore every area, but to look in detail at what is relevant to the presenting issue. Although it is always important to keep the child's whole world in mind.

Engaging parents in the assessment process

'Parents are the most significant influence on children' (C4EO, 2010: 8) and how children are parented has significant consequences for their future. As we recognised in Chapter 4, children benefit most when they are offered consistent support by their primary caregivers, usually their parents (Tickell, 2011). Sensitive and responsive parent–infant interaction is recognised as imperative to a child fulfilling their physical, cognitive and emotional potential (Axford et al., 2015). Effective parenting is key to preventing emotional and psychological difficulties in early and middle childhood, which are associated with behavioural problems and negative outcomes in adulthood (Lindsay et al., 2010). Early help interventions are carried out on a voluntary basis, working in partnership with parents and carers to identify areas of concern and agree support plans to promote the welfare of their children. Child-centred social workers must seek to build positive working relationships with parents and carers, as working in co-operation is more likely to enable positive change and enhance the well-being of the child (NSPCC, 2014).

Supporting parents in developing effective parenting skills is an important preventative strategy, promoting positive outcomes for children and young people (Frost et al., 2015). However, there is a fine balancing act between forming supportive relationships with parents and becoming overly absorbed by adult needs, so that attention is diverted from the child owing to the family's difficulties. To secure better outcomes for vulnerable children and their families, child-centred practitioners must retain a focus on the needs of the child whilst also carrying out a holistic assessment that takes account of the wider context. This means co-ordinating support from children's and adults' services, and mobilising community and informal networks of support. Circumstances affecting parents and carers also directly affect the children, 'so the focus needs to be on the whole family rather than any one individual within it' (NCB, 2010: 26). In some instances, early help interventions may focus on work to enhance parenting capacity, such as enabling parents to access drug or alcohol treatment or to attend parenting skills groups. Even where the work is solely undertaken with the parents, child-centred practitioners will remain mindful of the needs and best interests of the children in the family, working to enhance the well-being of parents and children (Mainstone, 2014).

The phrase 'hard to reach' is often used to describe families who choose not to access services; however, in reality there are often a range of organisational and personal barriers to overcome, meaning that in many instances, it is the 'services that are hard to reach for some parents' (NCB, 2010: 18). Many parents feel anxious about seeking help, fearing that they may be judged or criticised. The initial experience a family has will affect their confidence in using a service, and practitioners need to reflect on their initial contact with families to ensure this is a positive and engaging process. Positive working relationships between families and professionals which are based on respect, trust, openness and responsiveness are crucial to the success of early help assessments and interventions (Frost et al., 2015).

Engaging children in the assessment process

We have noted the importance of engaging with parents whilst also retaining a focus on the child. Ruch (2014) has emphasised the importance of meaningful contact with children and young people referred for assessment and has acknowledged the obstacles that may hamper this seemingly simple objective. Apart from scheduling issues and the reticence of children and young people around meeting with a stranger, in particular a social worker, parents may be reluctant to 'involve' their children; adults may wish to protect children from knowledge about family problems. Nevertheless, an assessment that fails to engage with and take account of the perspectives of the child will be partial, imbalanced and likely to miss important information. The ensuing intervention will be similarly compromised. Professionals working to engage families in an assessment will need to explain this and agree with parents the information that children might need to know. Children and young people often have concerns and confusions about complex family situations; early help assessments provide valuable opportunities to work together with families to respond to children's questions and to present their concerns to their parents. Section 17 of the Children Act 1989, amended by section 53 of the 2004 Act, is unequivocal in setting out the duty to ascertain the child's wishes and feelings where an assessment is made and supportive services provided. As emphasised in Chapter 2, the ethical imperative is clear also; children have a right to be involved in discussions and matters pertaining to their lives. They may choose not to be involved, but the obligation is upon professionals to enable them to make this choice.

Many practice tools have been developed that are useful in working with children and families, some of which we explored in Chapter 5. In the early stages of an assessment process, the use of genograms and ecomaps are crucial tools for gaining a full picture of the family, their potential sources of support and any risk factors in relation to the family and community network. In tragic cases which have been the focus of child abuse inquiries, it has become apparent that social workers have lacked basic knowledge about the family network of the child. For example, in the case of Victoria Climbie, it was not known that she was living apart from her parents in the care of her great-aunt. In the case of Baby Peter, it was not known that the mother's boyfriend and his brother were part of the household, or that Peter's father may be a protective factor in his life. Genograms and ecomaps are formal tools that can be drawn up by professionals to map the nature and strength of family relationships (DH, 2000b). A genogram has been provided for the Smith–Jones–Khan family on page 143; it provides a pictorial representation of what is known about the structure of the family at the point of referral for social work assessment. Ecomaps are in some sense simpler diagrams, with the child placed in the centre and names of significant others placed around them, to demonstrate the strength or otherwise of the support network for the child. Here is an example of an ecomap that might have been drawn by Hanif (from our case study) with support from his social worker (Figure 10):

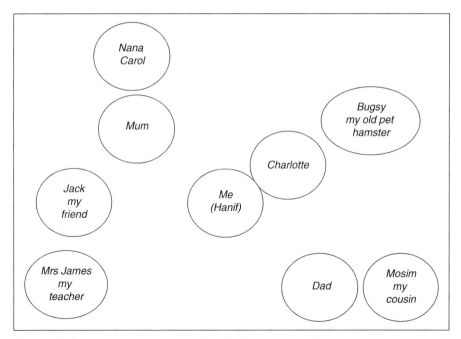

Figure 10 Ecomap – example based on Hanif (case study)

In this ecomap Hanif was able to identify people (and also a pet who died some time ago) who mattered in his life. The circles for each person are placed around Hanif in a way that denotes the closeness of the relationship.

Both genograms and ecomaps can be used as creative practice tools to work with families together or with children on their own to explore family relationships.

Focus on Practice

The Social Care Institute for Excellence has developed a range of interactive learning tools that are useful for social work practice. One of these includes a focus on genograms and ecomaps as creative methods of gathering information during the assessment process.

Further guidance can be accessed at:
www.scie.org.uk/assets/elearning/communicationskills/cs04/resource/html/object4/object4_7.htm#slide01

A Creative Genogram

A genogram is a way of structuring a family tree, providing a useful way of learning about the generations of the family, the key parental and sibling relationships, what is known and where the gaps are. As well as designing a formal diagram, part of an assessment session can be organised with a child or family to draw their family tree on a large piece of A3 or flipchart paper. This can be a picture of an actual tree – with important grandparents or ancestors in the roots, parents forming the main branches and children as smaller branches or leaves. Using coloured pens or sticking on simple drawings of people or faces (depicting each family member) can make the session interesting and informal, creating space to talk about the family in a safe way.

A Creative Ecomap

This can be a large picture, starting with the child in the middle (just their name or a simple drawing of them). The child can then have control over who or what else they choose to put in their ecomap – to denote the people and things that are important to them. Their diagram might include family pets, friends, hobbies and interests, people who counted in the past as well as the present. They can then be encouraged to draw lines between themselves and each item, denoting the strength of the bond and whether it is positive or stressful for them. The lines can be in different colours or broken, zigzag or wiggly, depending on how the child wishes to denote these different relationships.

Other forms of ecomaps can be made with a child using a selection of buttons (actual buttons of all shapes, colours and sizes) or jelly babies (sweets that can be eaten later as a treat for the child) arranged to denote different people and relationships. Or toys can be used, such as small, plastic animals; again each toy can relate to a person or aspect of the child's ecomap. It is important that adult interpretations are not placed on children's ideas in this process. For example, a child might choose a big toy spider to depict their father, not because he is scary, but because they love spiders and their dad has long legs. Listening to the child as they build their ecomap will be a valuable way of learning about how they understand the relationships that matter to them. A photograph can be taken of the final arrangement for the child to keep and a copy could be uploaded to the child's file with the notes of the session.

These creative approaches to making genograms and ecomaps are child-friendly and may enable children and families to participate in a relaxed way in discussions about their family and relationships. The process of drawing or playing, listening to the descriptions and meanings of the child, is as important as the final product. Such creative approaches enable children to share their views about their family and their support network safely and to contribute to the assessment process.

Recognising the needs of vulnerable children and children in need

Early intervention ensures that universal or targeted services can be channelled to address the particular needs of vulnerable children and to support families who may be struggling. In order to explore principles of child-centred practice in more depth, we will focus on two groups of vulnerable children, namely children with disabilities and young carers. These groups of children will be discussed in relation to their specific needs, recognising that these particular issues are relevant to the case study, which will then be examined.

Working with children with disabilities

Children with disabilities are not a homogeneous group. The particular needs and developmental progress of a child with a disability will be unique and may conform little to normative patterns of development. A child affected by a condition such as Down's Syndrome may be able to participate independently alongside their peers in all aspects of daily life, or they may have additional health problems or a severe speech or learning impairment that hinders their capability and opportunities. For many families raising a child with a disability, there are additional challenges to face. The Barnardo's report on disability and inclusion (Barnardo's 2016a) notes that many families are affected by poverty: 'it costs on average twice as much to raise a child with a severe impairment as it does to raise a non-disabled child.' Children with disabilities are also more likely to be excluded from educational and leisure activities that other children take for granted. Careful and comprehensive assessment of the individual needs of the child is essential to ensure appropriate early intervention to support the family and enable children to reach their full potential.

In recent years the legislative framework for child-centred practice has been strengthened to more effectively address the needs of children with complex needs. The Children and Families Act 2014 specifically relates to disabled children and states that Local Authorities have a responsibility to:

- ascertain the wishes and feelings of the child;

- ensure children participate as fully as possible in decision-making;

- provide the child and their family with information to enable them to make decisions;

- ensure support is provided to achieve 'the best possible educational and other outcomes'.

(Children and Families Act, 2014, Part 3, s. 19(d))

In addition, the Convention on the Rights of Persons with Disabilities (United Nations, 2008) is a human rights treaty which provides that parties to the convention promote, respect and ensure equal rights for disabled people. Article 23 emphasises that a disabled child has the right to live a full and decent life with dignity, and, as far as possible, independence, and to play an active part in their community. In response to this treaty, governments must do all they can to support disabled children and their families. Furthermore, according to article 7:

> Children with disabilities have the right to express their views freely on all matters affecting them, their views being given due weight in accordance with their age and maturity, on an equal basis with other children, and to be provided with disability and age-appropriate assistance to realize that right. (United Nations, 2008)

Despite the abundance of policy and guidance supporting the principle of enabling children with disabilities to participate in assessment and decision-making, in many aspects of daily life there is a distinct lack of the disabled child's voice in comparison to their non-disabled peers (Curran, 2010; Franklin and Knight, 2011). This may be due to communication difficulties, access issues or perceptions of professionals regarding the child's abilities (Bailey et al., 2015). 'All children are able to communicate their views in some way' (Dalzell and Chamberlain, 2006: 6), and disabled children, including those with additional communication needs, should not be excluded. It is essential that professionals see the child first, rather than the disability, and recognise the ways in which children can be enabled to participate. Capabilities and achievements need to be recognised and 'celebrated within the context of the child's abilities and potential' (Sloper et al., 2009: 276). In research carried out by the Children's Commissioner for England, one young person with a disability explained: 'I think people could treat us as not simply disabled, or people could treat you as the next person, as if you're completely normal. But then, yes, we have got these issues, obviously you've got to put that aside ... and not be, oh, you can't do this and you can't do that because you're disabled' (Davey, 2010: 33).

Practitioners need to be alert to barriers which impact on a disabled child's participation and ability to achieve their potential. Maximising a child's ability to communicate and ensuring children have appropriate equipment and accessible environments will provide greater opportunities for children to participate in assessment and decision-making processes. This may then have the knock-on effect of increasing opportunities for socialising, learning new skills and promoting independence. In carrying out work with children with special needs, it is crucial again to recognise that 'achieving many desired outcomes requires parents' support' – this is not only support from the parents for their children, but also support for the parents from professionals and supportive services (Sloper et al., 2009: 276).

Practitioner Testimonial

The team I supervise support children who are receiving treatment from one of the following medical departments: oncology and haematology, liver, renal, cystic fibrosis and the Paediatric Intensive Care Unit.

Children are central to our work and often ascertaining the wishes and feelings, views and decisions of the children we work with can be challenging. This is due to a variety of reasons – the child is too unwell, the child has limited communication or the social worker has limited opportunities to see the child alone. Child-centred practice means that the social worker must not state these barriers as a reason for lack of direct engagement with the child but must endeavour to develop skills to overcome these barriers. This often takes time and patience. I support the social workers to think about attachment, child development, to use the tools that are available to them (books, toys and so on) as well as work sheets and Makaton symbols, to undertake direct work and to observe the child's interactions.

In supervision, social workers will often talk about the child's diagnosis, treatment plan and how they are supporting the parents from an emotional and practical level. Whilst this is an important part of their role, I will often direct them back to focusing on the child – to ask how children are coping, not just from a medical perspective, but emotionally, psychologically and spiritually. I challenge the social workers to think about how the child's health issues may have changed their understanding of the world around them, changed their ability to play, engage and learn potentially for the rest of their lives and how they will need support to understand and come to terms with this. Plans are then devised about how support is to be offered and by whom.

Hilary Suddes, Social Worker and Team Manager, Children with complex health needs.

Listening to children with disabilities

The social model of disability emphasises that disability is socially constructed by physical and social barriers within society. This model promotes the acceptance of difference, and looks at ways of removing barriers to enable independence, equality, choice and control. This requires that we seek to overcome obstacles to children's participation and listen to disabled children, taking their views on board in any decision-making process that affects them (Dickens, 2011). When working with children with complex needs, listening is 'an active process of receiving (hearing and observing), interpreting and responding to communication, and includes all the senses and emotions' (Dickens, 2011: 2). Listening is therefore not limited to speech. This is especially important to remember when working with children who may have a communication impairment or be non-verbal.

Time to engage with a disabled child can be challenging in social work settings (Curran, 2010), therefore careful preparation and consultation with those who know the child well and are attuned to the child's ways of communicating are required to enable participation. Marchant (2008: 155) has noted that professionals seeking to carry out an assessment involving a child with a disability should not be asking: '"does he talk?" or "does she communicate?". A more useful starting point is an assumption that all children communicate, and thus the question is "how does he communicate?"' Social workers with heavy caseloads may not have specialist skills in different forms of communication, such as sign language or Makaton. However, bringing a positive, child-centred approach to the involvement of children with disabilities is the first step in overcoming obstacles. Parents may be well placed to provide guidance and colleagues, such as teachers and carers, may be able to facilitate opportunities to listen to the child, thus forming an effective partnership, a team around the child, in the assessment and intervention process.

Learning from Research

The National Society for the Prevention of Cruelty to Children (NSPCC) (October 2014) carried out a review of the literature and a held a series of meetings with disabled young people in order to compile a report focused around listening to children and preventing abuse. Young people cited in this report pointed out the struggles they experience at times in seeking help from professionals:

● *'It can be difficult to say something in private when you need someone to help you communicate.'*

● *'People don't listen to you if you have a communication impairment.'*

- *'Some disabled people get treated badly, get treated like a kid. They get isolated in their thoughts and minds. They could even self-harm. You need to give them more freedom.'*

(NSPCC, 2014: 6; 17)

The report highlights that children with disabilities are at greater risk of abuse and that barriers exist to their effective safeguarding. The NSPCC advocates that children with disabilities have a right to equal protection and that agencies and professionals need to promote opportunities for inclusion.

VIPER stands for Voice, Inclusion, Participation, Empowerment and Research and is a group developed by the council for disabled children. Working with agencies such as the National Children's Bureau (NCB) and the Children's Society, groups of young people with disabilities have developed and contributed to research and policies aimed at promoting the involvement of their peers and developing understanding of what works for young people's participation. Their Report *Hear Us Out* (VIPER, 2013) includes the views of young people with disabilities about participation in decision-making processes:

- *'It should not matter whether a young person can speak, they should be asked for their views – they can express themselves using body language and expressions.'*

- *'If [you're] not involved in decisions about your own life, then this is wrong – [non-disabled] people are.'*

(The Council for Disabled Children, 2013: 14)

Children with disabilities have rights and opinions, and are able to contribute to complex decisions if supported and enabled to do so. In some cases, the input of advocacy services will be both enabling and supportive. However, it is acknowledged there may be barriers in relation to access to advocacy services, including limited professional understanding of the role and a lack of resources and funding. Research carried out by Franklin and Sloper (2009) found that limited contact with their social worker impacted on whether children with disabilities were able to build rapport with them and understand the purpose of their intervention. This research found that disabled children enjoyed taking part in decision-making, feeling listened to and enabled to make choices, especially when creative and fun methods were used. The involvement of advocates can bridge the gap and ensure that children's voices are heard and properly represented in decision-making processes. In a study by Franklin and Knight (2011), one young person highlights the value of advocacy support: 'It's like other people we meet and I'm just sat there and like they're all talking about things but he [the advocate] doesn't talk about me, he talks to me. All the others are sat at table talking about me. But now he's started coming to meetings they listen to me.' (Peter, age 15, in Franklin and Knight, 2011: 62).

Points for Reflection

● What do you think might be the needs of a child with a disability, such as Down's Syndrome?

● How would you seek to involve a child who has learning disabilities in the assessment and intervention process?

Commentary

In any assessment of the needs of a child with a disability it is important not to generalise about certain conditions or make assumptions. Each child is a unique individual and will have their own priorities about what is important to them and the kind of support they need.

Some children use augmentative and alternative communication (AAC), deploying a range of specialist resources to support or replace verbal communication, including Makaton, sign language, communication boards and digital aids. Some children use methods personal to them, such as gestures or facial expressions that are understood by those closest to them. The child-centred practitioner will work in partnership with those who know the child best, to consider and facilitate ways to enable their participation.

Young carers

Young carers were first legally defined in the Carers (Recognition and Services) Act 1995, giving them the right to be formally assessed separately from the person they are providing care for. Legislation, policy and guidance have developed to improve assessment, promote multi-agency working and protect young carers, with the implementation of the Care Act 2014 and the Children and Families Act 2014. A young carer is defined as: 'a person under 18 who provides or intends to provide care for another person (of any age, except where that care is provided for payment, pursuant to a contract or as voluntary work)' (ADASS et al., 2015: 4).

It is reported in the 2011 census that there are 166,363 young carers in England. This is likely to be an underestimation. Young carers are *hidden* from official statistics for a number of reasons, including 'family loyalty, stigma, bullying, and not knowing where to go for support' (Hounsell, 2013: 4). Young carers come from a wide variety of backgrounds and 'their individual experiences remain poorly understood' (Doutre et al., 2013: 33). Children and young people providing care to a loved one may not recognise themselves as carers viewing their situation as a 'normal' family relationship (Smyth et al., 2011).

Children as young carers take on many roles and responsibilities for parents, relatives or siblings, including house work, personal care, interpreting for non-English-speaking relatives and managing finances (Dearden and Becker, 2004). Research shows young carers are more likely than their counterparts to 'come from a poorer background, have a special educational need or a disability, and come from black, Asian or minority ethnic families' (Hounsell, 2013: 18). Excessive caring responsibilities can have a negative impact on the child's education, as children miss school or have little time for homework. Young carers can also experience isolation, as children feel unable to invite friends to their home and have few opportunities for socialising with their peers. There is increasing evidence highlighting the necessity for professional support and intervention to enable children to be relieved of the burden of caring in order to prioritise their own needs and fulfil their potential. However, children and young people have also highlighted positive experiences through caring such as life skills, pride, confidence, motivation, greater maturity, improved political awareness, experience for potential future employment and strong attachment to the person needing care (Doutre et al., 2013; Heyman and Heyman, 2013). Being a young carer can increase the resilience of some children, enabling them to develop skills and coping strategies beyond their years. It is important, therefore, that professionals coming into contact with young carers do not make assumptions but recognise that the young person may draw positives from their situation, as well as having particular vulnerabilities. A child-centred approach 'allows time for listening to the details of an individual's life experiences, non-judgementally, to reduce the risk of problematising normative familial processes' (Doutre et al., 2013: 31).

Learning from Research

Wayman and colleagues (2016) completed qualitative research with 45 young carers, aged between 9 and 23 years. The study highlights the difficulties they face in accessing support from professionals, for reasons including feeling misunderstood and judged, being too proud to seek help, or fearful of repercussions. The following views are in the words of the young carers themselves:

> 'I don't think most people that I know would understand my situation because all their family are healthy. They wouldn't understand. They might think, "oh that's what you'd normally do as an older sister". But it's not.' (Alex, 15)

▶

'You don't want them to say "stop that caring".' (Bobby, 9)

'My mum had a real fear of social workers, so the rule in our house was what happens in these walls stays in these four walls ... she thought they would take us away.' (Selina, 21)

'Sometimes I feel like there's no point. People don't really care. They just ask for no reason ... Like in college I feel like that most of the time – when they ask me about stuff at home, I feel like they don't really care.' (Billie, 18)

'What if they find out that I am caring for my mum, and my mum doesn't do anything? What are they going to do – take me away?' (Samayya, 16)

The research emphasises how services and professionals can better respond to young people and take account of their perspectives. This includes having an awareness and sensitivity to the needs of young carers, recognising when young people are caring and providing useful information. A theme which resonated with young people, irrespective of their age or circumstances, was 'having an appropriate stake in what happened about care and support' (2016: 90). Some young people reported positive experiences; however, more frequently, young people reported feeling disillusioned. They emphasised practitioners failing to include them in decisions or not taking the time to explain things in a child-centred way. Young people stated:

'To be honest, even if I wanted to, no one actually listens to what I want. If a social worker comes and talks to my mum, sometimes my mum doesn't even know what I want, I just keep quiet. But it's not always what I want.' (Baruk, 11)

'I get blanked out, like we don't exist. Just because we are children, we don't know what's happening. But the fact is that we do know a lot of stuff that is happening.' (Samayya, 16)

(Wayman et al., 2016: 73–91)

Practitioners, at the first point of contact, have a responsibility to identify young carers, and ascertain from the child, as well as the adult, what caring tasks they are undertaking and how this impacts on their lives. As 'young carers and families are experts on their own lives', a whole family approach should be adopted (ADASS, 2015: 5), recognising the family as a system that provides a network of emotional and practical support for each other, including for the young carer. In respect of assessing the needs of the child or the adult, one young carer recognises: 'Both [needs] are equal – if you meet the child's needs they can help the parent and if you meet the parent's needs, they can care for the child' (Ofsted, 2009: 15).

Points for Reflection

- How do you think children might be affected by being a young carer in their family?

- What do you think might be the risks and the benefits for the young carer in taking a caring role?

Commentary

It is important for practitioners to be aware of the research about the effects upon children of being a young carer. Each case is unique and the social worker will need to listen to the child and explore with them how they manage their day-to-day life and what support would be of benefit to them and their family. They need to recognise the struggles and also the rewards for some children of caring for family members. Where caring responsibilities are constraining the opportunities and life chances of young people, for example by limiting engagement in school and leisure activities, this should be discussed with the family. Social workers need to understand their legal duties in relation to supporting people with disabilities and long-term conditions and advocate on behalf of the rights of young carers.

Case study analysis

It is useful to apply the learning from this chapter by considering the Smith–Jones–Khan family, introduced on page 143. At this stage, the family has been referred to the social worker based in the local Children's Centre for an early help assessment. We used a formal genogram in the introduction to Part II, to consider the structure of the family known to social workers at the point of referral. This highlights some of the important relationships for family members and also the losses experienced by them, due to bereavement or divorce. There is also much that is not known, such as any remaining links for Jade to her mother's family and how integrated Hanif may be within his paternal extended family. It may be helpful for a professional seeking to engage the family in an early help assessment to work with them to design a creative ecomap for each of the children. We have provided an example of Hanif's ecomap in Figure 10. This may help to fill some of the gaps and to explore who might be part of the network of support for the family. As noted above, the process of carrying out creative work together is also valuable as a means of listening to children and gaining insights into their perspectives about who and what matters to them.

Children's voices

It is helpful to reflect upon how the children may see their family. In the following, we imagine what might be the thoughts and concerns of the children in this family.

Charlotte's Story:

> 'I love mum and Dad. I love my Hanif. Jade don't play with me. "I'm off out … I'm off out" she says.'

Hanif's Story:

> 'I like Charlotte best – she's my favourite person in the world. My favourite time is reading bedtime stories with her. Mum says it's the best way to get Charlotte settled down. Sometimes I just snuggle down with her and go to sleep as well. I like Dad a lot as well, but I don't get to see him much.'

Jade's Story:

> 'Fiona's always nagging and moaning at me. Hanif's alright, but a bit irritating. I like playing with Charlotte, but Fiona annoys me cos she says I'm too rough with her. God, just cos she's got Down's, she thinks she might break. I never see Dad anymore – he's always down the pub. I can't wait till I'm old enough to leave home. I'll go and live with my boyfriend as soon as I turn 16 that's for sure.'

Case Study Analysis

With reference to the assessment framework and 'my world triangle' on page 150.

- Select one of the children from the case study.
- Identify the needs of the child with consideration to the three domains of the assessment triangle.
- How would you work with the children to ascertain their wishes and feelings?
- What kind of support do you think should be part of an early help plan?

Analysis of practice issues

In considering the needs of the children, the following factors may be important:

- In relation to Charlotte, it is important to recognise her need to thrive and remain healthy and to reach milestones that take account of the impact of Down's Syndrome on her growth and development. Fiona and Mick may benefit from meeting other parents caring for children with disabilities.

Charlotte should be assessed as a 'child in need', as she may require specialist support in order to attain her full potential as she grows up.

- Hanif may be taking on too much responsibility in his family as a young carer, supporting his mum and caring for Charlotte. This would need to be discussed with Hanif and Fiona. The family may benefit from links to local services for young carers. The issues around bullying need to be addressed by the school. Hanif may need more interaction with and support from his father, Nadir, and this may help him to gain a positive sense of his religious and cultural identity.

- In relation to Jade, with reference to the parenting capacity domain of the 'my world triangle' ('what I need from the people who look after me'), it will be important that Mick and Fiona are supported to provide consistent boundaries for Jade, enabling her to develop positive peer relationships that do not place her in situations of risk or exploitation. Mick has an important role to play in enabling Jade to retain positive memories of her mother, Jackie, and find ways to cope with her loss.

- There are several issues impacting on Mick and Fiona, which may be affecting their ability to parent and meet the needs of their children. They are experiencing pressures around Fiona's mental health and Mick's unemployment and drink problem. There is family conflict and inconsistent parenting. Work with the parents to explore their understanding of how these issues might impact on the children and their motivation to address the concerns will be crucial. The support of parent's groups at the local Children's Centre may be helpful.

- Completing genograms and ecomaps with the family will provide opportunities for family members to acknowledge losses and changes in their lives and to identify their most important relationships and sources of support. Such creative tools may also be helpful in exploring relationships in the extended family that could be built upon or re-established in order to provide a stronger support network for the children.

Conclusion

A key role for child-centred practitioners is to engage with children and to work in partnership with parents and other local professionals in order to assess and address the needs of vulnerable children. There are many challenges in fulfilling this role, in particular building collaborative relationships with parents and carers who are the main facilitators of their children's well-being. In this chapter, we have explored some of the issues around carrying out early help assessments in order to ensure effective, early intervention to meet the needs of vulnerable children. We have identified useful practice tools and analysed some key practice issues with reference to the case study. We will go on, in ensuing chapters, to analyse in more depth some of the complexities of child-centred practice in relation to managing risk and safeguarding children.

Recommended reading and resources

- The Department for Education have published a Research Briefing, written by Turney and colleagues (2011), that provides a useful overview of the literature about assessment processes, collating the key messages from research about good practice in assessment of children in need.

- The textbook by Ruth Dalzell and Emma Sawyer (2016), *Putting Analysis into Child and Family Assessment*, provides a valuable toolkit for practice, including ideas to promote analytical thinking and creative approaches to involving children and young people in assessment processes.

- The Social Care Institute for Excellence has developed some useful interactive learning tools and one of these focuses on assessment. The following website explores the use of genograms and ecomaps as creative methods of engaging families and gathering information:
www.scie.org.uk/assets/elearning/communicationskills/cs04/resource/html/object4/object4_7.htm#slide01

- Chapter 5 (by Anita Franklin), of the Research in Practice text (edited by Mark Ivory): *Voice of the Child* (2015), focuses on the importance of involving children with communication difficulties in assessment and decision-making processes.

- The Council for Disabled Children has carried out research and other important work to promote the participation of children with disabilities. Their website provides useful information about their work:
https://councilfordisabledchildren.org.uk/about

- *Born to be Different* is a series of documentaries filmed by the director and producer Anna Stickland on an annual basis since the early 2000s. The films follow the lives of several children with disabilities, depicting their struggles and achievements. They provide fascinating and candid insights into the lives and perspectives of the children and their families. Many episodes are available on:
www.channel4.com/programmes/born-to-be-different

7

WORKING WITH CHILDREN AND YOUNG PEOPLE AT RISK OF ABUSE AND NEGLECT

Introduction

In child protection work, where the child or young person is rarely a voluntary service user, there is often the challenge of how to balance the rights of the child with their safety and well-being. Children and young people at risk of abuse and neglect come to the attention of social workers primarily referred by concerned professionals, family members or friends, where abuse or neglect has been witnessed or is suspected. Disclosures made by children seeking help remain relatively rare (Jobe and Gorin, 2013). Although child-centred practice is ideally 'set to the child's pace rather than driven by adult or service-centred timescales' (Lefevre, 2010: 26), there are instances where the social worker has limited information in their first interaction with a young person and needs to act without delay. More often, the social worker is involved in longer-term interventions in order to assess and manage risk, maintaining a focus on the overall welfare of the child as well as their immediate safety. Ensuring child-centred practice is hugely challenging in this complex area of work.

This chapter considers how to work effectively with children and young people at risk of abuse and neglect. We explore risk factors that impact on the welfare of children and in some cases constitute child abuse. We draw learning from serious case reviews, where risks were not identified or adequately addressed leading to tragic consequences. We recognise that some children are particularly vulnerable to abuse and exploitation due to a range of factors, including their age and circumstances. We explore the challenges of child-centred practice, using the case study as a springboard to analyse specific aspects of practice, with a focus on domestic violence.

Who are children and young people at risk of abuse and neglect?

Local Authorities have a duty to safeguard and promote the welfare of children in their area. This is made explicit in the Children Act 1989 and Children Act 2004. Under section 47 of the 1989 Act, Local Authorities are specifically required to pay due consideration to the wishes and feelings of children and young people who are suffering, or *likely to suffer*, significant harm before making decisions to protect them. 'Harm' is defined as the 'ill-treatment or the impairment of health or development'. As amended by the Adoption and Children Act 2002, the definition of harm also includes 'impairment suffered by hearing or seeing the ill-treatment of another'.

Child protection is governed and managed through a range of policies, procedures, court processes and performance standards. At times when many agendas are running simultaneously, it is 'easy to lose sight of the child in these processes and allow other interests to dominate' (Winkworth, 2002: 5). Children are a key source of information about their lives and therefore not to engage with them directly is 'at best puzzling' (Munro, 2011: 25). To encourage children and young people not only to engage with social work professionals regarding decisions affecting their lives, but to actively participate and contribute to these decisions, is a crucial part of safeguarding practice. This can be demanding; the onus is on the social worker to find creative and resourceful ways to establish rapport, even when children are involuntary service users.

Children and young people living with parents who experience issues such as substance misuse, domestic violence, mental illness and learning disabilities are at an increased risk of abuse and neglect (Cleaver et al., 2011). That is not to say all parents who experience these factors present a risk to their children, but as Brown and Ward (2013:17) note: 'these factors interlock in complex combinations which substantially increase the likelihood of maltreatment'; where two or more of these factors exist, children are more vulnerable to their future life chances being impaired. Research has shown a correlation between these risk factors and cases of child death and serious injury (Brandon et al., 2008, 2012). The most recent triennial review of serious case reviews (Sidebotham et al., 2016), has emphasised the cumulative impact of risk, in particular where domestic abuse overlaps with parental mental illness or substance misuse. There is also recognition that other factors in the family situation interact to create potentially harmful environments for children, including a history of violent crime in the family and where parents are enmeshed in acrimonious separations. The term 'toxic trio' has been used to describe circumstances where substance misuse, parental mental ill health and domestic violence feature simultaneously. These cases can be particularly complex and social workers need to work closely alongside specialist colleagues in order to undertake assessments and intervene effectively to address multiple and overlapping needs (Wonnacott and Watts, 2014).

Children affected by domestic abuse

The Home Office defines domestic abuse as:

> Any incident or pattern of incidents of controlling, coercive or threatening behaviour, violence or abuse between those aged 16 or over who are or have been intimate

partners or family members, regardless of gender or sexuality. This can encompass but is not limited to the following types of abuse:

- Psychological

- Physical

- Sexual

- Financial

- Emotional

(Home Office, 2013: 2)

This revised definition raises awareness about the nature of domestic abuse, involving not only acts of physical violence but also intimidation and coercive control.

The charitable organisation SafeLives (www.safelives.org.uk 2014/2015) has collated information about the extent of the problem in England and Wales; the statistics are staggering:

- Each year around 2.1 million people suffer some form of domestic abuse – 1.4 million women and 700,000 men.

- Women are much more likely than men to be the victims of high-risk or severe domestic abuse.

- Seven women a month are killed by a current or former partner.

- 130,000 children live in homes where there is high-risk domestic abuse.

- On average high-risk victims live with domestic abuse for 2.6 years before getting help.

- 85% of victims seek help five times, on average, from professionals in the year before they get effective help to stop the abuse.

Domestic abuse is widely recognised in the literature as a significant risk factor for children and young people (Stanley and Humphreys, 2015). Being exposed to domestic violence in the home falls within the definition of emotional abuse set down in *Working Together* (HM Government, 2015: 92–93), recognising the likelihood of this experience leading to 'severe and persistent adverse effects on the child's emotional development'. Children and young people who witness domestic abuse not only suffer emotional harm through experiencing distress and fear; they may also incur physical injuries. Stanley (2011: 6) notes 'cumulative exposure over time produces profoundly serious problems which can be resistant to change'. Although domestic abuse can happen in any family, research indicates it is most common amongst those also suffering social and economic disadvantage. Stanley (2011) has drawn together the findings from various studies to estimate that almost a quarter of young adults witnessed domestic abuse at some point during their childhood; those children experiencing domestic violence in the family were three to four times more likely to also suffer physical abuse and neglect.

Learning from Research

Stanley and colleagues (2012) conducted research which captured the views of parents and children who had experienced domestic violence. The participants valued professionals who listened to and validated their accounts. The research highlighted the following key messages to assist in undertaking child-centred practice with children who have experienced domestic violence:

- Those professionals who appeared ineffective when faced with domestic violence could reinforce the victim's sense of powerlessness.

- Professionals need to engage with the emotional content of disclosures.

- Separate sessions with children are valuable so that they can feel safe to share their story and their voice can be heard.

- Rather than seeing the end point of intervention as separation of the adult couple, social workers need to consider the dynamics of the separation and how this might impact on children and young people.

Swanston and colleagues (2014) carried out research in order to hear the voices of school-age children who had experiences of domestic violence. They found that children were often aware of much more than their parents believed in terms of the violence in the home and that they were resourceful in seeking out ways to protect themselves and family members. Comments of the children included:

> 'I was always thinking about what had happened, what was going to happen next.'

> 'Like it feels really annoying cos you just like want to be like a normal family with a nice dad, a nice mum and all that.'

> 'My mum's come up screaming, like proper screaming, so I've locked my bedroom door to keep her in there so he don't hurt her.'

Social workers and other professionals concerned about domestic violence need to listen to children's accounts in order to understand the full picture and develop an effective plan to safeguard children.

Taking a child-centred approach to addressing domestic abuse means recognising the intense pressure and risk that many mothers experience as they seek to keep themselves and their children safe. Seeing mothers as secondary perpetrators who fail to protect their children is not an effective strategy and can lead to women feeling blamed and disengaging from professional input (Stanley and Humphreys, 2015). Furthermore, in those cases where the abuser is also the father or playing a parental role in the family, interventions that ignore the role of the perpetrator and his relationship with and responsibilities to the children are imbalanced and ineffectual. Featherstone (2007) has argued that interventions that challenge violent men are supportive to women and children, and offer possibilities to nurture non-violent parenting where children wish to retain a relationship with their father. Child-centred approaches, therefore, involve empowering mothers, challenging perpetrators, and listening to and safeguarding children.

Children affected by parental substance misuse

Parents who misuse legal or illegal substances can experience 'erratic mood swings, paranoia and hallucinations, feelings of elation and calm, diminished concentration, memory impairment and a loss of consciousness' (Brown and Ward, 2013: 24). This can have a detrimental impact on the safety and well-being of their children. As Howe notes: 'heavy use of alcohol and drugs distort, disrupt and disturb parent-child relationships' (Howe 2005: 184). Having said that, misuse of drugs and alcohol is not tantamount to child abuse and professionals should avoid pathologising parents. It is important to assess how parents manage their substance use and how this impacts on children in their care. As illicit substances are against the law and often shrouded in denial and secrecy, it is difficult at times to make this assessment and to estimate the number of children living with parents who misuse drugs (Cleaver et al, 2011). It has been estimated that there are between 250,000 and 350,000 children of 'problem drug users' in the UK (Advisory Council on the Misuse of Drugs, 2003). Problem drug use is 'characterised by the use of multiple drugs, often by injection', and is 'typically chaotic and unpredictable' with adults experiencing serious health and social problems (ACMD, 2003: 10). This affects children at every stage of development, from conception through the life cycle. The definition of neglect in *Working Together* (HM Government, 2015: 93) recognises that a child's health and development may be seriously impaired as a consequence of maternal substance misuse in pregnancy.

It is important to recognise that alcohol misuse negatively affects the lives of more children than illegal substances, with alcohol misuse being much more common. It is estimated that 2.6 million children are living in the UK with parents who are drinking hazardously (Turning Point, 2011). Alcohol misuse is too often not taken as seriously as illicit substance misuse, in spite of alcohol being 'addictive, easier to obtain and legal' (Adamson and Templeton, 2012: 4).

Learning from Research

In research conducted by O'Connor and colleagues (2014) with 27 families (including 84 children and 34 parents or stepparents) who had experience of parental substance misuse, neglect was highlighted by both children and their parents as a common experience. Families reported a high number of accommodation moves, changes in primary carers, sibling separations and childhood behavioural issues. The majority of participants disclosed the daily experience of living with tension, worry and sometimes fear. One child reports harassment and bullying from the local community stating:

> 'People kept beating up my mother and beating up me ... for no reason ... They poisoned my dad's dog ... we couldn't go nowhere without them causing trouble ... we were just living in fear.'

(quoted in O'Connor et al., 2014: 69)

The report for the Children's Commissioner (2012) – *Silent Voices: Supporting Children and Young People Affected by Parental Alcohol Misuse* – discusses the findings of focus groups with 23 children, young people and young adults aged from eight years of age to the mid-twenties, who had been directly affected by parental alcohol misuse. Teenage participants in the research were asked to brainstorm and rank the potential barriers to accessing support. They produced the following list (ranked greatest barrier to least):

1 Lack of confidence

2 Lack of personal direction (explained by young person as not knowing where to go to get help)

3 Parents finding out

4 Feeling comfortable enough/at ease with someone to tell them

5 Worried about brother/sister

6 Didn't want school friends/acquaintances to know

7 Fear of it going further, for example, to the police.

(Adamson and Templeton, 2012: 22)

Older young people were asked for one key message to present to the Children's Commissioner. These were individuals who had lived with parental alcohol misuse throughout childhood, had remained 'silent' and had not sought help until their late teens or early adulthood. Their key messages include:

'Don't patronise us/children of alcoholics. Don't see us as victims. We will just retreat further into our shells.'

'Appreciate the complexity and individuality of children.'

'We lost our childhoods and had to grow up quickly.'

'It's got to be the child's decision to speak, but we need to let them know it's okay to speak.'

'I need somewhere safe to go quickly when mum starts drinking and cutting herself but where can I go?'

(Adamson and Templeton, 2012: 28)

Literature on resilience highlights that children experiencing parental substance misuse can become 'well-functioning adults without developing serious psychological or behavioural difficulties' (O'Connor et al., 2014: 67). Factors positively contributing to resilience are the presence of a non-using adult, a supportive family network and access to supportive environments, including school and community-based activities (O'Connor et al., 2014; Jenkins and Cook, 2012). Social workers need to mobilise a network of support around the child, as well as seeking to work effectively with parents. Supporting parents to reduce or manage their problematic substance use is crucial in order to safeguard children (Forrester and Harwin, 2011). The child-centred social worker will seek to ensure that the needs of the parents do not overwhelm or distract from the paramountcy of the children's needs.

Children affected by parental mental illness

The UK charity the Mental Health Foundation reported in 2015 that one in four adults experience mental health problems in any one year. Many of these adults are also parents. Although poor parental mental health has been associated with poor outcomes in children, not all children of parents who have mental health problems are at increased risk. There are several biological, social, psychological and cultural contexts to consider which might provide protective factors for children or conversely might increase the risks (Mental Health Foundation, 2015). Parental mental health problems can range from moderate or 'common' difficulties such as depression and anxiety to chronic and enduring conditions such as severe depression, bipolar disorder or schizophrenia. The seriousness of the parental problem is less relevant than the level to which the child is directly affected by their parent's ill health; however, if the condition is entrenched it is more likely to impact upon the child over time. It is important to note that parental mental health issues are rarely static; they fluctuate, may be short or long term and are influenced by a variety of stresses (Tunnard, 2004). In addition, Cleaver and colleagues highlight that nearly half of those attending mental health services also report alcohol or drug issues, and nearly a quarter of male perpetrators of domestic violence are depressed, half have a history of alcohol misuse and one-fifth a history of illicit drug misuse (Cleaver et al., 2011: 48).

Social workers need to acknowledge and understand the relationship between the child and the parent where parental mental health is of concern if they are to successfully support the family. Many children and young people show great maturity when caring for their parent, for example dealing with emergency situations or assisting with medication (Evans and Fowler, 2008). Recognising the experiences of children and young people, and hearing their voices positively, contributes to more effective interventions (Aldridge, 2006).

Points for Reflection

- Consider one of the key risk factors noted in the paragraphs above – how do you think children and young people might be affected by living in a family exposed to domestic violence, substance misuse or mental health problems?

- How would you seek to engage with a family affected by these issues?

Commentary

It is important not to generalise or make assumptions about the impact of the risk factors we have discussed on a child. Research indicates that a significant proportion of children brought up in families with these problems show no long-term behavioural or emotional consequence. In some families, parental problems are managed and protective factors, such as supportive extended family networks, minimise the impact upon the child. Nevertheless, it is important that the particular implications for the individual child are properly assessed. This can only be achieved by listening to children in order to understand how their lives are affected by the problems of their parents. It is important to appreciate that families affected by serious risk factors may be difficult to engage due to fears of losing their children or other legal consequences (such as convictions related to illegal drug use). Children also may be anxious about what to say to professionals or feel pressure to maintain their family's privacy. Child-centred practice involves seeking to build trust in order to work with children, parents and carers. It may be helpful for the children's social worker to be introduced to the family by a worker they already know and trust, such as their drugs support worker. Social workers should be honest about their role and their paramount concern for the welfare of the child. Working to support parents to address their problems so that risks are managed and families can stay together is the initial aim of any intervention.

Vulnerable groups of children and young people at risk

There are specific groups of children who are particularly vulnerable to abuse and neglect, and ensuring child-centred practice can be more testing in these cases. These groups include babies and younger children who cannot verbally communicate and seek help, and (as noted in Chapter 6) children with additional physical or learning needs (Brandon et al, 2012). Also, teenagers at risk of abuse and neglect are often not prioritised by professionals in comparison to younger children (Stein et al., 2009; Hicks and Stein, 2010). Some young people may be particularly hard to reach, having disengaged from parental and professional contacts, but formed strong and exploitative bonds with abusive adults.

Very young children

The evidence suggests that children's very early life experiences have far-reaching effects over the course of a child's lifetime (Tickell, 2011). The child's experiences and environment during the first three years of life have the greatest impact into adulthood (Brown and Ward, 2013). Child abuse, neglect or trauma, including witnessing domestic abuse, 'alter normal child development and, without intervention, can have lifelong consequences' (Cuthbert et al., 2010: 14). In addition, early attachment forms the groundwork for many aspects of social functioning later in the child's life such as attainment, well-being and resilience (Winkworth, 2002; Tickell, 2011).

However, there are many parental problems that impact on the well-being of babies and very young children. The NSPCC report *All Babies Count: Prevention and Protection for Vulnerable Babies* identified that in the UK:

- 19,500 babies under 1-year-old are living with a parent who has used Class A drugs in the last year.

- 39,000 babies under 1-year-old live in households affected by domestic violence in the last year.

- 93,500 babies under 1-year-old live with a parent who is a problem drinker.

- 144,000 babies under 1-year-old live with a parent who has a common mental health problem.

(Cuthbert et al., 2010: 5)

Babies born to mothers using drugs or alcohol during pregnancy are likely to have serious health needs and may be at risk of neglect; interventions should be planned to safeguard the welfare of the child prior to and after birth. Children under the age of one year are nearly three times as likely to be the subjects of child protection plans due to physical abuse, and over twice as likely to be the subjects of child protection plans for neglect (Brown and Ward, 2013). Of the 471 serious case reviews evaluated by Ofsted between 2007 and 2011, 210 children were babies under the age of one (Ofsted, 2011).

It is clear then that professionals need to be aware of the particular vulnerability of our youngest and most dependent children. To work in a child-centred way with this age group requires a sound knowledge of child development and especially of emotional development (Brandon et al., 2012). Social workers work closely with multi-agency colleagues, and therefore do not need to be 'experts in child development themselves, however, they do need to be able to recognise patterns of overall development, to promote optimal child development and to detect when such development may be going off track' (Brandon et al., 2011: 20).

As babies are pre-verbal and cannot communicate their wishes and feelings directly, observation of attachment relationships, care within the family and physical and emotional development is integral to ensuring child-centred practice. This means taking a step back and observing interaction between a child and their parent or caregiver, preferably in the home environment. Observation of the parent–child dynamic is essential to assess actual parenting, as opposed to caregivers themselves describing how they parent (Fauth et al., 2010). Practitioners need to be able to observe and reflect on the child's responses to their caregivers; for example, what happens during feeding 'provides powerful clues to emotional development' (Brandon et al., 2011: 8). If the carer acts differently whilst the social worker is present, the child is likely to appear surprised or confused.

Focus on Practice

Observation of a child in the home environment

It can be useful to arrange to observe a parent with their child engaged in a playful activity. This can be particularly valuable as a precursor to exploring with parents how they interact with their baby or toddler, encourage their play and nurture positive attachment relationships.

Allow 30–40 minutes to complete the observation, explain the purpose to the carer and the child, age appropriately, and seek their consent. Sit where you can clearly see the interaction between the child and their carer. Do not engage with the parent or child during the observation, which includes avoiding smiling or small talk. This can be more difficult than it sounds. Use the following prompts:

▶

Ask the carer to be with the child whilst they play, but not to join in.
How engaged is the carer? Does the child approach them for interaction? How does the child respond?

Ask the carer to play with their child.
Does the carer allow the child to take the lead? Does the carer take over? Does the carer support the child? Is the carer enabling or critical? How do they communicate with each other? Is there eye contact?

Ask the carer to look at a picture book with their child.
How comfortable is the child within close proximity of their carer? Does the child attempt to move away? How does the carer respond? Does the carer talk about the pictures and engage the child with the book?

At the end of the observation, it is important to allow parents to share their views about how the play session went. Observers should take care to model a strengths-based approach by emphasising examples of positive interactions, as well as sharing constructive feedback to encourage positive play where needed.

Butler (2015) provides useful guidance about applying observational methods in practice.

Child-centred social workers need to make analytical, evidence-based and timely decisions for young children to ensure the best outcomes. Research shows that parents affected by problematic substance misuse who were able to provide nurturing homes and achieve lasting change for their babies did so within the first six months of the birth of their baby. Pregnancy and birth are often a catalyst for parents to address problematic and harmful behaviour (Ward et al., 2012). Children who remain with parents who have not made significant changes within the first few months of birth may continue to experience abuse or neglect for prolonged periods (Ward et al., 2012). Therefore, pregnancy and birth are a huge window of opportunity for social workers and health professionals to work collaboratively with parents to harness the motivation for change and to promote the safety and well-being of their children.

Points for Reflection
_____

- Why do you think babies and toddlers are particularly vulnerable and what risks might they be exposed to?

- How would you seek to assess the needs of a very young child and consider what might be their 'wishes and feelings'?

Commentary

Infants are dependent upon their parents and carers in order to survive and have their basic needs met. Babies are particularly vulnerable and need nurturing and sensitive care. The development of the baby's brain and skull in the neonatal period means that shaking and rough handling can have serious or tragic consequences. The arrival of a new baby can be a source of joy and also stress and anxiety for families. Many families need support and guidance to respond to the needs of their baby.

Assessing the needs of very young children will involve working closely with parents and carers, who are likely to know their child better than anyone else. Observation of parent–child relationships and daily care routines will help to form a picture of the needs of the child and parental capacity to respond to those needs. Child-centred practice involves liaising closely with health professionals, such as midwives and health visitors, in order to form a team around the child to offer integrated and targeted support.

Older young people

Knowledge has increased over recent years regarding the vulnerability of older young people, and how they are often regarded as resilient by virtue of surviving into their teens (Stein et al., 2009; Rees et al., 2010). Older young people are often categorised by their challenging behaviour, and are seen as rebellious or hard to reach (Ofsted, 2011). Young people may present with risk-taking behaviours, mental health issues, homelessness or be misusing substances in response to the difficulties they may be experiencing (Rees et al., 2010). Sadly, risk-taking is often seen as a choice, rather than recognising where this is a consequence of abuse and neglect. Social workers are faced with the challenge of seeking to understand the young person's presenting behaviour and the underlying causes (Sidebotham et al., 2016).

Young people who have experienced abuse or neglect for several years and have previously received professional input that they have found difficult or unhelpful are less likely to recognise when they need support or to disclose abuse or neglect (Cossar et al., 2013). This is described by Cossar and colleagues (2013: 105) as 'a vicious circle which could encourage extreme self-reliance and compound the effects of abuse, being labelled as a problem rather than a young person with problems'. Older children 'who felt that their needs were repeatedly unrecognised, ignored or misunderstood were likely to become distressed, angry and desperate' (Brandon et al., 2012: 94). Young people have stated they do not disclose information due to fear. This is fear of not being believed and fear of being placed in Local Authority care; there are also anxieties about repercussions for loved ones or the abuse escalating (Rees et al., 2010). Children and young people may have a deep sense of loyalty to their parents and consider social work involvement to be stressful for the family; they may find disclosure uncomfortable or humiliating

(Stanley et al., 2010; Brandon et al., 2012). In some cases, they may take steps to hide negative experiences to avoid stigmatisation, experiencing conflict between wanting others to know and keeping the 'family secret' (Adamson and Templeton, 2012: 34). Anna (17 years) describes how she would hide the abuse she was experiencing and resist the need to build trust with her social worker:

> 'Cos me and my mum used to cover it up. I used to have bruises, the lot, and we just used to make up stories and just … so at the same time it's what the child wants to tell you and it's what the parent wants to tell you. Because things can easily get covered up … because if the child really is hurting and they do need someone to talk to, then you've got to get their trust first before they'll do that. Like cos social services just used to walk into my house and think I'm just going to tell them everything and it's not like that.'
>
> (Rees et al., 2010: 43)

Social workers need to be mindful that building a relationship of trust with young people may take time and patience. It is important also to gain a full picture of how family difficulties may have impacted on a young person over time. In some cases, where young people have struggled with experiences of chronic neglect for many years, with intermittent periods of agency involvement, it is helpful to take the long view and consider whether change is possible in the family (Sidebotham et al., 2016). Completing a chronology of social work involvement and significant issues in the family will assist in the process of planning how best to address risk and support the young person in the present.

Focus on Practice

Use of Chronologies

A chronology is the sequential story of the significant events in the life of a child and their family. The information is recorded in date order, is factual, clear, precise and concise. Accuracy is vital, as mistakes can infiltrate records and be repeated. Although a chronology is not an assessment, it is a tool to inform assessment. A good chronology will provide a comprehensive overview of the child's life and experiences. This includes positive changes and achievements for the child, as well as risks and concerns.

The chronology keeps the child in mind and at the forefront of planning. Its purpose is to assisting in evidence-based, analytical decision-making by:

- Seeking to understand the cumulative impact of risk factors;

- Identifying and making sense of patterns of events or behaviours;

- Recognising whether change has occurred, is required and is likely; and

- Enabling reflection and analysis.

▶

A chronology is particularly useful where there is a plethora of information to process or where progress in a case is minimal. Review and analysis of the chronology are essential to effective assessment. A chronology that is not analysed and reviewed regularly serves very little, if any, purpose (Social Work Inspection Agency Scotland, 2010).

Social workers can use a chronology creatively in practice in the following ways:

- **In assessment sessions:** The chronology can be used to explore family history with a young person and their parents or carers, especially if there has been long-term or intermittent social work involvement. As the information is presented, it enables families to reflect on their past life experiences, the impact of these experiences on the children and whether their circumstances are now different.

- **As a visual tool:** The chronology can be colour-coded to provide a visual impact for the social worker, the child and family. This is especially useful in cases where there are a number of complex issues and it is difficult to establish patterns. Each area of concern can be highlighted in a separate colour, for example domestic violence incidents in blue, the child going missing in green. Protective factors can also be highlighted, for example the child's achievements in yellow. Patterns can be identified more clearly, aiding analysis.

- **As a creative timeline:** Using a roll of wallpaper or lining paper, work with the child to consider what they feel are the most significant events in their life from birth to the present day. The social worker may suggest some events from their formal chronology, but the aim will be to enable the young person to plot on their timeline the moments that mattered to them, or had greatest impact on their life or family, from their perspective. Katie Wrench (2016: 37) describes the value of working creatively with a child to draw a 'self-esteem timeline'. It is certainly important to commence this piece of work by seeking to plot the child's highlights and positive memories.

Children and young people at risk of sexual exploitation

Several high-profile public inquiries regarding child sexual exploitation across the UK have raised national awareness of this widespread problem and attracted significant media coverage. In Rochdale and Rotherham there were grave criticisms of both the police and the social work departments owing to the lack of timely interventions to protect victims. Professional responses have been hampered by the perception that engaging in such abusive sexual relationships was consensual. The impact of historical allegations of sexual exploitation by celebrities and adults in positions of power, such as Jimmy Savile and Rochdale MP Cyril Smith, has heightened the concerns. Media coverage has given a voice to victims of abuse and encouraged a change in public attitudes towards victims and offenders (Jones and Florek, 2015). Every Local Authority is now required to have a multi-agency strategy to prevent sexual exploitation, identify and support victims and target action against perpetrators. Professionals and society, as a whole, are 'all adjusting to a new and welcome re-discovery that young people have rights and deserve respect, whatever their background, circumstances and behaviour' (Jones and Florek, 2015: 66).

Practitioner Testimonial

I am a social worker working for the Local Authority. My role is working with young people who have been assessed as at medium or high risk of Child Sexual Exploitation. At times, young people do not wish to engage with a service, for some young people they have had many interventions in their lives. As practitioners, we have to recognise their autonomy and the stage of development they are at. What works with one young person doesn't necessarily work with another young person. It is important that young people have an understanding of what the concerns are and have the opportunity to agree, disagree or challenge this.

Young people need time to build up relationships and trust. It is important that their voices and views are represented in all of our work and there are a variety of ways in which this can be achieved. Wherever possible young people should be part of their meetings and this may mean that meetings are adapted to suit their needs, for example made shorter. It can take many weeks of phone calls, texts and visits before young people will agree to discuss what is going on for them and it is likely they will only share a snapshot of their lives. I have met young people in the park, taken them to appointments, seen them at their home or at their boyfriend's, met them on their street and spent time with them in fast-food restaurants. To be a child-centred practitioner with young people requires patience, understanding and persistence. We have to consider interventions with young people that meet their individual needs and that they feel are useful, while also fulfilling our safeguarding responsibilities.

Jacqueline Perrins, Social Worker, The Safe Project

The current definition of child sexual exploitation was created by the UK National Working Group for Sexually Exploited Children and Young People (NWG) and is used in statutory guidance for England. This states:

> Sexual exploitation of children and young people under 18 involves exploitative situations, contexts and relationships where young people … receive 'something' (e.g. food, accommodation, drugs, alcohol, cigarettes, affection, gifts, money) as a result of them performing, and/or another or others performing on them, sexual activities. Child sexual exploitation can occur through the use of technology without the child's immediate recognition; for example, being persuaded to post sexual images on the Internet/mobile phones without immediate payment or gain.

In all cases, those exploiting the child/young person have power over them by virtue of their age, gender, intellect, physical strength and/or economic or other resources. Violence, coercion and intimidation are common, involvement in exploitative relationships being characterised in the main by the child or young person's limited availability of choice resulting from their social/economic and/or emotional vulnerability. (DCSF and Home Office, 2009: 9)

The Child Exploitation and Online Protection Centre (CEOP) has reported that young people at risk of sexual exploitation frequently go missing or run away from home, are often disengaged from school and many victims are reported to be children who are looked after. These young people are particularly vulnerable and more likely to be susceptible to the grooming methods of perpetrators, including being shown attention and affection, and being coerced and isolated from other support networks. Research undertaken by CEOP (2011) highlights that victims are unlikely to disclose exploitation voluntarily due to fear of or loyalty to perpetrators, and a negative perception of authority figures. Often young people do not recognise that they have suffered abuse at the time and disclose later in life. One young person in this study highlights the lifelong effects of such abuse: 'What most people don't realise is that it scars you for life. It still affects you years later' (CEOP, 2011: 17). Research also highlights the risks posed to children and young people due to their immersion in digital worlds.

Learning from Research

Whittle and colleagues (2014) collated the findings of research to conclude that between 13% and 33% of young people have been approached sexually online. For some of these young people online grooming leads to experiences of exploitation and abuse, in the virtual or in the real world, that are traumatising. The researchers carried out a study with eight adolescents who had experienced online grooming resulting in sexual abuse online and/or offline. They found that grooming experiences included manipulation, deception, regular/intense contact, secrecy, sexualisation, kindness and flattery, erratic temperament and nastiness.

Young people reported the following experiences:

- *'Genuine, as he seemed like the nice person everyone wants ya to go out and be with, he just seemed really nice to me.'* (Mona, 14)

- *'We were like puppets, once we were under his control, anything he said would make me, would make me do it.'* (Shelley, 13)

▶

- *'Because you know you'd done it once or twice they just expect it all the time and then if you try and say like oh I don't want to talk about that or whatever, he'd like threaten or black(mail), like I'll send your Dad all the chat logs if you don't.'* (Chloe, 12)

This research found that even where young people felt pressured or uneasy, they found themselves enmeshed in a relationship they found it very hard to escape from.

Child protection and safeguarding procedures tend to focus on the home environment, working with the child and their caregiver. However, in direct contrast, child sexual exploitation frequently involves wider social circles, including online social networks, outside of the family environment and away from professional oversight. Young people are frequently manipulated by their peers or criminal gangs, actively resisting the notion that these 'friends' are 'undermining their interests' (Jones and Florek, 2015: 78). There are particular challenges for child-centred practitioners in seeking to respect the rights and agency of young people, whilst also recognising that they may be vulnerable to the manipulation and exploitation of abusers. In the past professionals have failed to take seriously the risks posed by this form of child abuse, emphasising the rights of young people to engage in relationships of their own choice, even to embark on a career selling sex. Recognising that we are dealing with sexual exploitation and not child prostitution, and that articulate, capable young people might be victimised by skilfully manipulative offenders, is the starting point for effective intervention.

Points for Reflection

- What particular risks do you think older young people might be exposed to?
- How would you seek to engage with a young person who you know to be at risk but who is also wary of professional intervention?

Commentary

Promoting the rights of young people to self-determination does not mean failing to ensure their protection when they are being manipulated and abused by adults or those able to exert power over them. The child-centred social worker will seek to build a relationship of trust with a young person who may be a victim of sexual exploitation. They will work closely with other adults, such as parents or foster carers, learning mentors or youth workers, to ensure a strong support network is available for the young person. They will liaise with the police who will seek to target and disrupt the exploitative actions of perpetrators.

Overcoming barriers to child-centred practice with children at risk

Barriers to working in a child-centred way with children and young people at risk of abuse and neglect are multifaceted. We will examine three key areas in which social workers can be proactive in ensuring the child is at the heart of their work, namely ensuring the child is 'visible', working effectively with resistant families and using supervision as a critical and analytical tool.

The invisible child

A persistent criticism of professionals in serious case reviews is that they did not pay attention to the child or speak to the child directly (Brandon et al., 2012; Cossar et al., 2013). A poignant example is the tragic death of Daniel Pelka, a 4-year-old child of Polish origin who starved to death in 2012. His mother and partner were subsequently charged and imprisoned for murder. Despite the child being the focus of concern by various professionals, there was no record of direct interaction with Daniel regarding his experiences at home and in school or his relationships with family members. As this case shows, simply 'seeing' a child is not protection against harm. The report, completed by the Coventry Local Safeguarding Children Board, noted: 'Daniel appeared to have been "invisible" as a needy child against a backdrop of his mother's controlling behaviour. His poor language skills and isolated situation meant that there was often a lack of a child focus to interventions by professionals' (2013: 6). Domestic abuse, parental mental ill-health and substance misuse were all risk factors in this case.

Ascertaining the wishes and feelings of a child where English is a second language is additionally challenging for practitioners, and interpreting services are always required. More than this, the child not only needs to be actively listened to, but truly heard. Victoria Climbie, an 8-year-old girl originating from the Ivory Coast who died at the hands of her great-aunt and her great-aunt's partner in 2000, was not hidden from services. As the inquiry into her death observes, she was known to two housing authorities, four social work departments, two child protection police departments, a specialist centre managed by the NSPCC and two different hospitals where deliberate harm was suspected (Laming, 2003). As Lord Laming states in his inquiry report: 'The dreadful reality was that these services knew little or nothing more about Victoria at the end of the process than they did when she was first referred' (Laming, 2003: 12). There were several concerns observed by workers prior to her death, including her poor physical presentation, her behaviour and the relationship with her primary carer. Despite these indicators of possible harm, direct conversation with Victoria was 'limited to little more than "hello, how are you?"' (Laming, 2003: 67). It may be that avoiding meaningful engagement with children in cases where there are high levels of concern reduces emotional connection with the child and enables avoidance of professional anxiety (Butler, 2015). Such an approach increases the risks for the child and means they remain invisible.

Resistant families

Working with adults who are aggressive, avoidant or resistant during safeguarding enquiries and assessments can be very stressful, and social workers need to be tenacious to ensure children are not only seen alone, but their views heard (Radford, 2010). As noted in many serious case reviews, parents or caregivers who appear uncooperative, anti-social and even dangerous present many challenges for professionals. Victoria Climbie's great-aunt was described as 'forceful and manipulative' (Laming, 2003: 86). She did not allow Victoria to answer any direct questions from professionals and social workers suspected Victoria's reactions were 'coached'.

Parents and carers can be superficially compliant, elusive and dishonest at times. Social workers are faced with the challenge of identifying these parents and carers amongst the majority who are struggling, anxious and ambivalent (Haringey LCSB, 2009). Social workers may be fearful of such adults, distracted by them or deliberately diverted away from the child or young person. This presents a significant barrier to child-centred practice. Reflexivity and self-awareness are vital so that practitioners know when to seek support in order to maintain professional confidence and avoid collusion when dealing with complex and dangerous family situations.

Supervision

Supervision, as described by Lord Laming in his inquiry into the death of Victoria Climbie, is 'the cornerstone of good social work practice' (Laming, 2003: 12). Supervision should provide a focus on the needs and welfare of the child in complex family situations. Although good supervision is always important in social work, it is especially significant when:

- practitioners feel overwhelmed or lack confidence;
- practitioners experience direct threats or actual violence; or
- when child protection work evokes strong emotions (Radford, 2010).

Good supervision undoubtedly does happen; however, there has been extensive criticism due to inconsistency and the increasing dominance of managerial and performance agendas. This is often to the detriment of critical reflection, case analysis and emotional support for the worker (Morrison and Wonnacott, 2010). Supportive space needs to be prioritised in the busy workplace to enable practitioners to analyse the challenges of practice and to explore and make sense of children's experiences and communications. To see and hear the child, so that they do not remain invisible, and to manage the anxiety of working in high-risk situations, practitioners need to be offered containing, reflective spaces. This is essential to the process of providing 'the emotionally engaged interpersonal relationships children want and need' (Lefevre, 2010: 21), so that they can begin to trust professionals and share their concerns. Supervision is a two-way process. Social workers of all levels and experience need to ensure supervision is regular and prepare thoroughly, remembering that 'supervision is part of the intervention for service users' (Morrison and Wonnacott, 2010: 3). Child-centred practitioners need the support of organisations that are committed to child-centred approaches and professional supervision.

Points for Reflection

- What barriers have you experienced in seeking to carry out child-centred practice with children at risk of abuse and neglect?

- How can effective supervision support practitioners to carry out effective work with children and families?

Commentary

The child-centred practitioner will prioritise supervision and ensure they seek the support they need to explore cases that present challenges due to the demands or complex needs of service users. Critical reflection will enable social workers to recognise when certain cases raise their anxieties or evoke strong emotions, leading to avoidance of some aspects of the work or over-identification with family members. Exploration of these personal and professional responses will enable the practitioner to manage the work more effectively, to plan their intervention with increased confidence and to maintain a focus on the needs of the child.

Case study analysis

It is useful to consider our case scenario in order to apply some of our learning to a practice situation. We are continuing to focus on the case of the Smith–Jones–Khan family, who were introduced on page 143, where we provided a case history and genogram. We discussed some of the issues in the case at the end of Chapter 6 in order to explore the importance of assessment and early intervention.

Some time has passed in this case and there have been developments in the following areas:

> The family have recently moved house. The police have been called to the house due to an incident of domestic violence, reported by concerned neighbours. Mick and Fiona acknowledged that they had argued about financial problems. Mick had been drunk at the time but denied any violence. Fiona told the police Mick had hit her but she did not want to take the matter further.
>
> The police decided not to bring charges but referred the family to the Children's Social Work Service as they were aware that the children were in the house when this episode took place, and that both Hanif and Charlotte were distressed.
>
> Fiona has recently stopped taking her medication for depression as she is worried about the effects on her unborn child. She is struggling with her mental health.
>
> Jade is staying out all night on occasions and her behaviour is a cause for concern.

Children's voices

A creative approach to assessment includes hypothesising about what might be the concerns and perspectives of the children in the family. We might imagine that an initial meeting with the family provides an opportunity for each of the children to share their views:

Jade shares:

I hate this house. My Dad said we had to move to be nearer to Carol and it would be good cos I'd have my own bedroom instead of having to share with Charlotte. But it's damp and smelly and more like a cupboard. I can only just get my bed in it. And it's further away from my mates now which is a pain. But that's not so bad cos my boyfriend comes round for me in his car. It makes me feel really special when he picks me up after school and we go to his place. Sometimes we have parties with all his mates, but I prefer it when it's just us two. Hanif told me the police came round the other night cos of Dad and Fiona fighting. I just keep out of the way. I can't stand it when they are on at each other and it's all the time now.

Hanif tells you:

I like our new house cos it's got a yard at the back. Me and Charlotte have moved school, but it's okay. I've got some mates. But it's further from my Dad's which is a pain. We have to get two buses now back to his. It's getting worse at home. The other night I had to take Charlotte out to the shed round the back cos I couldn't stand the shouting. It's not fair. Charlotte cries. I sneaked back in to get our duvets and some candles and I made it nice and cosy.

Charlotte says:

I've got fairies on my new duvet. There's my old cot for when baby comes. Nana Carol comes now. She's my big fairy. I like the shed with Hanif. Nice and cosy.

Points for Reflection

- In relation to Jade or Charlotte, complete a risk and resilience matrix, adapting the table we have used for Hanif in Table 2.

Table 2 Risk and Resilience Matrix for Hanif (adapted from Daniel, et al, 2010).

Sources of Vulnerability:	Sources of Resilience:
• Experience of family breakdown and missing Nadir and paternal extended family • Primary caregivers might not fully meet Hanif's cultural and religious needs	• Close relationship with Charlotte • Attachments to his parents and grandmother • Able to problem-solve and seek safety • Able to take responsibility and provide care
Risk Factors:	**Protective Factors:**
• Being a young carer and carrying too much responsibility for Charlotte's care • Having been bullied at school • Mick's alcohol use and Fiona's depression • Experience of domestic violence	• Time with Nadir and paternal extended family • Opportunities to build a cultural and religious identity through involvement in the mosque • Carol's support for the family • Friendships and opportunities in the new school

Commentary

The risk and resilience matrix (Daniel et al., 2010, discussed in Chapter 4) is a useful tool to use in supervision. The matrix assists in focusing on the relevant issues in the case and analysing how they positively or negatively impact on the child. The tool is useful in identifying the vulnerabilities and risk factors that need to be addressed and in exploring how the protective factors might be strengthened in order to safeguard the child and promote their resilience. In a family like the one in our case study, the matrix enables us to appreciate that each child is different. We have used the matrix to consider an assessment of Hanif and his family situation (Table 2).

Analysis of practice issues

- A thorough and holistic assessment is needed that addresses the needs of each of the children and the risks posed to them; incorporating their views, wishes and feelings; building on but not duplicating the work undertaken when the early help assessment was carried out.

- Sensitive work will be needed by a consistent child-centred worker seeking to engage with Jade, to enable her to recognise the risks and exploitation inherent in some of her relationships with peers and her older 'boyfriend'. It will be important to work alongside Mick in particular in this work, as Jade's father and a consistent male role model in Jade's life.

- It is important to discuss with Mick and Fiona the current risks within the family situation and to raise their awareness of the likely impact on their children. This will include agreeing action needed to alleviate the immediate dangers, such as removing candles and matches from the reach of the children and providing a torch for Hanif instead. It is essential to challenge Mick about the evidence of domestic violence and to support Fiona to consider her options in order to be safe. It would be useful to talk with the whole family about long-term risks to the welfare of each child and identification of protective factors.

- It will be important to recognise that the problems and concerns of the parents need to be acknowledged if they are to be supported and enabled to provide the nurture and care their children need. This includes mobilising resources to address Fiona's depression and Mick's alcohol use.

- A multi-agency plan will be developed with the family. Depending on the response of Mick and Fiona and how protective factors can be strengthened in this family, this may be a 'child in need' plan. The aim will be to work cooperatively with the parents to encourage Mick to engage with interventions to address his violent behaviour and excessive drinking. It will be important that Fiona works with appropriate agencies to access support and treatment for her depression. Any additional support that could be made available to the children by Carol, Hanif's father and other family members should be assessed and harnessed. If the risk factors remain of significant concern, a child protection plan may be needed.

Conclusion

This chapter has emphasised that child-centred social work practice with children at risk is immensely complicated and demanding, usually with multiple, interrelated social issues impacting on parenting capacity. Sadly, serious case reviews have highlighted that it is easy to lose sight of the child, sometimes with tragic consequences. Complexity in case work can be overwhelming for practitioners and mask the needs of and risks to the child. The use of reflective supervision, as a two-way process, is vital to explore these challenges.

There are vulnerabilities across the life cycle, from conception through to adulthood. We have recognised groups of children who are at increased risk of abuse and neglect, namely very young children and older children, and have highlighted the developing knowledge regarding children at risk of child sexual exploitation. We have acknowledged that children may be unable or apprehensive about disclosing abuse or neglect. Therefore, a positive, trusting relationship between the child and the social worker is essential to ascertain their views. Practitioners need to work effectively and collaboratively with parents, the wider family network and multi-agency colleagues, whilst always ensuring the child's needs are paramount.

As demonstrated within the case study, the child's experiences evolve and change over time, and situations can deteriorate quickly. Practitioners need to revisit the child's wishes and feelings regularly, especially in light of a change in circumstance or crisis within the family. This is to ensure safeguarding plans are appropriate. Chapter 8 explores child-centred practice within safeguarding processes, with a focus on directly engaging children and building on strengths within family networks.

Recommended reading and resources

- Research by Cossar and colleagues (2013), entitled 'It Takes a Lot to Build Trust' Recognition and Telling: Developing Earlier Routes to Help for Children and Young People, is useful in examining children and young people's perception of abuse and neglect, and how they seek help from formal and informal networks.

- Cleaver and colleagues (2011) in *Children's Needs – Parenting Capacity: Parental Mental Illness, Learning Disability, Substance Misuse and Domestic Violence*, explore in detail complex issues which impact on parenting capacity and the safety and well-being of children.

- Gill Butler's (2015) book *Observing Children and Families* provides information about the importance of child observation and valuable guidance around setting up opportunities for observation in an ethical and evidence-based manner.

- Ofsted (2011) carried out a thematic analysis of a series of Serious Case Reviews and summarised key findings in relation to the importance of the voice of the child:
www.gov.uk/government/uploads/system/uploads/attachment_data/file/526981/The_voice_of_the_child.pdf

- The Ofsted publication (2011) *Ages of Concern: Learning Lessons from Serious Case Reviews* highlighted the vulnerabilities specifically of babies under the age of one year and young people aged over 14 years.

- Wonnacott and Watts (2014) offer a comprehensive analysis and progress report on the death of Daniel Pelka entitled *Daniel Pelka Review: Deeper Analysis and Progress Report on Implementation of Recommendations.* There is much to learn from this tragic case about the importance of a multi-agency commitment to child-centred practice.

- The Research in Practice website has an interesting video of Marion Brandon and Peter Sidebotham discussing the key findings of their most recent triennial review of Serious Case Reviews, published by the Department for Education (Sidebotham et al., 2016). There is also a link to the publication: http://seriouscasereviews.rip.org.uk/

- Each Local Authority publishes serious case reviews in their area. It is useful to access your Local Children's Safeguarding Board website and read a serious case review that has been undertaken in your area. This will give an overview of a specific case and raise lessons to be learned for local practitioners. It is valuable to consider how professionals have undertaken more effective safeguarding by paying attention to, engaging with and listening to children. The NSPCC also provides access to a wide range of serious case reviews published in England, with links also to the equivalent reports produced across Scotland, Wales and Northern Ireland:
www.nspcc.org.uk/preventing-abuse/child-protection-system/england/serious-case-reviews/

- A group of young people with experience of sexual exploitation have worked with a local voluntary organisation, Basis Yorkshire, to develop a video that provides advice to children, parents and professionals. This is a powerful resource that can be used to raise the awareness of children at risk of exploitation. The video is called *Breaking Through: Moving On from Child Sexual Exploitation* and can be accessed via YouTube:
  www.youtube.com/watch?v=AltnP55q54c

8

INVOLVING CHILDREN AND YOUNG PEOPLE IN SAFEGUARDING PROCESSES

Introduction

There are a number of safeguarding processes that can be implemented when children have been abused or are at risk of significant harm to protect them from future abuse. These include initial enquiries and child protection investigations, child protection conferences and family group conferences, and court proceedings. This chapter addresses the nature, incidence and prevalence of abuse and neglect and the impact of these experiences on children. There is a focus on what research tells us about working with children and young people in safeguarding processes and how social workers can ensure they are child-centred, despite the pressure and demands of the statutory child protection role. Finally, there is discussion regarding the engagement of children and young people in safeguarding processes, including the importance of speaking to the child alone and relationship-building with young people.

Categories of abuse and neglect

There has been an upward trend in recent years in the number of children made subject to child protection plans (Department for Education, 2015). The number of section 47 enquiries increased by 12% in 2015 compared to 2014, resulting in 71,140 initial child protection conferences taking place across the UK (Department for Education, 2015). In March 2015, 49,700 children were the subject of a child protection plan, compared with 39,100 in March 2009 (Department for Education, 2015). Despite these increases in known cases, it is estimated that for every child subject to a child protection plan, there are approximately eight other children who have suffered abuse or neglect, as maltreatment is very often hidden from view (Harker et al., 2014). Many children carry their experiences of abuse as a secret that engenders shame and confusion for many years, often into adulthood. Professionals working with children need to be alert to the signs of abuse and create the conditions that enable children to disclose about their experiences.

There are four main categories of abuse which are used as the basis of intervention and planning to safeguard children, namely physical abuse, sexual abuse, emotional abuse and neglect.

Physical abuse

Physical abuse is defined as:

> A form of abuse which may involve hitting, shaking, throwing, poisoning, burning or scalding, drowning, suffocating or otherwise causing physical harm to a child. Physical harm may also be caused when a parent or carer fabricates the symptoms of, or deliberately induces, illness in a child. (HM Government, 2015: 92)

There were 6,800 children identified as in need of protection from physical abuse in 2015 (NSPCC, 2015a). Physical abuse can be, but is rarely, a single event (NSPCC, 2014). Many children who suffer a significant injury, such as abusive head trauma, have also suffered from other episodes of physical harm. The child may have been subjected to a range of injuries varying in severity over time. Physical abuse can be fatal or have lifelong disabling consequences for the child.

Recognising physical abuse is not easy. Children who are mobile will inevitably obtain cuts and bruises as part of normal play, with accidental bruising usually occurring over bony parts of the body (NSPCC, 2009a). Alarm bells should ring when immobile children, namely young babies or those with a disability, have physical injuries which they could not have caused themselves. Any delay in presentation to medical services can also be a cause for concern. However, caution is advised, as some injuries might become more apparent over time, for example blistering developing in burns (NSPCC, 2009a). Social workers and health professionals need to take into consideration the explanation given, the child's developmental stage and the child's medical and social history.

The physical chastisement of children is not illegal in the UK, and the NSPCC and other children's rights campaigners continue to call for the law to be changed. In some cultures and families the physical chastisement of children is still regarded as normative behaviour. Therefore, identifying and responding to physical abuse becomes a complex issue in a diverse and multicultural society (Davies and Ward, 2012). Physical chastisement must be considered in relation to the physical and emotional impact on the child, in the context of their day-to-day lived experiences within their family, to assess whether significant harm has occurred. Chastisement that causes a physical injury could be deemed an assault, leading to a safeguarding investigation and a possible criminal charge. It is important for parents to understand the impact of physical chastisement on children and to be supported to use more effective and appropriate means of behaviour management.

Sexual abuse

Sexual abuse involves forcing or enticing a child or young person to take part in sexual activities, not necessarily involving a high level of violence, whether or not the child is aware of what is happening (HM Government, 2015: 93).

It is estimated that nearly a quarter of young adults have been sexually abused by an adult or a peer during their childhood. This includes children experiencing contact abuse, such as penetrative abuse and inappropriate touch, and non-contact abuse, including grooming, exploitation and coercion (Radford et al., 2011b). Disabled children can be particularly vulnerable to sexual abuse (NSPCC, 2013).

Sexual abuse is largely hidden and there are often no clear physical signs. Sometimes the only chance of uncovering abuse is by disclosure. Many victims wait years before telling anyone about their experiences. The delay in disclosing childhood sexual abuse, due to fear, shame and not expecting to be believed, is well documented (Allnock and Miller, 2013), and has implications for child protection, mental health and criminal justice. Early disclosure is needed to ensure the child, and other children, can be protected, therapeutic intervention can be offered and a criminal investigation can proceed (McElvaney and Culhane, 2015).

For victims of sexual abuse and sexual exploitation, the psychological and emotional impact can have serious and long-term repercussions (NSPCC, 2013). Depression, eating disorders, self-harm, post-traumatic stress and difficulty coping with relationships and emotions are well-documented effects. Victims can blame themselves, struggling with guilt and shame, which further impacts on disclosure. Professionals need to be attuned to the social, emotional and behavioural signs of children experiencing sexual abuse or who are vulnerable to sexual exploitation, and be willing to open up discussions of these sensitive topics to enable children to disclose.

Neglect

Neglect is the most common form of child maltreatment in the UK and is the primary reason for children being made the subject of child protection plans (NSPCC, 2015b; Brandon et al., 2014). Neglect is defined as:

The persistent failure to meet a child's basic physical and/or psychological needs, likely to result in the serious impairment of the child's health or development. Neglect may occur during pregnancy as a result of maternal substance abuse. (HM Government, 2015: 93)

Neglect means that the child's needs of physical care, love and safety are not being met, to an extent that could cause them serious or lasting harm. Neglect may occur when a parent or carer fails to provide adequate food, clothing and shelter; to protect a child from physical and emotional harm or danger; to ensure adequate supervision; or to ensure access to appropriate medical care or treatment (NSPCC, 2015b).

There is no set standard or consensus about 'acceptable care', which makes identifying and intervening in neglect cases problematic for professionals (Action for Children, 2010: 8). Although social issues such as poverty and poor housing undoubtedly impact on children and increase the likelihood of all forms of child abuse, neglect does not always happen in deprived or marginalised families. Children in more affluent families, who appear provided for materially, may be experiencing neglect, for example by being left unsupervised by caregivers or deprived of consistent care and attention.

The effects of neglect are far reaching, often cumulative and especially damaging in the early years of a child's life. For some children, neglect can be fatal (Ofsted, 2014). This is usually a result of negligence resulting in a tragic accident, such as a house fire, accidental poisoning or infant death through co-sleeping; persistent neglect can also be a feature in adolescent suicide (Davies and Ward, 2012). In Chapter 3, we recognised that the early years of childhood are the formative period for physical, social, emotional and neurological development; neglect at this time can compromise development throughout childhood. Those experiencing neglect in infancy, impacting on their attachment relationships, might later display behavioural or emotional issues that hamper positive relationship-building. The effects of neglect might be internalised and expressed as depression, lack of self-esteem or being withdrawn; or the consequences might be externalised, through aggressive, acting out or impulsive behaviour (Brandon et al, 2014).

The neglect of adolescents is a major issue which often goes unnoticed (Hicks and Stein, 2015). Long-term effects described by young people are missing school, selling their own possessions, depression, self-harm, bullying and being bullied. Neglect in childhood is also linked to mental health issues in adulthood. However, one young care-leaver expresses how neglect can lead to the development of coping mechanisms in some resilient young people: 'Depends on the person, [neglect] can make you stronger, it might not always have a negative impact. It could lead to positive achievements' (Hicks and Stein, 2015: 227).

The problems or vulnerabilities of parents or adult caregivers can often overshadow the child's needs in neglect cases. When professionals fail to consider the child's lived experience, children can become 'lost in the assessment in the same way in which they are lost within their own families' where complex adult issues dominate (Ofsted, 2014: 19). Neglect cases are often managed with the threat of court processes being invoked, with social workers aware of how difficult it can be to argue that a case has reached the legal threshold for care proceedings (Farmer and Lutman, 2014: 270). Maintaining a focus on the child and whether professional intervention is significantly improving the life of the child is crucial, for example evaluating how attendance at a parent's support group is making a difference for the child's health and development.

Emotional abuse

Emotional abuse is defined as:

> The persistent emotional maltreatment of a child such as to cause severe and persistent adverse effects on the child's emotional development. (HM Government, 2015: 92)

This can involve conveying to the child they are unloved, worthless or inadequate. Parents and carers may not give the child opportunity to share their views, by deliberately silencing or ridiculing them. Parents may have unrealistic expectations of children, or overprotect them and limit their exploration, learning and social interactions. Emotional abuse can involve the child hearing or seeing the ill-treatment of another, perhaps through domestic violence, causing the child to feel frightened and worried. Although emotional abuse can occur alone, it can be argued that emotional abuse is involved in all other forms of child maltreatment. Emotional abuse can be demonstrated passively, by a parent ignoring the child or being emotionally unavailable. It can also be active, through rejecting, exploiting, isolating or terrorising the child (Barlow and Schrader-McMillan, 2010).

Emotional abuse, much like neglect, is a chronic condition (Davies and Ward, 2012). It can occur over months or years without leading to the type of crisis which demands immediate, authoritative professional intervention. Sometimes without such a crisis, it is difficult to argue that the threshold for child protection processes, such as a child protection plan or court action, has been reached. It is the persistence, frequency and scale of these behaviours which make them abusive. Therefore, a comprehensive chronology that enables social workers to critically analyse the impact of emotional abuse on the child over time is vital. Sometimes the child's experience is difficult to pinpoint, quantify and clarify, which makes engaging with the child and understanding what life is like for them crucial to the comprehensive assessment.

Points for Reflection

- How might you respond in your professional role if you were concerned that a child might be a victim of child abuse?

Commentary
Child-centred practitioners should be aware of the effects of child abuse and the possible indicators of abuse and be alert to paying attention when they observe these in their work. It is important not to jump to conclusions, as some aspects of children's behaviour or presentation may be indicative of abuse or responses to other social factors, such as stress. However, it is important to keep an open mind to the possibility of abuse, and not

to avoid the topic as too difficult or distressing. Professionals need to be willing to open up conversations that give permission to children to share their worries and disclose about abusive experiences. It is important for social workers and childcare professionals to attend child protection training to keep up to date with developments in knowledge about signs and indicators of child abuse.

Learning from Research

In research conducted by Allnock and Miller (2013) involving 60 young adults aged 18–24 years who had experienced abuse and neglect in childhood, participants felt strongly there were missed opportunities by professionals, especially teachers and social workers, to identify abuse. Many of these young adults 'wished they had been asked directly about abuse', especially when they were struggling with symptoms of maltreatment such as depression, suicidal ideation or self-harm (2013: 15). The police and social workers were already involved in the lives of several of these young people, for reasons such as domestic violence and neglect. This was described by the young people as an 'ideal opportunity' to identify other forms of abuse, and they felt disappointed that professionals were 'only interested in the specific issue they were investigating and were uninterested in them [as people]' (2013: 51).

The research found that 80% of participants had tried to tell someone about their experience of abuse at the time it was occurring. However, they struggled to tell and to be heard, so that their disclosure was significantly delayed, on average by a staggering 7.8 years. The younger the child was when the abuse started, the longer it took to disclose. Below are some of the views of the young men and women in relation to disclosing abuse:

> *'I don't know when I first told people, but like, in the years before I left, I increasingly … it was increasingly obvious that I was really acutely miserable. And, kind of, was … seeking attention and somebody to try and sort it out.'* (Female, abused physically and emotionally by her mother up to the age of 16)

> *'The first time I told, I told my teacher, and then a social worker came and two police officers, and umm, they wanted me to talk about it, what happened. But they invited my mum and dad and sat them in the room with me. And then they asked me what happened, and so I denied it and said no, nothing's happening, 'cause I could just see my dad in the corner and I just thought, oh my god.'* (Female, sexually abused by father who facilitated abuse by other men, from age 7 to 14)

> *'I didn't understand what was wrong and I never went and asked for help, but no one ever asked me if I needed help and I think, looking back it was, like, I don't know, kind of the indicators you get if someone's being abused were there.'* (Female, sexually abused by older cousin, from age 8 to 12)

'I didn't want to cause anyone any distress, and I certainly didn't want to be err, found out. I suppose. And so, that's why I only told them a very small part of the story to start with. And that, the reaction to that was bad enough, so I umm, I would never have considered police involvement.' (Male, sexually abused by babysitter, from age 9 to 11)

Child-centred practice is about making sure that children are listened to when they may be trying to tell us about their experiences of abuse through their behaviour or disclosures.

(Allnock and Miller, 2013)

Intervention in child abuse cases

As we are aware from previous chapters, legislation and guidance over the last 25 years have provided the statutory rights for children to participate in decision-making and service development, with the duty placed upon Local Authorities to ascertain the wishes and feelings of children and young people and to fully consider their views (Dillon et al., 2016). Children who become subject to safeguarding processes are 'amongst the most vulnerable in society' (Atkinson in Cossar et al., 2011: 4), dealing not only with the impact of abuse which has led to the safeguarding intervention, but also with the stress and upheaval of the intervention itself. These vulnerable children have uncertain and unpredictable lives (Bijleveld et al., 2015). This places a further responsibility upon professionals to seek to ensure that our interventions have a positive impact. As Munro succinctly states: 'For children and young people who have been maltreated by their parents or carers, it is especially important that the professionals trying to help them do not add to the feelings of being powerless and vulnerable' (Munro 2010: 18).

Points for Reflection

- How do you feel about child abuse and your professional responsibility to safeguard children?
- How should social workers intervene in cases of child abuse in order to effectively safeguard the rights and welfare of children?

Commentary

The weight of responsibility to safeguard children from abuse can feel daunting. It is important to recognise that social workers do not carry this responsibility alone – it is the responsibility of everyone to safeguard children and young people from abuse. We work most effectively to protect children when we listen to children and promote their rights, work in partnership with parents and carers and collaborate with our multi-agency colleagues. Child-centred practitioners work hard to engage and involve children every step of the way, as they fulfil their statutory duties to assess the risks, identify protective factors and develop a safeguarding plan.

Initial response

The reality of the initial referral process in child protection work is highly pressurised and often hurried (Woolfston et al., 2010). A decision must be made within one working day of the referral being received about the nature of the response that is required. For children in need of protection, action should be taken as soon as possible after the referral, with the maximum time frame for completing an assessment being 45 working days (HM Government, 2015). The participation and involvement of children in child protection processes is not only regarded as a fundamental right, but is also good practice. However, it is concerning that research continues to highlight 'low levels of meaningful involvement' (Dillon et al., 2016: 70).

Children and young people have expressed their unhappiness about inconsistent relationships with social workers during the referral process, such as seeing their allocated social worker irregularly, for short periods of time, or encountering a number of different social workers (Jobe and Gorin, 2013). They often have inadequate information in the initial stages about the child protection process, leading to fear and anxiety, especially about the possibility of being separated from their family (Woolfston et al., 2010). For many children, family members are the main source of information and at times this is inaccurate or misleading. Cossar and colleagues (2014: 107) noted that the children in their study: 'seemed to be trying to piece together bits of information and struggled to fill in the gaps.' Confusion and misunderstandings heightened their distress. In research by Woolfston and colleagues (2010), the first few hours after the child protection process commenced proved most challenging psychologically for children and young people. Children knew least about what was happening at this stage, and information given could be confusing or even forgotten with emotions running high. Sadly, in some cases highlighted by the research, initial plans were not implemented and promised actions not realised, creating feelings of isolation and distrust. One young person who involved child protection services through her own disclosure stated that she regretted doing so, and the 'lack of action made her feel abandoned' (Woolfston et al., 2010: 2081). Child-centred practitioners should ensure that information is given fully and clearly during their initial interaction with a child or young person, and repeated on subsequent visits, with a child-friendly leaflet also proving helpful. Social workers should take care not to make promises they cannot keep, but should be honest and reliable in their communications with children during this anxiety-provoking period.

Child protection conferences

Practitioner Testimonial

As a child protection Chair, child-centred practice means making safe plans that elicit the child's wishes and feelings – about their situation now as well as plans and hopes for the future. My role is to review the plans and progress that the multi-agency team around the family are managing, ensuring that they are achievable, timely and responsive to the individual needs of the children. I expect that practitioners will provide children with honest and accurate information about their situation and that future actions and interventions to support them and their family network are shared and explained.

As Missing Children Co-ordinator, part of my work is with the 'return interview' service. This is an independent service aimed to provide children and young people who go missing and their families and carers with high-quality responses, support and guidance. The basis of this is to ensure that children and young people understand the risks associated with going missing, they are provided with an opportunity to share their experiences, and plans are implemented to support and prevent future missing episodes. The information should be utilised to inform best practice so that children's voices inform knowledge, understanding and future service delivery.

Claire Ford, Safeguarding Conference Chair and Missing Children Co-ordinator.

Child protection conferences were introduced in the UK in the 1970s, following the death of Maria Colwell, as a way for professionals to share information to identify abuse and protect children. Case conferences are inter-agency meetings convened to consider the safety and well-being of a child who has been the subject of a child protection investigation and is deemed 'at risk of significant harm' under section 47 of the Children Act 1989. Professionals consider what action is required to safeguard and promote the child's welfare and if a child protection plan should be formulated (Appleton et al., 2015). Professionals working with the family form a core group to implement the plan, which is reviewed regularly.

Since the introduction of the Children Act 1989, child protection conferences have striven to achieve partnership between professionals and families, with parents routinely in attendance. In recent years, increasingly children and young people are invited to attend case conferences, and may be accompanied or represented by an advocacy worker (Jelicic et al, 2013). However, there are several criticisms of traditional child protection conferences. Professionals can focus on the impact of issues, such as how substance misuse affects the parents and their parenting, rather than analysing the effects on the individual child. Discussion, decision-making and planning are often driven by professionals. Children and parents have both expressed they find such meetings daunting and intimidating (Ghaffar et al., 2012; Appleton et al., 2015). Child protection conferences also tend to be problem-based rather than solution-focused, and there remains concern regarding poor engagement with fathers in the process (Goff, 2012). It is therefore no surprise that children rarely attend child protection conferences or core group meetings (Horwath and Tarr, 2015). It can be argued that where processes are not managed in a sensitive and child-centred way, 'there is a danger that attendance at child protection meetings might be harmful', contributing to the child's experience of powerlessness (Cossar et al., 2011: 13).

Learning from Research

In a study undertaken in Norway, Vis and Thomas (2009) found that a major factor affecting whether children were able to actively participate in decisions about their future during child protection processes was their attendance at meetings. Those young people who attended important multi-agency meetings were three times more likely to influence the outcomes than those who had just been consulted. The researchers conclude that resources should be channelled towards enabling the effective involvement of children in important meetings, such as case conferences.

In a study conducted with young people involved in child protection processes in Scotland, participants wanted the opportunity to attend or be represented at child protection conferences. There were a number of children in the study who were unaware they were even subject to child protection plans. Children made the suggestion of having fewer professionals present at a conference to make them feel more comfortable about attending (Woolfston et al., 2010).

In research by Cossar and colleagues (2014), 18 children were aware of formal reports about them; however, only six of these children stated they had seen all or part of these written documents. Dominic, aged 12, shared his frustration:

'They just put it in the report and they don't even tell our family what they're going to write, so that's what I don't like about the social.'

Ten children had attended a child protection conference or core group meeting, but they 'rarely felt able to ask questions' and some children and young people felt they were not supported or prepared well. The following views were documented:

'I did go once but it was awful … they were just all talking and I didn't understand what they were saying. It was about me. I didn't really enjoy it that much.'

'Every time I went to speak, someone interrupted me and that really annoyed me so I was like right I'm going, I've got to get to school.' (Heather,15 years)

(Cossar, et al., 2014: 103–112)

In an attempt to overcome the barriers to participation for children and families in the child protection process, the 'strengthening families' model recognises the positives in the family situation, as well as examining the concerns about the welfare of the child, and takes seriously the value of the contribution of the family to child protection conferences (Appleton et al, 2015). This model builds upon the 'signs of safety' approach developed by Turnell and Edwards (1997, 1999), which seeks to work in partnership with families to acknowledge both the risks and the protective factors that exist in the present situation, and to collaborate in order to set goals for change and enhanced safety. The model is based on the theoretical framework offered by solution-focused therapy. Based on principles of empowerment, power is shifted from the professionals to families, and more mutual communication takes place (Appleton et al., 2013). Employing the 'strengthening families' approach, case conferences are organised in a more flexible and informal manner. The Chair of the conference meets with family members to ensure they understand the process and supports them in making their contribution during the meeting. Children and young people are seen as participants, rather than victims, and are supported by an advocate so that they are able to decide whether to attend and how to present their views.

These important developments are crucial to the promotion of child-centred practice in child protection processes. Nigel Parton has emphasised: 'If we are serious about wanting to ensure that children feel safe, it seems that it is not simply that the voices of children and young people have to be heard, but that they have to be given more control about what happens to them once they have raised their voice' (2006: 186). Enabling the genuine participation of children in the meetings where the big decisions are made during child protection processes is central to promoting children's rights and enabling them to take back some control over their lives at the very time they might be seen as most vulnerable.

Family group conferences

Families are complicated. The majority of cases dealt with by children's social workers are based on a network of often unconventional and complex relationships 'built up as a result of divorces, separations, remarriages, new partners and their families entering the family's networks' (Saltiel, 2013: 15). A lack of vocabulary for complex relationships can often lead to reluctance by professionals to accept and understand what they mean for the safety and well-being of the child (Saltiel, 2013). The extended family network, irrespective of what form this takes, can be invaluable in offering protection to a child at risk of significant harm. Originating from New Zealand in the 1980s, a family group conference is a strengths-based, task-centred process of planning and decision-making for a child at risk, led by the child's family, alongside significant family friends or neighbours.

A family group conference is completely voluntary and families cannot be forced to have one (Family Rights Group, 2016). This model consists of four separate yet interconnected stages: preparation, information giving, private family time and planning (Frost et al., 2014a). The family group conference enables and encourages families to find their own solutions to problems. The family are the primary planning group, rather than professionals, with an independent co-ordinator meeting with all family members separately, prior to the conference taking place. The role of the social worker is to provide accurate, jargon-free, accessible information for the family to digest (Frost et al., 2014a). Other professionals are not involved in the meeting and the family develop the plan to address the concerns and ensure the safety and welfare of the child.

Children and young people are directly involved in their family group conference, often with the support of an advocate. Research with children and young people suggests they are more actively involved in decision-making and more likely to be given a voice in family group conferences than in child protection conferences. Some children feel much more in control amongst their family and are able to contribute more freely or even chair the meeting. However, care and attention is needed to ensure children are not adversely affected, especially if the conference becomes a forum for family disagreements or for airing disapproval about the child's behaviour (Frost et al., 2014a). Some studies have emphasised that attendance does not equate to participation, and being listened to is not the same as being influential (Morris and Connelly, 2010). Professional skill is required to fully engage and empower children.

Family group conferences provide a bridge between the formal, professional safeguarding system and the family system. The research evidence indicates that family group conferences are no less effective in producing plans to safeguard children than traditional child protection conferences. Furthermore, family group conferences are often experienced as more positive processes for participants, being family-centred, strengths-based and actively promoting partnership working (Frost et al., 2014b). However, it can be difficult to balance the participatory discourse of family group conferencing with the bureaucratic and procedural discourse of child protection, where social workers are increasingly under public scrutiny and may inadvertently influence agendas (Ney et al., 2011). If child protection processes and procedures dominate, then voice and participation is denied; ultimately, 'a child-centred practice is lost' (Ney et al., 2011: 186). Nevertheless, the evidence suggests that family group conferences provide opportunities for effective participation and safeguarding for children and can enhance child-centred practice in child protection processes. This model of practice is also valuable at earlier stages of professional intervention, such as planning for children in need or in youth justice cases.

Care proceedings

Local Authorities initiate care proceedings when it is considered that there are such serious concerns for a child's safety and well-being that a court order is required to safeguard the child. Care proceedings are not disputes between parents and Local Authorities regarding the care of a child, 'rather they are a court-supervised, multi-party enquiry into the child's current circumstances and future care needs' (Pearce et al., 2011: 4). During care proceedings, a child is entitled to independent legal representation. A children's guardian is appointed and they report directly to the court in respect of the child's wishes and feelings. The children's guardian makes recommendations regarding the child's best interests (Berricka et al., 2015), and has a unique role to ensure child-centred practice within the court arena. The role of the court is to make decisions regarding whether the threshold test is met in relation to the legal definition of significant harm and what care or supervision orders, if any, are required in the best interests of the child (Pearce et al., 2011).

Children and their families have historically endured excessive delays, and have struggled to understand court proceedings (Family Justice Review, 2011a). Children and parents can feel bewildered by legal processes and feel their views are not sufficiently taken into consideration. Decisions made in court can have a dramatic effect on a child's life, and children want to be heard and involved.

Learning from Research

When children and young people have been asked for suggestions on how their voice could be heard in court, they have stated: speaking directly to the Judge either inside or outside court; writing to the judge; appearing in court by telephone or video link; or having their views expressed through a third party (Family Justice Review, 2011a). Young people have expressed the following views about the need to be heard:

'The judge should just make sure that he/she hears every party that will be affected by his/her decision. For example, I remember having few, if any, of my views making it into the files. Also I was never extended an invitation to court. So every avenue that can ascertain the views of the young person should be explored.'

'I found "the judge" was mentioned and how he was going to make the decision of who I lived with. And not being boastful, but this court was about me. So why couldn't I see him?'

(Family Justice Review, 2011a: 47)

The Family Justice Review (2011b) emphasises the importance of social workers understanding what the court expects in relation to the information they need to present. This includes high-quality assessments 'that set out a clear narrative of the child's story' (2011b: 13). There are likely to be different and conflicting views about the best interests of the child, and information for the court needs to present a balanced account of the varying perspectives. Recognising and clearly including the voice of the child, social workers and other professionals with responsibility for safeguarding the child will increase the accuracy of their assessment and the validity of their recommendations. This will result in a more timely and successful outcome for the child (Macdonald et al., 2008).

The Public Law Outline (2010, revised 2013) requires the court to consider what work has been undertaken with the child's family prior to the issue of care proceedings, except in emergency situations, and encourages parties to use alternative dispute resolution options, which can include family group conferences. Social workers need to ensure they consider how the wider family can be involved in ensuring the safety and welfare of the child, including providing possible alternative placements for children or shared care arrangements, to avoid unnecessary legal proceedings (Family Rights Group, 2011). Compulsory intervention into family life through care proceedings should only be considered if it is the necessary means to ensure that the safety and welfare of the child is protected.

Engaging children in safeguarding processes

Social workers have the challenge of balancing a commitment to child-centred practice with a number of constraints, including managing an evolving caseload, meeting organisational targets and fulfilling statutory duties within official timescales. It can be extremely difficult to create space for the 'creative planning, relationship building, reflection and emotional processing' which is required to respond empathetically and authoritatively to a child who may have experienced trauma (Lefevre, 2015: 205). To build rapport and gather meaningful information from a child, or from each of the unique individuals that make up a sibling group, is demanding during any child protection process (Horwath and Tarr, 2015). However, there are steps social workers can take to ensure they make the most of the, sometimes limited, time they spend with children.

Prioritise and plan

Lord Laming, in his inquiry into the death of Victoria Climbie, recommended that no home visit should be undertaken without a clear purpose and clarity about the kind of information to be gathered (Laming, 2003). Even during section 47 enquiries, which require an immediate response, social workers must consider the information received and what response is required. This includes some pre-liminary consideration of how to engage with the child. Checking the social work system for any previous intervention and speaking to a professional who knows the child well, such as a teacher or health visitor, are practical and useful steps to complete before any initial visit. Information regarding the child's personality, developmental stage, likes and dislikes can be helpful in preparing to speak to the child alone. There will be situations where the child has not been known previ-ously to social work services, and a professional who knows the child is not avail-able prior to the visit. Social workers can consider the information on the referral such as age and gender of the child, and if they have a disability or any special needs. Discussion with a manager or colleague prior to the visit can clarify and focus the social worker's mind on what information needs to be obtained, and how tools and resources may be used to engage with the child and family.

Focus on Practice

A day in the life of a child

Child protection investigations involve interviewing children and seeking information through a range of methods. As discussed in Chapter 5, social workers should consider what methods may appeal to the child, such as discussion, use of toys and games, or art and craft activities. The following questions indicate the type of detailed information social workers may require in order to understand what life is like for a child or young person:

Question	Factors to Consider
What are mornings like in your family?	Is the child expected to get themself up? Does the child take responsibility for parents/siblings? Is there a regular routine?
Do you have anything to eat?	Is there usually food in the house? Who takes responsibility for preparing breakfast? Is the child given money to buy food?
What happens about getting dressed?	Are clothes clean, in a good state of repair and avail-able? What happens about washing? Does the child wash and brush their teeth?
What happens on a school day?	How does the child get to school? Is the child respon-sible for other children? What are the child's relation-ships like with other children, teachers and staff?
What happens on a weekend/holiday?	Does the child look after other children? How do they spend their time? Are they left unsupervised or allowed to undertake inappropriate activities?
What happens after school?	Are they collected from school? Is anyone home when they return? Is food available for the child?

| What happens in the evening? | What does the child eat in the evening? Where does the child spend their time? Is the child left alone? |
| What happens at bedtime? | Does the child have a bedtime? Where does the child sleep? Do they wash and brush their teeth? Is the child ever left alone or expected to care for other children? |

Based on Horwath (2007: 178)

Speaking to the child alone

As we have noted, it is important that the child, of sufficient age and under-standing, should be seen on their own by their social worker to ensure they have opportunity to share their concerns, wishes and feelings during child protection processes. However, in research conducted by Ferguson (2014), children were only seen alone by social workers during 15 of the 71 visits undertaken as part of child protection investigations. The study found that children were usually seen for between 5 and 16 minutes and the child's bedroom was the most popular room in which to speak to the child alone. Social workers felt that the availability of toys and photographs could be used as aids in communication, with the bedroom seen as 'essential to experiencing the child's inner world' (Ferguson, 2014: 4). Some workers avoided interviews in the child's bedroom and preferred to arrange meetings outside the home. Only seeing children with their parents is unhelpful, as the latter may dominate conversations and the child's experience may be either ignored or not fully explored. If a child is very young, observation of the parent and child together is vital to assess family interactions and relationships (as discussed in Chapter 7).

Points for Reflection

● If you received a referral that required an investigation of child abuse how would you prepare to talk to the child/children alone?

Commentary
It is important to think about the age and stage of development of the child and how to enable the child to feel at ease during a first meeting. If possible, the social worker should gain information from the person making the referral about the child, their abili-ties, interests and personality. This will help the social worker to consider how to build

rapport. The nature of the concerns shared in the referral will also prompt consideration of whether to meet with the child in their home or to organise a quiet room elsewhere. It can be problematic for children to be open about their experiences with parents in close proximity, and if abuse has occurred in the home, this may create further anxiety for the child. This is a particular issue for children who have been sexually abused and talking in their bedroom would not be appropriate.

There is value in seeking to locate a quiet space in a venue familiar to the child, such as their school, where you can be introduced to them by a trusted adult, such as their teacher or learning mentor. Taking along a bag of resources, such as paper and crayons, books and toy figures, can enable rapport-building and child-friendly communication. However, social workers need to be prepared to think on their feet. When making visits to the home, many factors may interfere with the best-laid plans, such as the presence of blaring televisions, visiting neighbours, distracting mobile phones and potentially dangerous dogs. Being confident to assert the importance of a quiet, private space for a conversation with parents and with children is an essential skill.

Using visual aids, activities and direct work tools can be helpful to ascertain and clarify information. Focusing on an activity can enable the child to express themselves more openly than being asked direct questions. There is important learning to be drawn from the serious case review of a 15-year-old young person known as Child P, who had experienced sexual abuse by her stepfather over a period of ten years, before finally being able to make a disclosure. A psychologist meeting with Child P asked her to write down her wishes and feelings. Child P provided a page and a half of information which triggered a section 47 enquiry into her sexual abuse. Sadly, this child had experienced years of professional involvement, including from social work services, prior to these disclosures. This was for several reasons, including her mother's alcohol misuse, her stepfather's criminal history, including sexual offences, her poor school attendance and self-harm. However, a simple technique used by this professional allowed Child P to express herself in a way which direct conversation or assessment interviews had not (Norfolk Safeguarding Children's Board, 2015). In Chapter 5, we noted that children often speak more openly on car journeys, for example to and from contact sessions, or during walks in the park, where the atmosphere is informal and relaxed. Social workers need to be mindful that any disclosures made by a child need to be written down, using the child's words, as soon as practicable after the event, as contemporaneous notes can be requested by the police during criminal investigation or by the court during care proceedings.

Focus on Practice

The 'Three Houses' tool is a creative approach used to interview children. It was created in New Zealand (Weld, 2008) and further developed by Turnell and colleagues (2009). It is highlighted as good practice by Eileen Munro (2011) in her review of child protection. The tool focuses on interviewing children using their own words and drawings in three areas, namely 'the house of worries', 'the house of good things' and 'the house of dreams' (Figure 11).

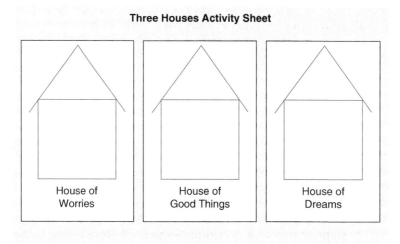

Three Houses Activity Sheet

House of
Worries

House of
Good Things

House of
Dreams

Figure 11 The 'Three Houses' tool (Munro, 2011: 30)

This technique helps the child to think about risks and strengths in their lives, and their hopes and dreams. It can be used individually or with sibling groups. Social workers, with the permission of the child, can use the finished work to explore with parents or carers the child's views. This can be a powerful and illuminating experience for parents.

Using three separate pieces of paper, the child is asked to draw their houses. Inside each house the child is asked to write or draw pictures to show what their values, beliefs, thoughts and feelings are about worries, the good things in their lives, and what their hopes and dreams for the future are. This provides the foundation for discussion, and social workers can identify risks and protective factors in the child's family and circumstances. Be cautious, however, of interpreting pictures or taking them too literally. Drawing is a way for children to share their experiences and also, at times, to express emotions or explore and process events in their life.

The importance of relationship in child protection practice

Partnership practice in statutory social work is extremely difficult to achieve and the ability to work collaboratively with parents 'appears to rely heavily on the relationship skills of the worker involved' (Platt, 2008: 301). In Chapter 1, we noted the importance of relationship-based practice as a basis for effective, child-centred assessment and intervention. Even in the context of conflictual, statutory processes, it is important for social workers to work towards developing mutual understandings and building shared problem-solving strategies (Smith, 2010). A trusting relationship between the individual social worker and the child is also crucial for active participation and effective safeguarding practice (Dillon et al., 2016; Cossar et al., 2014). Frost and colleagues (2014a: 487) remind us: 'social work is not an area where you can apply techniques and get the desired outcomes; outcomes are affected by relationships and experiences, which are in turn affected by the worker's attitude and skills.'

Children need to be treated with respect and seen as experts in their own lives. Every child, irrespective of age, has a story to tell. We need to remember that 'how this story is understood is not dependent on the age of the teller, but rather on the sensitivity of the listener' (CAFCASS, 2008). Reflecting on your own interactions with a child, or having a colleague observe and offer constructive feedback, can be a useful way of developing child-centred interpersonal skills.

Learning from Research

Research conducted by the Office of the Children's Commissioner (2010) with young people and their families who had been involved in safeguarding processes found that 'the personal attributes of social workers were more important than the agency or work role' (2010: 49). The majority of children and families consulted sadly reported feeling judged and blamed by social workers; they found practitioners to be unreliable; and changes in social work personnel meant service users had to constantly repeat their stories. The following comments are by young people expressing how the behaviour and attitude of individual social workers have a direct impact on their engagement:

'You would say to them about something that's happening or how you feel and they would always seem in a rush to get away or feel like you have to hurry the conversation.'

'How does she think her [the social worker's] constant lateness makes me feel? Worthless? Unimportant? Yes. If I am late – well, that's different. They do not understand then.'

'It works best for me when someone respects you, encourages you and has faith in you. My social worker did and it really helped.'

Cossar and colleagues (2014) completed qualitative research with 26 children and young people aged between 6 and 17 years. All participants were subject to child protection plans at the time. Children found minimal contact with their social worker unhelpful, and seven children reported not being seen alone at all by their social worker. Another participant felt interrogated and treated like 'a source of evidence'. The following children highlighted the importance of a trusting and honest relationship with their social worker:

'Because if you're not honest with her she can't really help you and like it'll make things harder, if you lie about something it will make things harder, because she does try and help you with it and if it's not the truth and that, it's not going to make things any easier, and she won't trust you either, because you've got to trust her and she's got to trust you. Otherwise there's no point.' (Louise, 15 years)

'It's annoying because like, if I'm having a good day then it's just like, because I know it's going to be the same old questions, is your dad still taking the stuff, and has he ever hit you, it's just like shut up.' (Amy, 13 years)

'The social worker that decides everything ... she doesn't really work with me much.'

(Cossar, et al., 2014: 103–112)

The research reinforces the importance of social workers having the skills and commitment to listen to children and to build supportive relationships, even, or especially, when carrying out pressurised and demanding child protection work. At times of enormous stress for young people, they want to engage with social workers who will listen to them and offer them reliable support. Relationships of trust enable children to share information about their lives and negotiate the complex systems and processes that are unleashed in response to child protection concerns.

Case study analysis

Consideration of our case study will enable us to explore child protection practice and apply some of our learning from research to practice. We will continue to focus on the case of the Smith–Jones–Khan family, who were introduced on page 143. In Chapter 7, there were increasing concerns about the case, due to domestic violence and other issues impacting on parenting capacity, including Mick's alcohol use and Fiona's mental ill-health. At this point, there has been a major incident that has precipitated a section 47 investigation and the need to convene an initial child protection conference (ICPC):

There have been ongoing concerns about domestic violence and the police have been called to the family home on several occasions. The most recent incident this week resulted in Fiona being admitted to hospital and experiencing a miscarriage. Hanif was also caught up in the violence when he tried to protect his mother, and has severe bruising to his shoulders and chest, consistent with being shaken and pushed. Mick is the subject of a police investigation and has been asked to live apart from the family home. Carol (maternal grandmother) has moved in to take care of the children. The police have also been involved over recent weeks when Jade was reported by the family as 'missing' – they brought Jade home in an inebriated state on two occasions in the early hours of the morning.

Children's voices

Although this is a fictional case, it is helpful to engage our curiosity and imagination in order to reflect upon what might be the views and concerns of the children at this time of extreme stress and upheaval. They are likely to have many worries about their family and what professional intervention might mean for them.

Hanif's feelings and concerns:

I'm still feeling a bit sore, but I'm glad. Someone had to stop it. I've told my Dad I'm sick of Mick and I want to go live at his. But then what will happen to Charlotte and Mum?

Charlotte's views:

Want my Mum. Want Daddy home. Hanif's a bit sore.

Jade's perspective:

Well it's all kicked off now. Carol won't tell me where Dad is, even though it's none of her business. Fiona never did learn to just keep out of his way when he was that way out. I am gutted about the baby though. I fancied having another little sister. I can't wait to be out of here. I might ask them to put me in Care. They say you can do what you want in Resi. Or I'll go stay at my boyfriend's. My social worker says that's not safe, but it's better than here. There's going to be this meeting conference thing. I'll tell them it needs sorting.

Points for Reflection

- Consider a way of explaining to each of the children what might happen next. Think about what each child needs to know and the kinds of questions they may have about their family situation and the child protection process.

- How would you work with Carol to enable her to provide support and reassurance to the children?

- If Hanif and Jade wish to attend the ICPC, what will you tell them about the meeting and how will you ensure they are prepared and supported to be able to participate?

Analysis of practice issues

● It is hoped that the social worker may have already got to know the children a little, through previous involvement due to Charlotte's disability, the concerns about Hanif, as a young carer, and also Jade, as a possible victim of sexual exploitation. Such previous contact will enable the worker to provide reassurance at this time of crisis. The social worker should seek to strengthen the team around the children, by ensuring other key professionals who know the family well (such as school staff members) are involved in providing ongoing support and contributing to safeguarding plans.

● It will be important to offer support to Carol, so that she can provide the stability that the children need during this time of upheaval. Carol may need guidance about what to tell Charlotte and how to offer her reassurance about the family situation. After she has had some time to recuperate, Fiona also will need advice and support to consider her options and to think about her children's needs and best interests. It will be important to work with empathy and compassion, mindful of her loss due to the miscarriage, her mental health problems and the possible breakdown of her relationship with Mick. It will be important also to engage with Mick, liaising closely with the police who may be conducting their own criminal investigations. It is likely that he will be asked to remain living apart from the family home, but enabling continued contact with his children, Jade and Charlotte, may be important in the long term.

● Engaging with other family members will be crucial at this stage. The social worker will have met with Nadir previously, when the earlier assessment of need was completed, as non-resident fathers are integral to this process. This will make meeting with Nadir now to discuss Hanif's abusive experience and plans for his future much more straightforward. It would be useful to convene a meeting with Hanif, Fiona and Nadir together, to talk about Hanif's welfare, family rights and the options for the future, including arrangements for Hanif's residence and family contact. The parents may wish to consult with solicitors or may be able to reach an amicable agreement.

● A family group conference to talk about short-term and long-term plans to ensure the welfare and safety of all the children could provide a useful way forward. This may provide a useful forum to mobilise support for the children from members of Hanif's paternal extended family and from Jade's maternal extended family.

● The social worker will need to talk with Hanif and Jade about the ensuing meetings and conferences, and to share the reports and recommendations that will be presented. Leaflets designed for children and young people that explain the process should be provided. Advocacy services should be consulted, to enable the children to seek separate, independent advice and support and to prepare for their contribution to or participation in the ICPC. Jade and Hanif may have different views about whether to attend meetings and about how to express their views. It is important that Hanif does not carry an inappropriate sense of responsibility for Charlotte and his mother. Play sessions with Charlotte, possibly alongside Carol or Fiona, may be helpful to explore changes in the family and Charlotte's wishes and feelings. It will be important to ensure that the views, wishes and feelings of all the children are presented at the ICPC.

● Sensitive long-term work is needed to build a relationship of trust with Jade to enable her to recognise the risks and exploitation inherent in her current relationships. It will be important to work with her to consider strategies for keeping safe. Working to identify and retain links with supportive adults in her family and to strengthen protective factors in her life, such as attendance at school, will be crucial in this time of change and upheaval.

Conclusion

Research indicates that many children have abusive experiences but only a small percentage of these come to the attention of social workers. It is crucial that all professionals working with children and young people demonstrate a child-centred attitude and willingness to hear when children disclose or seek help. All forms of abuse and neglect have far-reaching consequences for children and young people, impacting through childhood and into adulthood. Implementation of safeguarding processes can further impact on the child's emotional well-being. Children and young people tell us they want to be informed, they want to be involved and they want to participate in safeguarding processes.

The organisational culture underpinning child protection practice is based upon adult-centric, administrative and risk-averse priorities. Discourses of child rescue tend to take precedence over children's rights. It is perhaps, then, not surprising that children continue to struggle to have their voices heard. Nevertheless, children and young people consistently express a desire to be present or at least represented at formal meetings, and want to understand when, how and why decisions are made. It is the role of the social worker to ensure the child is central to all safeguarding processes, and that their day-to-day lived experiences and perspectives are fully explored and represented. With preparation and good supervision, social workers can focus and plan their interaction with the child, demonstrate empathy and build rapport. Interpersonal and listening skills are fundamental to child-centred practice, and creative tools can be used to encourage children to express their wishes and feelings and to actively participate in safeguarding processes.

Recommended reading and resources

- The NSPCC website includes a wealth of information about the different forms of abuse, how professionals should be alert to signs of abuse and the impact of abuse on children and young people. The following link provides a good place to start:
  www.nspcc.org.uk/preventing-abuse/child-abuse-and-neglect

- The NSPCC annual report entitled *How Safe Are Our Children?* provides a comprehensive overview of child protection in the four nations of the UK, collating and analysing child protection data. It enables identification of themes and exploration of progress in the changing landscape of safeguarding practice. The most recent report is available at:
  www.nspcc.org.uk/services-and-resources/research-and-resources/2016/how-safe-are-our-children-2016/

- Brandon and colleagues (2014), in *Missed Opportunities: Indicators of Neglect – What Is Ignored, Why, and What Can Be Done?*, provide a comprehensive overview of research in relation to neglect and the impact on children. It explores the barriers to intervention and how these can be overcome.

- The Children's Commissioner report *Don't Make Assumptions: Children's Views of the Child Protection System and Messages for Change* by Cossar and colleagues (2011) provides excellent insights, from the perspective of children, about child protection conferences and processes. Children and young people offer messages for social workers in relation to good practice.

- In their publication *No One Noticed, No One Heard*, Allnock and Miller (2013) explore the childhood experiences of 60 young men and women who experienced childhood abuse, as well as how they disclosed abuse and sought help. The study offers powerful insights to support better identification of abuse, reduce the barriers to disclosure and improve the experience of children at the point of initial investigation.

9

PROMOTING POSITIVE OUTCOMES FOR CHILDREN AND YOUNG PEOPLE WHO ARE LOOKED AFTER

Introduction

There have been ongoing debates amongst policy-makers, service providers and practitioners, and within the family justice system, regarding the best way to achieve permanence and stability for children who come into care from high-risk backgrounds (Schofield et al., 2011). There are a range of options available including reunification, kinship care, adoption and special guardianship; however, there will continue to be children whose needs are best served through positive, planned, stable and secure foster placements or residential care.

Children and young people who have been raised in the care system are accustomed to professional jargon and bureaucratic shorthand; however, there is no doubt that many feel confused and frustrated by the use of the acronym LAC – denoting looked-after children, but holding connotations of 'deficit' and 'deficiency'. Children and young people consistently highlight that being treated with respect is a key component of a positive care experience (Coram Voice, 2015). The language used with service users is powerful. In this chapter, the phrase 'children and young people who are looked after' will be used to refer to this population. After all, they are children and young people first, above any other attribute.

This chapter explores child-centred practice for children who are placed in the care of the Local Authority. We discuss the challenges for children who are looked after and for those providing care and support, particularly in relation to ensuring stability and planning for permanence. We recognise the importance of relationships that enable children who have experienced loss, trauma and upheaval to retain connections to the past, to thrive in the present and to achieve positive outcomes. The importance of care planning that enables the participation and enhances the resilience of the child is also discussed.

Children and young people who are looked after

The umbrella term 'looked after' encompasses a wide range of children and young people and a diversity of issues. It can include children severely disabled from birth, those whose parents have acute medical problems and children and young people who have suffered abuse or neglect, with placements ranging from foster care to residential care and young offender institutions. Children and young people may also be placed with birth parents under a care order, or family members and friends in kinship arrangements.

In England and Wales, the term refers to children and young people looked after by the State where the Children Act 1989 applies, including those subject to care orders or temporarily looked after through voluntary arrangements with parents and, in some cases, children having short breaks to provide respite for parents (NICE, 2010). The Local Authority is the child's 'corporate parent', which is a concept founded on the principle that the Local Authority, collectively with other relevant services, should provide the same kind of care and the same aspirations as any good parent would for their own children (Dixon et al., 2015).

The number of children and young people who are looked after has increased steadily over recent years and it is now higher than at any point since 1985 (Department for Education, 2016a). In England, there were 69,540 children and young people recorded as looked after in March 2015, compared with 52,020 in March 2011, a rise of 6%. The majority of these children and young people are placed in foster care. Of these children and young people, 73% are of White British origin, reflecting ethnicity in the general population; however, children of mixed ethnic background continue to be slightly over-represented and children of Asian ethnicity slightly under-represented in the care system. In terms of age, the number of younger children coming into care has reduced in recent years, and the number of children aged over ten has increased. The long-term plan for the majority of children and young people is reunification with their birth family. The figure for children and young people returning home from care was 10,062 in 2015 (Department for Education, 2016a).

There has been a significant reduction in the number of decisions made by Local Authorities in relation to pursuing plans for adoption, and in the number of placement orders made in the last few years (National Adoption Leadership Board, 2014). This appears linked to high-profile court judgements, notably the cases *Re B* and *Re B-S* in 2013, in which birth families appealed in the High Court against the making of placement orders in relation to their children where the Local Authority plan was adoption. Recognising that adoption permanently severs all ties with the child's birth family, these judgements emphasised that the legal test for adoption requires that it should be regarded as the 'last resort' (National Adoption Leadership Board, 2014: 3). This case law has led to more robust exploration and analysis of all other realistic options available to a child in terms of permanency, prior to Local Authorities applying for adoption or placement orders. The court continues to 'require expert, high quality, evidence-based analysis of all realistic options for a child and the arguments for and against each of these options' (National Adoption Leadership Board, 2014). The Local Authority, in ensuring such analysis has been carried out, can be confident presenting the case to court with a plan for adoption in the best interests of the child. The number of adoptions is now steadily increasing (Department for Education, 2016a).

Challenges for children and young people who are looked after

Children and young people enter the care system for a variety of reasons and many have suffered abuse and neglect (Department for Education, 2014a). Despite a national aspiration for children and young people to achieve their potential, and many policy developments focused on achieving this, there remain distinctive differences between children who are looked after and their peers. The poor long-term outcomes for children and young people who are looked after is well documented. Burghart (2012) reports shocking statistics regarding young people who have been in care, in comparison to their non-looked-after peers, including that they are:

- 50 times more likely to be imprisoned;

- 7 times more likely to misuse alcohol and illicit substances;

- 60 times more likely to experience homelessness; and

- 4 to 5 times more likely to commit suicide in adulthood.

It is important to emphasise that children who become looked after primarily do so due to a range of long-term, entrenched and complex problems, and therefore, this is expected to be reflected in the outcomes. Although the care system is not responsible for children entering care, it can be argued that, at times, the system fails to repair the damage of abuse and neglect (Harber and Oakley, 2012). Furthermore, for some children additional stress, insecurity and upheaval is experienced within the care system. Some children and young people, especially those who enter care later in childhood or suffer acute placement instability, suffer disproportionally in the long term (Burghart, 2012).

It must be acknowledged that being placed in care can be of great benefit to children and young people, especially those who have suffered abuse and neglect. At its very best, care is a place of healing and support, allowing children 'the opportunity to play, learn, grow and discover, and develop into adulthood' (The Who Cares? Trust, 2015: 6). The care system offers many opportunities and benefits, which is echoed by the voices of young people leaving care (NIACE, 2013):

> '*Support from social services effectively got me to where I am now … being in care in and of itself was a positive thing for me and helped me no end.*' (Dawud [NIACE, 2013: 27])

> '*I have met a lot of people who have changed my life from being in care and a lot of them have helped me to achieve better things. If I had not have been in care my life would have been completely different and I probably would not be the person that I am today.*' (Danielle [NIACE, 2013: 23])

> '*Being in care, though seen as a bad thing by lots of people, has opened so many doors for me.*' (Chelsea [NIACE, 2013: 40])

Mental health and emotional well-being

Nevertheless, the difficulties for some children of a poor start in life and poor experience of the care system are not easily overcome. Children and young people who are looked after are approximately four times more likely to have a mental health disorder than children living in their birth families (Bazalgette et al., 2015). The mental health needs of these children and young people are often not recognised and addressed, leading to poorer outcomes in areas such as educational attainment and placement instability. The reasons for mental health difficulties are complex, with many young people experiencing such problems at the point of entering care. However, mental health issues for this population are undoubtedly linked to exposure to and the duration of abuse and neglect in childhood.

Scientific research in relation to the neurobiological consequences of child abuse and neglect in the early years is highly relevant for exploring the diverse needs of children and young people who are looked after and those who are subsequently adopted (Woolgar, 2013). Such research highlights that the effects of child maltreatment are different for each individual child. Children and young people's mental health issues are at risk of blurring into a single type of service provision if their individual needs are not considered. Woolgar (2013: 239) reminds us that: 'real children are much more than just their brain structure, their physiology, their caregiving history, their attachments or their genetics in isolation.' Children who are looked after therefore need to be treated as individuals, with care plans developed to address their particular needs.

Learning from Research

Bazalgette and colleagues (2015) conducted fieldwork in partnership with the NSPCC, with children and young people who were looked after in four Local Authorities and those who had recently left care. The aim was to understand young people's views on how the care system supports emotional well-being and what changes they would like to see. Choosing the right placement was highlighted as key, with children and young people stating:

'Choose the right carers. That's all I can really say. Because some can be good and some can be bad. You've just got to make sure that they're able to cope and support that child in whatever they need.'

'I think the emotional understanding of foster carers varies massively. Some are excellent and are really tuned into those sorts of issues, and I think the opposite of others.'

'You don't have any input [with moves]. You just get put wherever the social put you really. Wherever there's space.'

One young person highlighted the importance of having a direct choice in the placement decision-making process:

'With me, I was taken out of my primary school, when I was little, and my social worker drove me round, looking at placements, and it was like "oh do you like that one?" And it was eventually that I met my mum and dad now and ever since then I've always been there. I got a choice.'

Children and young people expressed that they wanted social workers to ask them how they are feeling, take their views into consideration and recognise that behavioural difficulties may indicate that they are struggling:

'You can get social workers who will take your feelings and opinions into consideration, but you can also get the ones who say, "yeah, this is what's happening, this is how it's going to go". No feeling.'

'It's not always easy to respect or trust someone who is working on your case. They know what happened, in a chronological way, but they don't always take into account how you are feeling. They might not ask you how you feel.'

'When I was phoning and leaving messages and asking for help, it was obvious I just needed not to be alone. [...] When I cut all my hair off, my social worker should have referred me for counselling.'

There were examples of thoughtful and empathetic practice by social workers. For example, a 14-year-old young person highlighted the significance of the relationship with his social worker stating, 'we had a great relationship with each other'. When his worker was leaving, she and the young person completed a memory book together with pictures and photographs. It made a big difference for this young person knowing his social worker had considered the emotional impact of this important relationship ending.

(Bazalgette et al., 2015: 27–59)

Educational attainment

It has been consistently highlighted that children and young people who are looked after demonstrate low educational achievement and disproportionate exclusions, with few progressing to higher education (Brodie, 2010). This has serious implications for their future life chances.

The statistical comparison for educational attainment between young people who are looked after and their peer group is a cause for concern:

- In 2014, only 12% of children who were looked after achieved 5 A–C grades at GCSE in comparison to 56% of their peers (Department for Education, 2014b).

- 66% of looked-after children compared with 19% of peers were identified as having a special educational need (SEN). The most common type of SEN recorded for this group in 2014 was 'behavioural, emotional and social difficulties' (Department for Education, 2014b).

- Of the 26,330 former care leavers aged 19–21, 39% were not in education, employment or training (NEET) (Department for Education, 2015a).

- 43% of children with just a single placement during 2011–12 achieved more than 5 A–C grades at GCSE compared to 13% of those who had more than three placements (Department for Education 2013: 24).

The Children and Families Act 2014 amends section 22 of the Children Act 1989, and requires every Local Authority in England to appoint an officer to make sure that the duty to promote the educational achievement of looked-after children is properly discharged (Department for Education, 2014c). This officer is known as the virtual school head (VSH). All children and young people who are looked after must have an individual personal education plan (PEP) as part of their overall care plan (Department for Education, 2014c). This should reflect the identified educational needs of the child, raise aspirations and promote improved life chances. A multi-agency approach is necessary, with close working relationships between the social worker, the placement and the school, alongside birth parents as appropriate. A strong team around the child, with the input of the virtual school head, is vital to an effective care plan that enables the young person to achieve in school and to reach their potential (Ofsted, 2012).

There are several barriers which children and young people have identified from their personal experiences. Young people have expressed, at times, they feel professionals make assumptions about what being in care means for their educational attainment. This includes that they are not interested in school work, not academically able or are 'trouble makers' (Barnardo's, 2016b: 7). Children and young people have stated that they believe social workers and teachers should actively encourage them, acknowledge their achievements and praise them for small accomplishments. The evidence is clear that children and young people value individual support in relation to their education from all adults in their lives (Brodie, 2010). Support includes an everyday interest in educational issues such as homework; ensuring the child participates in wider school activities and discussion about school life; practical support in terms of equipment; and incentives, rewards and celebrations to mark achievements.

Points for Reflection

- Recognising that the majority of children who enter the care system do so for reasons of abuse, neglect or family dysfunction, what do you think might be the challenges for children who are looked after?

- What do you think children who are looked after need in order to do well and overcome the difficulties and traumas they may have experienced?

Commentary
It is important for the child-centred practitioner to recognise that children who come into the care system are children first and need the same secure, safe and nurturing environment that any child needs to be free to get on with the job of growing up. Due to their past experiences, they may also have additional needs and these should be identified and assessed, to ensure that the right support can be put in place, such as a learning mentor at school to enable educational progress or therapeutic work to promote coping skills and positive mental health.

Stability and resilience

Stability is arguably the most significant factor in determining well-being, positive outcomes and success for children and young people who are looked after (Stein, 2005). Achieving permanence for children and young people is a key national policy objective (Department for Education, 2012). Permanence means 'security, stability, love and a strong sense of identity and belonging' and is not connected to a specific legal status (The Care Inquiry, 2013). One route to permanence does not outweigh another, and adoption will only ever be the right permanence plan for a small number of children in care. It will almost always be in the best interests of the child to grow up in a family setting; however, for some children with high-level needs, a specialist residential setting may be the most appropriate long-term placement.

Despite changes in government, the commitment to improving permanence has remained a consistent priority of State policy. In 2013, the Department for Education collated statistics and guidance on this theme, to inform good practice in the placement of children who are looked after (Department for Education, 2013: 11–14). It was noted that in the year ending 31 March 2012:

- Two-thirds (67%) of all children looked after had one placement.

- 89% of children had up to two placements.

- 11% – a small but substantial number of children – experienced three or more placements.

- 240 children experienced ten or more placements.

Young people aged over 13 when they became looked after were most likely to experience multiple placements. Those children who entered care due to family dysfunction (as opposed to reasons such as abusive experience, family ill-health or acute stress) were far more likely to have ten or more placements. It is possible that these children's lives were characterised by lack of support and stability for many years prior to entering the care system. Skilled assessment is needed to address the needs of the child and develop a care package to provide therapeutic support, consistency and security that seeks to compensate for previous experiences of dysfunction and chaos.

Stability should ideally be a core theme spanning all aspects of the child's life. This is in relation not only to the child's placement, but to their educational experience and health care, and to their contact with family members, professionals and their peer group. Ensuring the right placement clearly has a direct impact on all other areas of the child's life. However, placement moves can be positive for some children. The policy objective to improve permanency planning must not present a barrier to serious reconsideration or change of placement for children who are unhappy or unsettled. Young people who wished to move placement have reported that no one listened to them, and no one was prepared to make radical changes to their care plan (Sinclair et al., 2007). This highlights the importance of listening to children and involving them in making and reviewing plans regarding their placement.

As we noted in Chapter 4, having a secure base in order to build strong and enduring attachments is a central factor in promoting resilience (Gilligan, 2000). This is of crucial importance for children in the care system who are likely to have already endured many stresses and setbacks and need every opportunity to nurture resilience. An integral factor for stability is a placement allocation that meets the needs of the child through a good match with the skills and expectations of the placement provider (Schofield et al., 2011). Such a placement will enable new attachments to evolve whilst maintaining important bonds with significant people from the child's past, ensuring continuity and connection.

Points for Reflection

- Think back to a time in your childhood that you can remember well and that stands out as a period of change. Recognising that every change incorporates some form of loss, what enabled you to manage that time of change?

- Imagine that for reasons beyond your control, you had entered the care system at that time (or reflect upon that time, if this was your actual experience). What would you need from the adults in your life in order to cope with the experience of change and upheaval?

Relationships matter

For children in the care system, their support network may be limited due to difficult or absent family relationships, or moves between several placements or geographical areas (Ryan, 2012). As we are aware, learning to form positive relationships begins through attachments in the early years. Children with negative early life experiences may have encountered broken or inconsistent relationships; they may have learned to fear closeness and developed insecure or disordered attachments; and they may lack confidence and skills in building new relationships.

Our lives are influenced and shaped by the people we are close to, those who encourage us, advise us and help us when things go wrong. For children who are looked after or leaving care, these relationships can be difficult to establish, short-lived and too easily fractured (The Who Cares? Trust, 2015). Social workers play an important role in supporting carers to provide stability and consistency when young people are experiencing difficulties and demonstrating challenging behaviour. The Care Inquiry (2013: 8) highlighted that: 'high-quality relationships matter more than anything else for children in or on the edge of care.'

The Care Inquiry was undertaken by a range of experts who consulted with children who are looked after, professionals and carers in order to develop positive practice to promote placement stability. The inquiry highlighted the quality and continuity of relationships as 'the golden thread' (2013: 8), enabling children to negotiate the challenges of the care system and do well. The report concluded that what really matters to children in the care system are relationships with people who:

- are always there for them;

- love, accept and respect them for who they are;

- are ambitious for them and help them succeed;

- stick with them through thick and thin;

- are willing to go the extra mile; and

- treat them as part of their family, or part of their life, beyond childhood and into adulthood.

(The Care Inquiry, 2013: 9)

Learning from Research

Julie Ridley and colleagues (2013) carried out a study examining the relationships of young people in care and care leavers with their key workers. They interviewed 169 children and young people and found some heartening results. The vast majority of interviewees were satisfied with the relationship with their key practitioner (social worker or personal adviser). In common with similar research, they highlighted the importance of being listened to and the value of professionals showing interest in them, their day-to-day interests and their concerns:

> 'He stops what he's saying and listens to what I have to say, like if I had a problem and he was talking about something else, he'd stop and then he's listen to what I was saying and so he, he obviously cares, he listens.' (10-year-old boy who is looked after)

The young people described workers who do their best for them and get things sorted out, for example providing practical support, doing the paperwork for passports and enabling choice around accommodation. Relationships of acceptance, warmth and encouragement counted for these young people:

> 'I don't know how to describe it, we're not mates, I know we're not mates because she's got to be professional. But, but at the same time like, I know I can talk to her about anything.' (16-year-old care leaver)

> The researchers noted the emphasis in policy and the organisational changes that underpin the provision of more consistent supportive relationships for young people in care and professionals. They recognised that for some young people, with strong networks of support provided by family, friends and carers, relationships with social workers may be more peripheral, but for those whose lives continue to be unsettled, their relationship with their key worker is vitally important.
>
> (Ridley et al., 2013: 60–62)

Positive relationships for children with family, friends, professionals and peers are highly significant. They can enable children to build a sense of security and belonging, and facilitate the opportunity for children to fully understand their past. Continuity of relationships is crucial to help children construct their identity, which develops through life, but is particularly important during childhood and adolescence, and essential for those who have experienced high levels of change and upheaval.

Contact with family and friends

The child's social worker has a vital role to play in continued work with the child's family and wider network when the child enters care. This is to sustain relationships throughout the child's period in care, and is essential if reunification is the plan for permanence. Contact with the birth family is always important, but is often a very challenging aspect of care planning (Schofield et al., 2011). This is especially the case if there is an expectation that relationships with a foster family will be become close and last into adulthood.

In contemporary society, children and young people across the board increasingly grow up with a wide range of connections and shifting family relationships, and this should not be any different for children and young people who are looked after. The Care Inquiry (2013: 9) posed the thought-provoking question: 'Why do we persist in breaking children's old relationships when we introduce them to future carers, despite knowing that so many children who do not happen to be in care manage to negotiate complex family relationships as they grow up?' Children and young people themselves have also highlighted the significance of maintaining relationships established before they entered care, with one child highlighting 'sometimes friends mean more than family' (Morgan, 2009). Children and young people with strong friendship networks feel more content, have improved life skills and social skills, and a positive sense of self-esteem (Dixon, 2008). Enabling children to keep in touch with old friends and to form new friendships with peers is an important aspect of care planning, and one that is sometimes neglected by professionals.

Learning from Research

In research carried out by Roger Morgan (2009), the Children's Rights Director for England, 370 children and young people were consulted about keeping in touch with family and friends during their period in care. The study highlighted that children were more likely to keep in touch with their birth mother than their father; and noted a concern that the longer a child remained in care the more likely they were to lose touch with parents and siblings. The vast majority of children (86%) felt it was important for siblings to be placed together.

Children emphasised that they wanted a choice about who they kept in contact with and the people they cited as wanting to keep in touch with included grandparents, uncles, aunts, cousins, nieces and nephews, in addition to their immediate family. Children also identified unrelated individuals, such as godparents, close friends of their birth family and previous carers, as people they would like to see. One child also identified that they missed contact with their very first social worker. Young people understood the importance of planning for safety and ensuring long-term networks of support:

> *'You might not always want contact with certain people because they might have something to do with the reason you were taken into care in the first place.'*

According to one young person, it is important to keep in touch because otherwise: *'later in life when you come out of care you've got no one to see because you've lost contact.'*

Some children were willing to take risks to maintain contact even when it was officially prevented, perhaps by running away to visit family members. However, one child had to run away because they wanted to avoid contact and their views had not been listened to.

Some children worried when they had no contact and missed people from their past. They emphasised the importance of receiving information about them:

> *'When there's no contact you always think the worst.'*

The views of the young people are summarised in the following comments:

> *'It's a big issue that needs to be taken seriously.'*

> *'If a young person doesn't want contact they shouldn't be forced to, if they do then a social worker should do something about it.'*

Each child has a unique experience and exploration is required through direct work to understand the significance of the child's relationships. Children have a right to be involved in decision-making about contact arrangements and to have a clear and honest explanation if changes have to be made.

Social workers need to think creatively about how to facilitate and maintain contact for children and young people with their family and friends, whilst considering their needs, wishes and personal safety. Contact is often thought to be direct visits, but can also be through email, letter, telephone and social media. Contact visits should be supervised only when necessary, to ensure children and young people can maintain relationships as naturally as possible. However, it is important to emphasise there will always be relationships which cannot be supported by professionals, even if the child requests these, if the child's safety and well-being is endangered. Professionals need to be open and honest about the reasons for this, and share the risk assessment undertaken with the child.

Child-centred care planning

Every child who is looked after should have a care plan that addresses their particular needs, including education and health, placement and contact arrangements, permanency planning and other aspects relevant to their individual well-being. In order to develop the plan, social workers consult with parents, persons with parental responsibility, carers and significant others in the child's life, including relevant professionals in the team around the child. It is a legal and ethical duty to involve the child in any decisions pertaining to the care planning process, in line with section 22 of the Children Act 1989. The statutory guidance and regulations for professional practice with children who are looked after, updated in 2015, emphasise the importance of enabling children and young people to participate in decision-making processes, taking proper account of their wishes and feelings.

Children may be safer and have their basic needs met when they enter the care system; however, their lives do not automatically improve – this is only the beginning of a journey requiring ongoing help and support (The Who Cares? Trust, 2015).

Practitioner Testimonial

Anyone who works with children and young people who are looked after should be a good listener; for example, always be open to hear the good and the bad. Always be consistent keeping appointments – this will help with building relationships and trust issues. Remembering young people have so many changes of workers so not having them repeat things over and over. Remember to acknowledge birthdays and celebrations. Not many looked-after children receive even a card or gift from biological families so a birthday card once a year from their social worker makes an impact. Go the extra

▶

mile. Always make recordings factual and backed up with evidence. Don't make assump-
tions when working with children and young people, everyone is an individual and differ-
ent and remember many young people will go back through adulthood to read their files.
Don't wear ID badges in front of young people in public, it's embarrassing. Encourage
children and young people to be confident and have a voice, encourage them to Chair
their reviews, remembering that in review meetings the child's voice can become lost in
amongst all the professionals making decisions about their lives. Make them aware of
their entitlements.

Mel Metcalfe, Care Leaver, Total Respect Trainer and Social Work Assistant.

Review meetings

Each child is appointed an independent reviewing officer (IRO) to provide oversight of the child's case. The IRO is responsible for ensuring the care plan reflects
the needs of the child and progress is made towards identified outcomes
(Department for Education, 2015b). Key decisions regarding care planning take
place at review meetings, chaired by the IRO and involving the young person,
their carers and social worker and significant others who play an important part
in the life of the child, such as parents or teachers. Reviews should consider
decisions from previous reviews and ensure appropriate action has been taken
to promote the safety and welfare of the child; if not, the IRO should take action
(The Care Inquiry, 2013).

Children and young people have expressed varied attitudes to the review
process (Schofield et al., 2011). They have described wanting to be involved,
but often worry about who might attend the meeting or feel embarrassed by
the attention. Children and young people have expressed they do not like
review meetings to take place in their educational establishment, as this may
mean they stand out as different from other children (The Care Inquiry, 2013).
They want reviews to be less formal and they feel they should have a say about
who is invited to attend.

As we noted in Chapter 4, an important component of resilience is the development of self-efficacy. Children who are able to declare preferences, make
choices and define outcomes for themselves are more likely to develop confidence in their own capability as they mature. For young people in the care
system, many choices have been taken out of their control and have been made
by parents or carers, the legal system or professionals. It is important therefore
that social workers and IROs seek to facilitate opportunities for children to regain
a voice in decisions about their own lives. Ensuring that reviews are child-centred
meetings, organised with or by the child, will enable young people to become
resourceful individuals, able to contribute to decision-making and planning
processes.

Life story work

Most children and young people in care have experienced a variety of parental figures and lived in a range of different family settings. To construct a sense of identity for themselves, the child or young person needs to make sense of their own memories, their family background and complex history (The Care Inquiry, 2013). Children and young people who have experienced separation from their parents may remain preoccupied with their birth family, feeling a sense of loyalty and connectedness to family members they rarely see or can barely remember (Biehal, 2014). This can impact on relationships with new parental figures. Feelings of uncertainty or confusion about past relationships can undermine their sense of security as they grow older. Identity develops through life, but is especially important in childhood. An understanding of the past is key to developing a sense of security in the present and confidence in the future. Life story work helps children and young people understand why they cannot live with their birth family temporarily or permanently and enables them to maintain their connections with the past whilst focusing on moving forward in the present.

Focus on Practice

There are many ways of carrying out life story work and the final product, which may be a life story book or album, a special box or digital file, can be revised and added to over time.

According to Rose and Philpott (2005) A life story book should include all the aspects that make up a human life: the stories and the anecdotes, ambitions realised and unfulfilled, family idiosyncrasies and cultural traditions, happy and sad memories.

A life story book will contain factual information that a diligent social worker may obtain from archived case files, important documents and court reports. This might be presented in the form of a family history or a life-line. A map could be printed or drawn with important places in a child's background. The process of making the map might involve travelling to significant places to pause for photographs or arranging visits to previous schools or carers. Life story work may involve learning about different parts of the world, or exploring cultural and religious customs and traditions significant to the child's ethnic identity. There will be stories about the past, including important memories or pictures of significant events.

The stories might be told through photographs or a narrative of an imaginary character (such as a favourite animal whose life has included similar events and experiences). For example, a social worker might consult with the present and previous carers of a child in order to find out about their likes and dislikes, and significant events in their lives. If a ▶

child loves cats, the worker might devise a story about a kitten who experiences some enjoyable events similar to those that the child has had, such as a holiday or outing. The story book or cartoon strip might then explain why the kitten has had to move to a new family, making links to the experience of the child. The child may be able to understand that it was not the kitten's fault that it's parents could not look after it, and through this gain some insights about their own experiences.

Life story work should include space to explore feelings and emotions, of the child or others, at the time events occurred or in the present looking back. The process of doing the work, sensitively and at the pace of the child, is as important as the final product, providing a therapeutic opportunity for making sense of the past and preparing for the future (Wrench and Naylor, 2013).

One of the tasks of life story work is to make connections between the chronological events of the child's life and their lived experiences. This work is an ongoing process rather than a 'one-off' event which requires reviewing and revisiting (NICE, 2015). This provides information for the young person, as well as supporting the carer to respond to questions from the child about their personal history. Life story activities need to be planned sensitively and focus on the needs of the child. Information delivered needs to be by a trusted person who considers timing, how much information is shared at one time, taking account of the emotional needs and developmental stage of the child.

Points for Reflection

- How would you make sure that childcare reviews are child-friendly meetings that enable the participation of the child or young person?

- Why is it important for children who are looked after to have a good understanding of their past and their family background?

Commentary

Reconstituting the childcare review meeting as the child's meeting, rather than an organisational or bureaucratic function, is a good place to start. Little things can make a difference, such as the child baking biscuits for the meeting or choosing the music they want to play as people arrive. Active ways of enabling young people to have more control include letting them set the agenda and send out the invitations or having the IRO step back and support the young person to chair the meeting.

Children who are looked after may need help to make sense of a complicated family history marked by disruption and upheaval. They may have fragmented memories or carry a sense of responsibility for events in their childhood that were outside their control. Life story work is an important way to explore the child's understandings and enable them to make sense of events, in a way that is appropriate to their age and stage of development. Life story work should be returned to at different points in the life of a child who is looked after or adopted, to enable further information to be shared and insights gained as the child matures.

Transition into adulthood

For many, being placed in care is a difficult and traumatic experience. However, leaving care can be just as hard, if not more so, as entering care (Duncalf, 2010). The relationship between the young person leaving care and their social worker is fundamental to ensuring a well-supported transition from care to independence (Children's Commissioner for Wales, 2011). It is essential that the social worker has the knowledge, skills and understanding to provide information and guidance on accommodation and housing options, employment and training, independent living skills and benefits. The social worker is responsible for ensuring the young person's care plan becomes a pathway plan as they move towards increasing independence and that the plan is delivered effectively. Young people reiterate the vital importance of consistent and supportive relationships with social workers to help them prepare for the transition from care to independence (Munro et al., 2010).

Every year in England, approximately 10,000 young people leave care aged 16–18 years (HM Government, 2013). In contemporary society, young people, on average, leave their parental home at the age of 24 years (Department for Education and Skills, 2007). The pressure to move on is not always explicit but related to a culture in which 16 is seen as a 'special age and a turning point' for young people (Scotland's Commissioner for Children and Young People, 2008). The age of 16 is often reinforced as the age where everything changes, both legally and in terms of service entitlements and additional rights acquired. Although a child is no longer *looked after* from the age of 18 years, they are provided with ongoing support from the Local Authority until they are 21 years, and if they remain in full-time education, up to 25 years.

Many young people have expressed that living independently is 'scary' (Children's Commissioner for Wales, 2011). The journey to independence is 'often shorter, steeper and more hazardous' in contrast to the extended transitions of young people in the general population (Stein, 2005: 1). Many young people feel they have no choice regarding the timing of their transition, as one young person expressively states:

'I didn't want to go. I still had to go anyway. I didn't have a choice … I was moving out at eighteen, end of discussion, and the bit that really pissed me [off] is [that] they chucked me out on my eighteenth birthday.' (Care leaver quoted in Munro et al., 2010: 21)

Such an approach is not child-centred and fails to fulfil in any meaningful way the corporate parenting responsibilities of the Local Authority. Young people who move on from care in a positive way are likely to have been prepared gradually, and left care later, in a planned way. The research of Professor Mike Stein found that young people leaving care who managed this challenging transition successfully had:

- stability and continuity in their lives, including a secure attachment relationship;
- made sense of their family relationships so they could psychologically move on from them;
- achieved some educational success before leaving care.

(Stein, 2005: 19)

Transition should not be seen as something which happens suddenly, but as a gradual preparation process that happens over many years. Fundamental to a successful transition to adulthood is ensuring that the focus is on the needs of the child, their level of maturity and capability, rather than their age (Fauth et al., 2012). Planning should begin early and be collaborative, fully involving the child and those who support them. Continuity of workers and carers is an important factor in providing stability and security while preparing young people for independence. Once again, the value of a positive working relationship between the young person and their social worker is highlighted as key to success (NCB, 2015).

Case study analysis

Referring to our case study enables application of some of the key issues discussed in this chapter to an evolving and realistic practice situation. It is evident that thorough assessment and timely intervention are effective for most families, avoiding the need for children to enter the care system. Nevertheless, in some cases, despite the best efforts of families and professionals, acute difficulties or crises occur that necessitate removal into care or placement change for some children. In the case of the Smith–Jones–Khan family, introduced on page 143, there have been escalating problems over a period of some time that have not been resolved. At this point, we are some months after the serious incident of domestic violence, which also involved physical abuse of 8-year-old Hanif (discussed in Chapter 8). Fiona has separated from Mick, who is awaiting a court date for criminal charges.

For a month, 14-year-old Jade continued living with her stepmother Fiona, often staying at her father's bedsit or her boyfriend's flat. She was then received into care, as her relationship with Fiona fractured and there were concerns about her safety, due to possible child sexual exploitation. Her emergency foster placement broke down owing to her challenging behaviour. Jade is currently living in a residential children's home where her behaviour is proving difficult to manage. She rarely attends school and often stays out all night. She regularly turns up at her father's place late at night. Fiona's mental health has deteriorated and she is struggling to cope. She has recently been admitted to hospital for treatment. Carol (the maternal grandmother) has taken on the care of Charlotte and this may become a permanent arrangement. Hanif is staying with his father, Nadir.

Children's voices

Working with a fictional case and considering the complexities of the evolving situation, is helpful as it allows us to take a step back and reflect upon the possible perspectives of the children and young people in this family:

Charlotte's thoughts:

Mummy's poorly and sad. Nana Carol don't like dad. Not got Hanif to play with anymore.

Hanif's feelings about his new situation:

It's pretty good at dad's really. I get to see my nana and papa and play with Mosim's Xbox. But I've not seen my mum for weeks now and I think Charlotte is really missing me. Dad says it's all okay now but I'm not sure.

Jade's perspectives:

It's alright here except that I never know who the staff are, they keep changing. I can do what I want, so I keep going to stay at my boyfriend's or my dad's. My social worker wants me to go live with a foster family again, but I didn't like that last one. She was right stuck up. Sometimes I just want to be like a family again with my proper mum and my dad – it was better then. It's not fair.

Points for Reflection

- Consider the needs of each of the children. Think about the kinds of questions and concerns they may have about their family situation and plans for their future.

- How would you work with Carol to enable her to provide support and reassurance to Charlotte?

▶

- What do you think is best for Hanif in the long term? How would you work with Nadir and Fiona to meet Hanif's needs for security and family contact?

- How would you work with Jade to develop a plan for permanence that will provide safety and stability?

Analysis of practice issues

- Depending on Fiona's mental health and the long-term prognosis, it may be that Charlotte's needs can be supported by an informal arrangement between Fiona and Carol. Alternatively Carol might seek legal advice about how best to provide security for Charlotte in the long term, possibly through a Special Guardianship Order or a Child Arrangements Order. It will be important for the social worker to maintain involvement to ensure stable care is provided for Charlotte, despite the recent upheavals. Arrangements for contact with father Mick may need supervision in the first instance, due to concerns about his substance misuse and violent behaviour. It will be important for Charlotte to maintain contact with Hanif and Jade, her half-siblings.

- Hanif's arrangement to stay with his father is a private matter, as Nadir has parental responsibility and has stepped in to care for his son. Nevertheless, the social worker may wish to offer advocacy on behalf of Hanif, to ensure that his voice is not lost, and to support the family to provide stability and security for him. The importance of his remaining in close contact with his mother and with Charlotte should be emphasised. Social work input may be required if the parents cannot ultimately agree on residence and contact matters, and Nadir or Fiona may seek a Child Arrangements Order.

- Jade's situation is the most precarious at this point. Her main long-term stability has been provided by her father, Mick, and it will be important to enable him to provide security and boundaries for Jade. It is necessary to assess how Mick can maintain contact with Jade safely, managing his substance use and violent behaviour. We have discussed previously the possible impact upon Jade of the loss of her mother; any links to members of her maternal extended family that could be renewed or strengthened could prove crucial at this time of change and upheaval.

- The risk of sexual exploitation remains an ongoing feature of Jade's life. Jade's care plan will need to address her safety, involving the police to gather evidence of exploitation and challenge or arrest the 'boyfriend'. The social worker will only be able to monitor Jade's safety and offer advice if a relationship of trust is built and maintained. It will be important to provide a consistent key worker in the children's home to build a relationship with Jade and agree with her appropriate boundaries around going out safely. The aim of the work will be to enable Jade to recognise the risks for herself and be involved in decision-making processes that improve her safety and welfare. Involving Jade in the care planning process will be crucial, therefore, which will include prioritising with Jade her education, including school attendance, and positive opportunities for leisure and peer relationships. Creative approaches to involve Jade in making decisions about her future placement, including being introduced to a potential long-term foster carer, will be important.

Conclusion

In this chapter, we have explored some key aspects of child-centred practice around social work with children and young people who are looked after. We have noted that, although the majority of children who pass through the care system return home to their birth family and some are adopted, there will always be a cohort of children and young people whose needs are best served by remaining in care. This can be of great benefit to children, especially those who have experienced trauma and difficulties in their birth family. Care allows time to heal and recover and can support a positive future and enhanced opportunities.

The key to a successful experience for the child throughout their journey in care is diligent planning by their social worker, working in partnership with carers and family members and the multi-agency team around the child, and fully involving the child in all aspects of their care. Children and young people repeatedly identify that having the right placement is essential for stability and resilience, and that they want to be involved in decision-making about their life and their future. Planning for leaving care needs to be undertaken gradually through the review process, to ensure the young person has the necessary life skills and support to make a successful transition.

It is clear that the role of the social worker is immensely important in ensuring positive outcomes for children and young people who are looked after. Practice based on child-centred principles will promote the rights of young people whilst recognising the importance of nurture, stability and consistent care. Social workers who engage with young people through challenging times, listening to their wishes and feelings, advocating on their behalf, and strengthening positive, secure relationships, can make a real difference. A positive and trusting relationship between child and social worker is essential to fully supporting young people and enabling a successful care journey.

Recommended reading and resources

- Bazalgette and colleagues (2015) in their research for the NSPCC entitled *Achieving Emotional Well-being for Looked After Children: A Whole System Approach* provides an excellent insight into young people's journey through the care system in relation to their emotional well-being. The report also visually charts the experience of individual children exploring their views and feelings, as well as the opinions of carers and professionals.

- The Research in Practice website is a valuable resource, providing information about fostering and adoption. Commissioned by the Department for Education in 2013, it brings together research on a range of relevant issues to build the skills and knowledge of social workers and foster carers involved in supporting children who are looked after. Sections 9 (communicating with children and young people) and 14 (placement stability and permanence) are particularly relevant to the themes in this chapter: http://fosteringandadoption.rip.org.uk/topics/

- The report completed by The Care Inquiry (2013) *Making not Breaking: Building Relationships for Our Most Vulnerable Children* provides an excellent overview of the challenges and some fresh thinking about ways forward in order to promote permanence and positive outcomes for our most vulnerable children and young people.

- The report *Children and Young People's Views on Being in Care: A Literature Review* published by Coram Voice in partnership with the University of Bristol in 2015, provides a valuable overview of the research that has explored the views of children and young people who have experience of the care system.

- Katie Wrench and Lesley Naylor (2013) have written an accessible textbook, full of creative activities for practitioners to use when undertaking life story work with children and young people: *Life Story Work with Children who are Fostered or Adopted.*

- The documentary 'Kids in Care', produced by *Panorama* for the BBC, follows several children from Coventry who are looked after. The programme highlights the challenges for the young people, their social workers and carers. Excerpts from the programme are available on YouTube. Available at: www.youtube.com/watch?v=mnzJT-6g9Us

- The Social Care Institute for Excellence has put together a series of films made by and about young people who have experience of the care system. The following films reinforce some of the themes of this chapter: *Care Experienced Young People* and *Being Heard and Getting Support.* The short films are available at: www.scie.org.uk/socialcaretv/topic.asp?t=lookedafterchildren

CONCLUSION

In this book, we have emphasised throughout the importance of child-centred practice. At the outset, in Chapter 1, we recognised that child-centred practice makes a difference for children and young people, it matters to children and it is sometimes a matter of life and death. In some senses, it is surprising and alarming that something as simple as listening to children, taking seriously what they say and involving them in decisions about their lives, should need to be emphasised at all. The rights of children have been enshrined in UK and international law for many decades, based upon the UNCRC published in 1989. Nevertheless, throughout this text, we have acknowledged that child-centred practice is neither simple nor straightforward. The role of the social worker is particularly complex, involved in assessing and managing complicated family dynamics, in the context of demanding and ever-changing social, organisational and legal duties. It is hoped that this textbook will go some way towards both reinforcing the ethical imperative of child-centredness and providing ways forward to support practitioners in navigating this challenging professional terrain.

In Part I, we explored the theoretical and ethical foundations of child-centred social work, developing a framework for practice consistent with ecological thinking and reflective-relational approaches. We emphasised the rights of the child, whilst also noting the value of the ethic of care, recognising that children are rarely autonomous, independent agents. Children need consistent care and nurture and are usually dependent upon their parents and family for many years in order to reach their full potential. We argued that an emphasis on child-centredness is not incompatible with think-family approaches that prioritise partnership with parents and the importance of family support. Children have a right to a private family life, as do adults, and their best interests are usually promoted most effectively within the context of the family. We have also acknowledged that the welfare of the child is the paramount concern for the social worker and the wider professional community; it is the justifying and organising principle of any intervention into family life. Children have a right to grow up in safety, free from harm and abuse. When families are unable to protect their children, or are the source of danger, professionals must intervene to safeguard the child and ensure that they retain a focus on the needs, safety and well-being of the child.

Through Part I, we focused on some key areas of knowledge that are fundamental to child-centred practice and in line with the 'Knowledge and Skills' statement for children's social work (Department for Education, 2014). We highlighted the ways in which theory and research about child development underpin good practice. Understanding normative stages of development enables social workers to understand children and to assess their needs, to support parents and carers to meet their needs and to recognise when problems may be occurring that are impacting on the welfare of the child. We also recognised the importance of understanding the family and environmental context of the child, to appreciate what life might be like for the child and what might be important for that unique young person. This included recognising the effects of social change and poverty in an age of austerity, and the impact upon young people of their immersion in digital worlds. In Chapter 5, we focused particularly on the importance of engaging directly with young people. Child-centred practitioners take responsibility to develop their skills to communicate effectively and creatively with children, and to find ways, even in challenging circumstances, to build relationships of trust with their young service users.

Throughout the book, we have sought to bring our discussions to life by including the testimonials of professionals who adopt child-centred approaches in their practice. This inclusion provides inspiration for students and assurance that many practitioners are rising to the challenges of child-centredness in their day-to-day work. Recognising the importance of reflexivity, to enable practitioners to address the complexities of child-centred work, we have included regular 'points for reflection', to encourage the reader to pause and consider how they might apply their learning to practice. At times, we have included commentaries that give examples of relevant practice, additional guidance and prompts to enable the reader to reflect further upon significant issues. The aim of the book is to enable the application of theory and research to inform ethical child-centred practice.

In Part II we examined social work practice at different stages of intervention, and introduced a case study to examine more directly the knowledge and skills required for different aspects of professional practice. Although in most cases there is good evidence to suggest that social work works – that is, early intervention strategies and safeguarding processes are effective for many families, meaning children are able to do well without extensive, long-term professional involvement – nevertheless, for some children, social work involvement becomes part of the pattern of their lives, often associated with those aspects of their lives that are most stressful and over which they have least control. For these reasons, our case study (analysed throughout Part II) focused on a family whose situation deteriorates, despite the best efforts of all involved, such that it required social work input over a considerable period, with one child becoming looked after. The case study reminds us that, for children and young people involved with social workers as involuntary service users, the opportunity to actively participate in decision-making processes led by professionals, and regain some sense of self-efficacy, is crucial to their safety, well-being and resilience. The case study enabled the reader to analyse some key aspects of social work practice in complex, evolving and realistic scenarios, in order to apply learning from each chapter and to consider the application of child-centred principles in practice.

The chapters in Part II move through the stages of professional intervention in family life, from voluntary offers of early help through more targeted support to statutory interventions to protect children from harm, with the final chapter examining the role of the corporate parent in supporting children who are looked after. Whilst not claiming to address social work in every field of practice, the chapters explore some key aspects of the everyday work of professionals in the UK, presenting the evidence base for good practice and focusing on child-centred approaches. Each chapter highlights creative techniques that aim to enhance the toolkit of students or practitioners as they build their skills and competence in direct work with children, young people and families.

Covering a wide range of themes and areas of practice, this book cannot provide a comprehensive analysis of every practice issue. We have ensured the reader is directed to relevant books, websites and resources for further study to enhance professional knowledge and capability. We have endeavoured to bring together in one book a wide range of research that gives voice to the child. It is by listening to the views, wishes and feelings of children and young people, expressed through this research, that practitioners can gain the understanding and empathy required to work in a child-centred way. Listening to children reminds us that children have a valid and valuable contribution to make.

Most parents know that good parenting is not about allowing, or abandoning, children to do what they want, when they want. Parenting is about respecting and valuing the child as a unique individual, providing care to enable them to reach their developmental milestones and nurturing their capacity to become increasingly independent. Similarly, child-centred practice is about taking responsibility to work in the best interests of the child at all times, promoting their rights and ensuring their welfare. It is about recognising the child's right to be involved and their capability to contribute to decision-making processes. Where children need support to participate, it is about enabling this through advocacy and child-friendly approaches. Child-centred practitioners support children and young people to make their own decisions, whilst ensuring that when this is not possible it is for ethical reasons, in the interests of the child and that this is fully and clearly explained. Taking a child-centred approach does not diminish the challenges and tensions inherent in social work practice, but it does ensure more effective practice to safeguard and promote the rights and welfare of children and young people.

REFERENCES

Action for Children (2010) *Neglecting the Issue: Impact, Causes and Responses to Child Neglect in the UK.* London: Action for Children.

Adamson, J. and Templeton, L. (2012) *Silent Voices: Supporting Children and Young People Affected by Parental Alcohol Misuse.* London: Office of the Children's Commissioner for England. Available at: http://dera.ioe.ac.uk/15497/ (accessed on 26/6/2016).

Advisory Council on the Misuse of Drugs (2003) *Hidden Harm: Responding to the Needs of Problem Drug Users.* London: Home Office.

Ainsworth, M.D.S. and Bell, S.M. (1970) Attachment, exploration and separation: Illustrated by the behavior of one-year-olds in a strange situation. *Child Development, 41,* 49–67.

Ainsworth, M.D.S., Blehar, M.C., Waters, E. and Wall, S. (1978) *Patterns of Attachment: A Psychological Study of the Strange Situation.* Hillsdale, NJ: Erlbaum.

Albert, D. and Steinberg, L. (2011) Judgment and decision making in adolescence. *Journal of Research on Adolescence, 21* (1): 211–224.

Alderson, P. (1983) *Children's Consent to Surgery.* Buckingham: Open University Press.

Alderson, P. (1992) The rights of children and young people, in A. Coote (ed.) *The Welfare of Citizens: Developing New Social Rights.* London: Institute for Public Policy Research.

Aldridge, J. (2006) The experiences of children living with and caring for parents with mental illness. *Child Abuse Review,* 15: 79–88.

Allen, G. (2011) *Early Intervention: The Next Steps.* London: The Stationery Office.

Allnock, D and Miller, P (2013) *No One Noticed, No One Heard.* London: NSPCC.

Appleton, J., Terlektsi, E. and Coombes, L. (2013) The use of sociograms to explore collaboration in child protection conferences. *Children and Youth Services Review, 35* (12): 2140–2146.

Appleton, J., Terlektsi, E. and Coombes, L. (2015) Implementing the strengthening families approach to child protection conferences. *British Journal of Social Work, 45*: 1395–1414.

Archard, D. and Skivenes, M. (2009a) Balancing a child's best interests and a child's view. *International Journal of Children's Rights, 17*: 1–21.

Archard, D. and Skivenes, M. (2009b) Hearing the child. *Child and Family Social Work, 14*: 391–399.

Aries, P. (1961) *Centuries of Childhood.* Harmondsworth: Penguin.

Arnstein, S.R. (1969) A ladder of participation. *Journal of the American Institute of Planners,* 35: 216–224.

Association of Directors of Adult Social Services (ADASS), The Children's Society, Association of Directors of Children's Services (ADCS) (2015) *No Wrong Doors: Working Together to Support Young Carers and Their Families* [online] http://www.local.gov.uk/documents/10180/11431/No+wrong+doors++working+together+to+support+young+carers+and+their+families/d210a4a6-b352-4776-b858-f3adf06e4b66 (accessed on 10/3/2016).

Axford, N., Barlow, J., Coad, J., Schrader-McMillan, A., Sonthalia, S., Toft, A., Wrigley, Z., Goodwin, A., Ohlson, C., and Bjornstad, G. (2015) *The Best Start at Home: What Works to Improve the Quality of Parent-Child Interactions from Conception to Age 5 Years? A Rapid Review of Interventions.* London: Early Intervention Foundation.

Axline, V.M. (1947) *Play Therapy: The Inner Dynamics of Childhood.* Houghton Mifflin.

Bailey, S.; Boddy, K.; Briscoe, S.; Morris, C. (July 2015) Involving disabled children and young people as partners in research: A systematic review. *Child: Care, Health & Development, 41* (4): 505–514.

Bandura, A. (1977) *Social Learning Theory.* Englewood Cliffs, NJ: Prentice Hall.

Barlow, J. and Schrader-McMillan, A. (2010) *Safeguarding Children from Emotional Maltreatment: What Works.* London: Jessica Kingsley Publishers.

Barnardo's (2016a). *Disability and Inclusion.* London: Barnardo's. Available at: http://www.barnardos.org.uk/what_we_do/our_work/disability.htm (accessed on 10/6/2016).

Barnardo's (2016b). *Failed by the System: The Views of Young Care Leavers on Their Educational Experiences.* London: Barnardo's. Available at: http://www.barnardos.org.uk/failed_by_the_system_report.pdf (accessed on 10/7/2016).

Barnes, V. (2007) Young people's views of children's rights and advocacy services: A case for 'caring' advocacy? *Child Abuse Review, 16* (3): 140–152.

Barnes, V. (2012) Social work and advocacy with young people: Rights and care in practice. *British Journal of Social Work, 42* (7): 1275–1292.

Baumrind, D. (1967) Child care practices anteceding three patterns of child behavior. *Genetic Psychology Monographs, 75* (1): 43–88.

Bazalgette, L., Rahilly, T. and Trevelyan, G. (2015) *Achieving Emotional Wellbeing for Looked After Children: A Whole System Approach.* London: NSPCC.

Bee, H. and Boyd, D. (2014, 13th edition) *The Developing Child.* Boston, MA: Pearson.

Bell, M. (2011) *Promoting Children's Rights in Social Work and Social Care: A Guide to Participatory Practice.* London: Jessica Kingsley Publishers.

Belsky, J. (1984) The determinants of parenting: A process model. *Child Development, 55*: 83–96.

Berricka, J., Dickens, J., Poso, T. and Skivenes, M. (2015) Children's involvement in care order decision-making: A cross-country analysis. *Child Abuse and Neglect, 45*: 128–141.

Best, P., Manktelow, R. and Taylor, B. (2014) Online communication, social media and adolescent wellbeing: A systematic narrative review. *Children and Youth Services Review, 41*: 27–36.

Biehal, N. (2014) 'A Sense of Belonging': Meanings of family and home in long-term foster care. *British Journal of Social Work, 44*: 955–971.

Biestek, F.P. (1961) *The Casework Relationship.* London: Allen and Unwin.

Bijleveld, G.G.van, Dedding, C.W.M. and Bunders-Aelen, J.F.G. (2015) Children's and young people's participation within child welfare and child protection services: A state-of-the-art review. *Child and Family Social Work, 20*: 129–138. doi: 10.1111/cfs.12082

Bion, W. (1962) *Learning from Experience.* London: Karnac Books.

Botti, S., Orfali, K., Iyengar, S.S. (2009) Tragic choices: Autonomy and emotional responses to medical decisions. *Journal of Consumer Research, 36*: 337–352. doi:10.1086/598969

Bowlby, J. (1953) *Child Care and the Growth of Love*. London: Penguin Books.

Bowlby, J. (1969) *Attachment and Loss: Vol. 1*. New York: Basic Books.

Boylan, J. and Dalrymple, J. (2011) Advocacy, social justice and children's rights. *Practice: Social Work in Action, 23* (1): 19–30.

Brandon, M., Belderson, P., Warren, C., Howe, D., Gardner, R., Dodsworth, J. and Black, J. (2008) *Analysing Child Deaths and Serious Injury Through Abuse and Neglect: What Can We Learn? (A Biennial Analysis of Serious Case Reviews, 2003–2005)*. London: Department for Children, Schools and Families.

Brandon, M., Sidebotham, P., Ellis, C., Baily, S. and Belderson, P. (2011) *Child and Family Practitioners' Understanding of Child Development: Lessons Learnt from a Small Sample of Serious Case Reviews*. London: Department for Education Publications.

Brandon, M., Sidebotham, P., Bailey, S., Belderson, P., Hawley, C., Ellis, C. and Megson, M. (2012) *New Learning from Serious Case Reviews: A Two-year Report for 2009–2011*. London: Department for Education.

Brandon, M., Glaser, D., Maguire, S., McCrory, E., Lushey, C. and Ward, H. (2014) *Missed Opportunities: Indicators of Neglect – What is Ignored, Why, and What Can be Done?* London: Department for Education.

Braye, S. and Preston-Shoot, M. (1995) *Empowering Practice in Social Care*. Buckingham: Open University Press.

British Association of Social Workers (2012, updated October 2014) *The Code of Ethics for Social Work – Statement of Principles*, London: BASW. Available at: http://cdn.basw.co.uk/upload/basw_95243-9.pdf (accessed on 22/9/2016)

Broadhurst, K., Wastell, D., White, S., Hall, C., Peckover, S., Thompson, K., Pithouse, A. and Davey, D. (2010a) Performing 'Initial Assessment': Identifying the latent conditions for error at the front-door of Local Authority Children's Services. *British Journal of Social Work, 40* (2): 352–370.

Broadhurst, K., White, S., Fish, F., Munro, E., Fletcher, K. and Lincoln, H. (2010b) *Ten Pitfalls and How to Avoid Them: What Research Tells Us*. London: NSPCC.

Brodie, I. (2010) *Improving Educational Outcomes for Looked After Children and Young People*. London: Centre for Excellence and Outcomes in Children and Young People's Services (C4EO).

Bronfenbrenner, U. (1979) *The Ecology of Human Development*. Cambridge Massachusetts: Harvard University Press.

Browne J., Hood A. and Joyce, R. (2013) *Child and Working-Age Poverty in Northern Ireland from 2010 to 2020, Appendix A*. London: Institute for Fiscal Studies.

Brown, R. and Ward, H. (2013) *Decision-making within a Child's Timeframe*. Loughborough: Childhood Wellbeing Research Centre.

Bruer, J.T. (1999) *The Myth of the First Three Years: A New Understanding of Early Brain Development and Lifelong Learning*. New York: Free Press.

Burghart, A. (2012) *A Better Start in Life: Long-term Approaches for the Most Vulnerable Children*. London: Policy Exchange.

Butler, G. (2015) *Observing Children and Families: Beyond the Surface*. Northwich: Critical Publishing Ltd.

Butler-Sloss, E. (1988) *Report of the Inquiry into Child Abuse in Cleveland 1987*. Presented to Parliament by the Secretary of State for Social Services by Command of Her Majesty: HM Stationery Office.

Bywaters, P. (2015) Inequalities in child welfare: Towards a new policy, research and action agenda. *British Journal of Social Work, 45* (1): 6–23.

CAFCASS (2008) *My Needs, Wishes and Feelings Guidance for Practitioners,* London: CAFCASS. Available at: www.cafcass.gov.uk/media/6616/Handbook%20for%20practitioners.pdf (accessed on 1/4/2016).

The Care Inquiry (2013) *Making Not Breaking: Building Relationships for Our Most Vulnerable Children.* Care Inquiry and Nuffield Trust. Available at: https://thecareinquiry. files.wordpress.com/2013/04/care-inquiry-full-report-april-2013.pdf (accessed on 25/4/2016).

Centre for Excellence and Outcomes (C4EO) (2010) *Grasping the Nettle: Early Intervention for Children, Families and Communities. A Practice Guide to the Challenges and Opportunities in Supporting Children, Families and Communities Through Early Intervention, Based on Effective Local, National and International Practice.* London: C4EO.

Centre of Excellence for Early Childhood Development. (2013) *Encyclopedia on Early Childhood Development.* Available at: www.child-encyclopedia.com/play (accessed on 22/3/2016).

Child Exploitation and Online Protection Centre (CEOP) (2011) *Out of Mind, Out of Sight: Breaking Down the Barriers to Understanding Child Sexual Exploitation, Executive Summary.* London: CEOP.

Child Poverty Action Group (June 2015) *Child Poverty Facts and Figures.* Available at: http://www.cpag.org.uk/child-poverty-facts-and-figures.

Children's Commissioner for Wales (2011) *Lost in Care.* Swansea: Children's Commissioner for Wales.

The Children's Society (2011) *4 in every 10 Disabled Children Living in Poverty.* Available at: www.childrenssociety.org.uk/4_in_10_reportfinal.pdf (accessed on 7/3/2016).

The Children's Society (2013) *A Good Childhood for Every Child? Child Poverty in the UK.* Available at: www.childrenssociety.org.uk/child_poverty_briefing_1.pdf (accessed on 7/3/2016).

The Children's Society (2014) *The Good Childhood Report.* London: The Children's Society. Available at: www.childrenssociety.org.uk/sites/default/files/The%20Good%20 Childhood%20Report%202014%20-%20FINAL_0.pdf (accessed on 7/3/2016).

Clark, A. and Moss, P. (2011) (2nd edition) *Listening to Young Children: The Mosaic Approach.* London: National Children's Bureau.

Cleaver, H. and Walker, S. (2004) *Assessing Children's Needs and Circumstances: The Impact of the Assessment Framework.* London: Jessica Kingsley.

Cleaver, H., Unell, I. and Aldgate, J., (2011, 2nd edition) *Children's Needs – Parenting Capacity: Parental Mental Illness, Learning Disability, Substance Misuse and Domestic Violence.* London: The Stationery Office.

Clifton J. (2014) *Children and Young People Giving Feedback on Services for Children in Need.* Principal Policy Advisor (Safeguarding) for the Office of the Children's Commissioner England. Available at: www.childrenscommissioner.gov.uk/sites/default/files/ publications/Feedback_on_services_for_children_and_young_people.pdf (accessed on 24/2/2016).

Cochran, N.H., Nordling, W.J. and Cochran, J.L. (2010) *Child-Centred Play Therapy: A Practical Guide to Developing Therapeutic Relationships with Children.* New Jersey: John Wiley and sons.

Cockburn, T. (2005) Children and the feminist ethic of care. *Childhood, 12* (1): 71–89.

Coleman, J.S. (1991) Prologue: Constructed social organisation, in P. Bourdieu and J.S. Coleman (eds.) *Social Theory for a Changing Society.* Oxford: Westview Press.

Coleman, J.C. (2011, 4th edition) *The Nature of Adolescence.* London: Routledge.

Coram Voice (2015) *Children and Young People's Views on Being in Care: A Literature Review.* London: Coram Voice and Bristol University.

Corder, K. et al (2015) Revising on the run or studying on the sofa: Prospective associations between physical activity, sedentary behaviour, and exam results in British adolescents. *International Journal of Behavioral Nutrition and Physical Activity.* Published online, September.

Cornock, M. (2010) Hannah Jones, consent and the child in action: A legal commentary. *Paediatric Nursing, 22* (2): 14–20.

Cossar, J., Brandon, M. and Jordan, P. (2011) *Don't Make Assumptions: Children's and Young People's Views of the Child Protection System and Messages for Change.* London: Office of the Children's Commissioner.

Cossar, J., Brandon, M., Bailey, S., Belderson, P., Biggart, L. and Sharpe, D. (2013) '*It Takes a Lot to Build Trust' Recognition and Telling: Developing Earlier Routes to Help for Children and Young People.* London: Children's Commissioner.

Cossar, J, Brandon M and Jordan P (2014) 'You've got to trust her and she's got to trust you': Children's views on participation in the child protection system. *Child and Family Social Work, 21* (1): 103–112.

The Council for Disabled Children, VIPER – Voice, Inclusion, Participation, Empowerment and Research. Available at: https://councilfordisabledchildren.org.uk/help-resources/resources/viper-report-what-we-found (accessed on 10/6/2016).

Coventry Local Safeguarding Children Board (2013) *Daniel Pelka Serious Case Review: Final Overview Report.* Coventry LSCB.

Crittenden, P.M. (2000) A dynamic-maturational exploration of the meaning of security and adaptation, in P.M. Crittenden and A.H. Claussen (eds.) *The Organization of Attachment Relationships: Maturation, Culture, and Context,* pp. 358–383. New York: Cambridge University Press.

Crompton, M. (2007) Individual work with children, in K. Wilson and A. James (eds) *The Child Protection Handbook: The Practitioners Guide to Safeguarding Children,* pp. 392–413. Oxford: Elsevier Limited.

Curran, T. (2010) Social work and disabled children's childhoods: A Foucauldian framework for practice transformation. *British Journal of Social Work, 40,* 806–825.

Cuthbert, C., Rayns, G. and Stanley, K. (2010) *Prevention and Protection for Vulnerable Babies.* London: NSPCC.

Cuthbert, C., Rayns, G. and Stanley, K. (2011) *All Babies Count: Prevention and Protection for Vulnerable Babies.* London: NSPCC.

Dahl, R.E. (2004) Adolescent brain development: A period of vulnerabilities and opportunities. *Annals of the New York Academy of Sciences, 1021* (1): 1–22.

Dalrymple, J. (2005) Constructions of child and youth advocacy: Emerging issues in advocacy practice. *Children & Society, 19* (1): 3–15.

Dalzell, R. and Chamberlain, C. (2006) *Communicating with children: A two-way process.* London: National Children's Bureau.

Dalzell, R. and Sawyer, E. (2016) *Putting Analysis into Child and Family Assessment: Undertaking Assessments of Need.* London: Jessica Kingsley Publishers.

Daniel, B., Wassell, S., Gilligan, R. and Howe, D. (2010) *Child Development for Child Care and Protection Workers*. London: Jessica Kingsley Publishers.

Davey, C. (2010) *Children's Participation in Decision-making: A Summary Report on Progress.* London: Office of Children's Commissioner and National Children's Bureau.

Davies, C. and Ward, H. (2012) *Safeguarding Children Across Services: Messages from Research*. London: Jessica Kingsley.

D'Cruz, H. and Stagnitti, K. (2008) Reconstructing child welfare through participatory and child-centred professional practice: A conceptual approach. *Child and Family Social Work, 13*: 156–165.

Dearden, C. and Becker, S. (2004) *Young Carers in the UK*. London: Carers UK and The Children's Society.

Department for Children, Schools and Families (2009) *Think Family Toolkit Improving Support for Families at Risk: Strategic Overview*. London: DCSF.

Department for Children, Schools and Families (DCSF) and Home Office (2009) *Safeguarding Children and Young People from Sexual Exploitation: Supplementary Guidance to Working Together to Safeguard Children*. London: Department for Children, Schools and Families (DCSF).

Department for Education and Skills (2003) *Every Child Matters*. London: Stationery Office.

Department for Education and Skills (2007) *Care Matters: Time for Change*. Norwich: The Stationery Office.

Department for Education (June 2011) *Positive for Youth: The Relationship Between Services for Young People and the Parents of Young People,* Discussion Paper. https://webcache. googleusercontent.com/search?q=cache:HdmHk_k7dk0J:https://www.gov.uk/ government/uploads/system/uploads/attachment_data/file/210374/the-role-of-parents-and-families-in-the-lives-of-young-people.doc+&cd=1&hl=en&ct=clnk&gl=uk] (accessed on 18/3/2016)

Department for Education (2013) *Improving Permanence for Looked After Children: Data Pack*. London: Department for Education. Available at: www.gov.uk/government/ uploads/system/uploads/attachment_data/file/264952/final_improving_ permanence_data_pack_2013_sept.pdf (accessed on 25/4/2016).

Department for Education (2014a) *Children in Care: Research Priorities and Questions.* London: Department for Education.

Department for Education (2014b) *Statistical First Release Outcomes for Children Looked After by Local Authorities in England as at 31 March 2014*. London: Department for Education. Available at: www.gov.uk/government/uploads/system/ uploads/attachment_data/file/384781/Outcomes_SFR49_2014_Text.pdf (accessed on 25/4/2016).

Department for Education (2014c) *Promoting the Education of Looked After Children Statutory Guidance for Local Authorities*. London: Department for Education.

Department for Education (2014d) *Knowledge and Skills for Child and Family Social Work.* London: HM Government.

Department for Education (2015a) *Children Looked After in England (Including Adoption and Care Leavers) Year Ending 31 March 2015. London: Department for Education.* Available at: www.gov.uk/government/uploads/system/uploads/attachment_data/ file/464756/SFR34_2015_Text.pdf (accessed on 25/4/2016).

Department for Education (2015b) *The Children Act 1989 Guidance and Regulations. Vol. 2: Care Planning, Placement and Case Review*. London: HM Government.

Department for Education (2015c) *SFR 41/2015: Characteristics of Children in Need: 2014 to 2015.* Available at: www.gov.uk/government/uploads/system/uploads/attachment_data/file/469737/SFR41-2015_Text.pdf (accessed on 14/4/2016).

Department for Education (2016a) *Children Looked After in England (Including Adoption and Care Leavers) Year Ending 31 March 2015.* London: Department for Education.

Department for Education (2016b) *Putting Children First: Delivering Our Vision for Excellent Children's Social Care.* London: Department for Education.

Department of Health (2000a) *The Framework for the Assessment of Children in Need and Their Families.* London: HM Government.

Department of Health (2000b) *Assessing Children in Need and Their Families: Practice Guidance.* London: HM Government.

Department of Health (2002) *National Standards for the Provision of Children's Advocacy Services.* London: HM Government.

Department for Work and Pensions (2013) *Households Below Average Income 2011/2012.* London: Stationery Office.

Devine, P. and Lloyd, K. (2012) Internet use and psychological well-being among 10-year-old and 11-year-old children. *Child Care in Practice, 18* (1): 5–22.

Dickens, M (2011) *Listening to Young Disabled Children.* London: National Children's Bureau.

Dillon, J., Greenop, D. and Hills, M. (2016) Participation in child protection: A small-scale qualitative study. *Qualitative Social Work, 15* (1): 70–85.

Dishion, T.J. (2016) Social influences on executive functions development in children and adolescents: Steps toward a social neuroscience of predictive adaptive responses. *Abnormal Child Psychology, 44* (1): 57–61.

Dixon, J (2008) Young people leaving care: Health, well-being and outcomes. *Child and Family Social Work, 13*: 207–217.

Dixon, J., Lee, J., Stein, M., Guhirwa, H., Bowley, S. and Catch 22 Peer Researchers (2015) *Corporate Parenting for Young People in Care: Making the Difference?* London: Catch 22.

Donaldson, M. (1986) *Children's Minds.* London: Harper Collins.

Donne, J. (2007) *Devotions Upon Emergent Occasions and Death's Duel, Literary Collection.* New York: Cosimo Classics.

Donnelly, C. (2010) Reflections of a Guardian Ad Litem on the participation of looked after children in public law proceedings. *Child Care in Practice, 16* (2): 181–193.

Doutre, G., Green, R. and Knight-Elliott, A. (2013) Listening to the voices of young carers using interpretative phenomenological analysis and a strengths-based perspective. *Educational & Child Psychology, 30* (4): 30–43.

Downie, A. (1999) Consent to medical treatment – Whose view of welfare? *Family Law Journal, 29.*

Duncalf, Z. (2010) *Adult Care Leavers Speak Out: The Views of 310 Care Leavers Aged 17–78.* Manchester: The Care Leavers' Association.

Eekelaar, J. (1994) The interests of the child and the child's wishes: The role of dynamic self-determinism, in P. Alston (ed.) *The Best Interests of the Child: Reconciling Culture and Human Rights.* Oxford: Clarendon Press.

Einav, S. and Robinson, E.J. (2012) When being right is not enough: Four year olds distinguish knowledgeable informants from merely accurate informants. *Psychological Science, 22* (10): 1250–1253.

Eldén, S. (2012) Inviting the messy: Drawing methods and 'children's voices'. *Childhood, 20* (1): 66–81.

Erikson, E.H. (1963, 2nd edition) *Childhood and Society.* New York: Norton.

Erikson, E.H. (1968) *Identity, Youth and Crisis.* New York: Norton.

Evans, J. and Fowler, R. (2008) *Family-Minded: Supporting Children in Families Affected by Mental Illness.* Barkingside: Barnardo's.

Family Justice Review (2011a) *Family Justice Review: Interim Report – March 2011.* London: Ministry of Justice.

Family Justice Review (2011b) *Family Justice Review: Final Report – November 2011.* London: Ministry of Justice. Available at: www.gov.uk/government/uploads/system/uploads/attachment_data/file/217343/family-justice-review-final-report.pdf (accessed on 30/3/2016).

Family Rights Group (2011) *Family Group Conferences in the Court Arena: Practice Guidance on the Use of Family Group Conferences for Children Who Are In, or Are On the Brink of, Care Proceedings.* London: Family Rights Group.

Family Rights Group (2016) *Family Group Conferences.* Available at: www.frg.org.uk/involving-families/family-group-conferences (accessed on 28/3/2016).

Farmer E. and Lutman E. (2014) Working effectively with neglected children and their families – what needs to change? *Child Abuse Review, 23*: 262–273.

Fattore, T. and Mason, J. (2005) *Children Taken Seriously.* London: Jessica Kingsley.

Fauth, R., Jelicic, H., Hart, D., Burton, S. and Shemmings, D. (2010) *Effective Practice to Protect Children Living in 'Highly Resistant' Families.* The Centre for Excellence and Outcomes in Children and Young People's Services (C4EO).

Fauth, R., Hart, D. and Payne, L. (2012) *Supporting Care Leavers' Successful Transition to Independent Living.* London: NCB Research Centre.

Featherstone, B. (2007) 'Letting them get away with it': Fathers, domestic violence and child protection. *Critical Social Policy, 27* (2): 181–202.

Featherstone, B., Rivett, M. and Scourfield, J.B. (2007) *Working with Men in Health and Social Care.* London: Sage Publications.

Featherstone, B. and Morris, K. (2012) The feminist ethic of care, in M. Gray, J. Midgley and S. Webb (eds) *The SAGE Handbook of Social Work.* London: Sage Publications.

Featherstone, B., White, S. and Morris, K. (2014) *Re-imagining Child Protection: Towards Humane Social Work with Families.* Bristol: The Policy Press.

Featherstone, B., Gupta, A., Morris, K. and Warner, J. (2016) Let's stop feeding the risk monster: Towards a social model of child protection. *Families, Relationships and Societies, 10* (10): 1–16. http://dx.doi.org/10.1332/204674316X14552878034622.

Fergus, S. and Zimmerman, M.A. (2005) Adolescent resilience. *Annual Review of Public Health, 26*: 399–419.

Ferguson, K.M. (2006) Social capital and children's well-being. *International Journal of Social Welfare, 15*: 2–18.

Ferguson, H. (2011) *Child Protection Practice.* Basingstoke: Palgrave Macmillan.

Ferguson, H. (2014) What social workers do in performing child protection work: Evidence from research into face-to-face practice. *Child and Family Social Work.* doi:10.1111/cfs.12142.

Field, F. (2010) *The Foundation Years: Preventing Poor Children Becoming Poor Adults.* London: The Stationery Office.

Folgheraiter, F. (2004) *Relational Social Work.* London: Jessica Kingsley.

Fook, J. and Gardner, F. (2010) *Practising Critical Reflection: A Resource Handbook.* Maidenhead: McGraw Hill/Open University Press.

Forrester, D. and Harwin, J. (2011) *Parents Who Misuse Drugs and Alcohol: Effective Interventions in Social Work and Child Protection.* London: Wiley-Blackwell.

Fosco, G.M., Caruthers, A.S. and Dishion, T.J. (2012) A six-year predictive test of adolescent family relationship quality and effortful control pathways to emerging adult social and emotional health. *Journal of Family Psychology, 26*: 565–575.

Foucault, M. (1980) *Power and Knowledge.* London: Bedminster.

Foucault, M. (1983) The subject and power, in H. Dreyfus and P. Rabinow (eds) (2nd edition) *Beyond Structuralism and Hermeneutics,* pp. 208–226. Chicago: The University of Chicago Press.

Franklin, A. and Knight, A. (2011) *Someone on Our Side: Advocacy for Disabled Children and Young People.* London: The Children's Society.

Franklin, A. and Sloper, P. (2009) Supporting the participation of disabled children and young people in decision-making. *Children and Society, 23*: 3–15.

Freeman, M.D.A. (1983) *The Rights and Wrongs of Children.* London: Frances Pinter.

Frost, N., Abram, F. and Burgess, H. (2014a) Family group conferences: Context, process and ways forward. *Child and Family Social Work, 19*: 480–490.

Frost, N., Abram, F. and Burgess, H. (2014b) Family group conferences: Evidence, outcomes and future research. *Child and Family Social Work, 19*: 501–507.

Frost, N. and Dolan, P. (2012) The theoretical foundations of family support work, in M. Davies (ed.) *Social Work with Children and Families,* pp. 40–52. Basingstoke: Palgrave.

Frost, N., Abbott, S. and Race, T. (2015) *Family Support.* Cambridge: Polity Press.

Gallacher, L.A. and Gallagher, M. (2008) Methodological immaturity in childhood research? Thinking through participatory methods. *Childhood, 15* (4): 499–516.

Galvan, A. (2010) Adolescent development of the reward system. *Frontiers in Human Neuroscience, 4* (6): 1–9.

Gardner, M. and Steinberg, L. (2005) Peer influence on risk taking, risk preference, and risky decision making in adolescence and adulthood: An experimental study. *Developmental Psychology,* 41, 625–635.

Ghaffar, W., Manby, M. and Race, T. (2012) Exploring the experiences of parents and carers whose children have been subject to child protection plans. *British Journal of Social Work, 42* (5): 887–905.

Ghate, D. and Hazel, N. (2002) *Parenting in Poor Environments: Stress, Support and Coping.* London: Jessica Kingsley Publishers.

Gibb, J., Rix, K., Wallace, E., Fitzsimons, E. and Mostafa, T. (2016) *Poverty and Children's Personal and Social Relationships.* London: National Children's Bureau.

Gillick v West Norfolk and Wisbech Area Health Authority (1985) UKHL7. British and Irish Legal Information Institute.

Gilligan, C. (1998) Hearing the difference: Theorising connection, in M. Rogers (ed.) *Contemporary Feminist Theory,* pp. 341–346. Boston, MA: McGraw-Hill.

Gilligan, P. and Manby, M. (2008) The Common Assessment framework: Does the reality match the rhetoric? *Child and Family Social Work, 13* (2): 177–187.

Gilligan, R. (1997) Beyond permanence? The importance of resilience in child placement practice and planning. *Adoption and Fostering,* 21, 12–20.

Gilligan, R. (2000) Adversity, resilience and young people: The protective value of positive school and spare time experiences, *Children and Society*, *14* (1): 37–47.

Gilligan, R. (2010) Promoting positive outcomes for children in need, in J. Horwath (ed.) *The Child's World* (2nd edition). London: Jessica Kingsley Publishers.

Godar, R. (2015) The hallmarks of effective participation: Evidencing the voice of the child, in M. Ivory (ed.) *Voice of the Child: Meaningful Engagement With Children and Young People.* Dartington: Research in Practice.

Goff, S. (2012) The participation of fathers in child protection conferences: A practitioner's perspective. *Child Abuse Review*, *21* (4): 275–284.

Golding, K.S. (2014) *Using Stories to Build Bridges with Traumatized Children.* London: Jessica Kingsley Publishers.

Gray, M. (2009) Moral sources and emergent ethical theories in social work, *British Journal of Social Work*, *40* (6): 1794–1811.

The Guardian, 'Right-to-die teenager Hannah Jones changes mind about heart transplant', *Guardian*, 21 July 2009. http://www.guardian.co.uk/uk/2009/jul/21/hannah-jones-heart-transplant (accessed on 22/6/2015).

The Guardian, '*Teenager who won right to die'. Guardian*, 11 November 2008. http://www.theguardian.com/society/2008/nov/11/child-protection-health-hannah-jones (accessed on 22/6/2015).

The *Guardian*, 'What I'm really thinking: The GCSE student', *Guardian,* 28 March 2015.

Guerney, L. (2000) Filial therapy into the 21st century. *International Journal of Play Therapy*, *9* (2): 1.

Habermas, J. (1984) *The Theory of Communicative Action, Vol. 1.* Boston: Beacon Press.

Handley, G. and Doyle, C. (2014) Ascertaining the wishes and feelings of young children: Social workers perspectives on skills and training. *Child and Family Social Work*, *19*: 443–454.

Harber, A. and Oakley, M. (2012) *Fostering Aspirations: Reforming the Foster Care System in England and Wales.* London: Policy Exchange.

Haringey Local Safeguarding Children Board (2009) *Serious Case Review: Baby Peter: Executive Summary.* Haringey: Local Safeguarding Children Board.

Harker, L., Jütte, S., Murphy, T., Bentley, H., Miller, P. and Fitch, K. (2014) *How Safe Are Our Children?* London: NSPCC.

Hart, R. (1992) *Children's Participation: From Tokenism to Citizenship.* Florence: UNICEF International Child Development Centre.

Heyman, A. and Heyman, B. (2013) 'The sooner you can change their life course the better': The time-framing of risks in relationship to being a young carer. *Health, Risk and Society*, *15* (6–7): 561–579.

Hicks, L. and Stein, M. (2010) *Neglect Matters: A Multi-Agency Guide for Professionals Working Together on Behalf of Teenagers.* London: Department for Children, Schools and Families.

Hicks, L. and Stein, M. (2015) Understanding and working with adolescent neglect: Perspectives from research, young people and professionals. *Child and Family Social Work*, *22*: 223–233.

HM Government (2013) *Care Leaver Strategy: A Cross-Departmental Strategy for Young People Leaving Care.* London: HM Government.

HM Government (2015) *Working Together to Safeguard Children – A Guide to Inter-Agency Working to Safeguard and Promote the Welfare of Children.* London: Stationery Office.

Holland, S., Renold, E., Ross, N.J. and Hillman, A. (2010) Power, agency and participatory agendas: A critical exploration of young people's engagement in participative qualitative research. *Childhood, 17* (3): 360–375.

Holt, J. (1975) *Escape from Childhood,* Penguin, Harmondsworth.

Home Office (2013) *Information for Local Areas on the Change to the Definition of Domestic Violence and Abuse.* London: Home Office.

Horwath, J. (2007) *Child Neglect: Identification and Assessment.* Basingstoke: Palgrave Macmillan.

Horwath, J. and Tarr, S. (2015) Child visibility in cases of chronic neglect: Implications for social work practice. *British Journal of Social Work, 45*: 1379–1394.

Hounsell, D. (2013) *Hidden from View: The experiences of young carers in England.* London: The Children's Society.

Howe, D. (1992) Child abuse and the bureaucratisation of social work. *The Sociological Review, 40* (3): 491–508.

Howe, D. (1997) Psychosocial and relationship-based theories for child and family social work. *Child and Family Social Work, 2*: 161–169.

Howe, D. (2005) *Child Abuse and Neglect: Attachment, Development and Intervention.* Basingstoke: Palgrave Macmillan.

Howe, D. (2010) Attachment: implications for assessing children's needs and parenting capacity, in J. Horwath (ed.), *The Child's World* (2nd edition). London: Jessica Kingsley Publishers.

Hughes, D. (2007) *Attachment Focused Family Therapy.* London: WW Norton and Company.

International Federation of Social Workers (2014) *Global Definition of Social Work.* http://ifsw.org/policies/definition-of-social-work/ (accessed on 22/6/2015).

Institute of Public Care (June 2012) *Early Intervention and Prevention with Children and Families: Getting the Most from the Team around the Family Systems.* Oxford: Institute of Public Care.

Ivory, M. (ed.) (2015) *Voice of the Child: Meaningful Engagement with Children and Young People.* Dartington: Research in Practice.

Jack, G. and Donnellan, H. (2013) *Social Work with Children.* Basingstoke: Palgrave.

Jagger, A.M. (1992) Feminist ethics, in L. Becker and C. Becker (eds.) *Encyclopaedia of Ethics,* pp. 363–364. New York: Garland Press.

James, A., Jenks, C. and Prout, A. (1998) *Theorising Childhood.* Cambridge: Polity.

James, A. and James, A. (2012, 2nd edition) *Key Concepts in Childhood Studies.* London: Sage.

James, A. and Prout, A. (1997) A new paradigm for the sociology of childhood? Provenance, promise and problems. In *Constructing and Reconstructing Childhood: Contemporary Issues in the Sociological Study of Childhood,* 7–33.

Jay, A. (2014) *Independent Inquiry into Child Sexual Exploitation in Rotherham, 1997 to 2013.* Rotherham: Rotherham Metropolitan Borough Council.

Jelicic, H., Gibb, J., La Valle, I. and Payne, P. (2013) *Involved by Right The Voice of the Child in the Child Protection Conferences.* London: National Children's Bureau.

Jenkins, M. and Cook, J. (2012) How parental substance misuse affects children's wellbeing. *Primary Health Care, 22* (5): 22–24.

Jobe, A. and Gorin, S. (2013) 'If kids don't feel safe they don't do anything': Young people's views on seeking and receiving help from Children's Social Care Services in England. *Child and Family Social Work, 18* (4): *429–438.*

Jones, D.P.H. (2003) *Communicating with Vulnerable Children. A Guide for Practitioners.* London: Gaskell.

Jones, D. and Florek, A. (2015) *Child Sexual Exploitation: A study of International Comparisons Desk: Review for the Department for Education.* Office for public management and Virtual Staff College. http://www.virtualstaffcollege.co.uk/wp-content/uploads/CSE_main_final_publish_1.0.pdf (accessed on 26/5/2016).

Jones, P. and Walker, G. (eds.) (2011) *Children's Rights in Practice.* London: Sage.

Kirby, P., Lanyon, C., Cronin, K. and Sinclair, R. (2003) *Building a Culture of Participation: Involving Children and Young People in Policy, Service Planning, Delivery and Evaluation.* London: Department for Education and Skills.

Kroll, B. (1995) Working with children, in Kaganas, F., King, M. and Piper, C. (eds.) *Legislating for Harmony: Partnership Under the Children Act 1989.* London: Jessica Kingsley Press.

Laming, H. (2003) *The Victoria Climbie Inquiry.* London: Stationery Office.

Laming, H. (2009) *The Protection of Children in England: A Progress Report.* London: Stationery Office.

Lefevre, M. (2010) *Communicating with Children and Young People.* Bristol: The Policy Press.

Lefevre, M. (2015) Becoming effective communicators with children: Developing practitioner capability through social work education. *British Journal of Social Work, 45* (1): 204–224.

Lilley, C. and Ball, R. (2013) *Younger children and social networking sites: A blind spot.* London: NSPCC. Available at: www.nspcc.org.uk/blindspot.

Lindsay, G., Strand, S., Cullen, M., Cullen, M., Band, S., Davis, H., Conlon, G., Barlow, J. and Evans, R. (2010) *Parenting Early Intervention Programme Evaluation.* London: Department for Education.

Lister, R. (2013) 'Power, not Pity': Poverty and human rights. *Ethics and Social Welfare, 7* (2): 109–123.

Little, M. and Sodha, S. (2012) *Prevention and Early Intervention in Children's Services.* Dartington: The Social Research Unit.

Livingstone, S., Olafsson, K. and Staksrud, E. (2011) Social networking, age and privacy: E U Kids Online: www.eukidsonline.net.

Llewellyn, A., Agu, L. and Mercer, D. (2015, 2nd edition) *Sociology for Social Workers.* Cambridge: Polity Press.

Local Government Association (2013) *Must Know 5: What You Need to Know About Early Help,* London: Local Government Association.

Lolichen, P.J. (2009) Rights-based participation – Children as research protagonists and partners in mainstream governance, in J. Fiedler and C. Posch (eds.) *Yes They Can! Children Researching Their Lives,* pp. 135–143. Austria: Schneider Verlag,.

Longfield, A. (August, 2015) *Internet Taskforce Press Statement.* Office of the Children's Commissioner for England.

MacDonald, A. (2008) The voice of the child: Still a faint cry. *Family Law, 38:* 648–653.

McElvaney, R. and Culhane, M. (2015) A retrospective analysis of children's assessment reports: What helps children tell? *Child Abuse Review.* doi:10.1002/car.2390.

Macionis, J. and Plummer, K. (2012, 5th edition) *Sociology: A Global Introduction.* Harlow: Prentice Hall.

Maclean, S. and Harrison, R. (2015, 3rd edition) *Theory and Practice: A Straightforward Guide for Social Work Students.* Lichfield: Kirwin Maclean.

McLeod, S.A. (2015) Jean Piaget. Retrieved from http://www.simplypsychology.org/piaget.html (accessed on 22/11/2015).

Main, G. and Pople, L. (2011) *Missing Out: A Child-Centred Analysis of Material Deprivation and Subjective Well-Being.* London: The Children's Society. Available at: http://www.childrenssociety.org.uk/missing_out.pdf.

Main, M. and Solomon, J. (1990) Procedures for identifying infants as disorganized/disoriented during the Ainsworth Strange Situation, in M.T. Greenberg, D. Cicchetti and E.M. Cummings (eds.) *Attachment in the Preschool Years,* pp. 121–160. Chicago, University of Chicago Press.

Mainstone, F. (2014) *Mastering Whole Family Assessment in Social Work: Balancing the Needs of Children, Adults and Their Families.* London: Jessica Kingsley Publishers.

Marchant, R. (2008) Working with disabled children who live away from home some or all of the time, in B. Luckock and M. Lefevre (eds.) *Direct Work: Social Work with Children and Young People in Care.* pp. 151–168. London: BAAF.

Martellozzo, E., Monaghan, A., Adler, J.R., Davidson, J., Leyva, R. and Horvath, M.A. (2016) *'I Wasn't Sure It Was Normal to Watch It.' A Quantitative and Qualitative Examination of the Impact of Online Pornography on the Values, Attitudes, Beliefs and Behaviours of Children and Young People.* London: NSPCC.

Masten, A.S. and Coatsworth, J.D. (1998) The development of competence in favorable and unfavorable environments. *American Psychologist, 53* (2): 205–220.

Mayall, B. (1994) Children in action at home and school, in B. Mayall (ed.) *Children's Childhoods: Observed and Experienced,* pp. 114–127. London: Falmer Press.

McMahon, L. (2012, 2nd edition) *The Handbook of Play Therapy and Therapeutic Play.* Hove: Routledge.

Mental Health Foundation (2015) *Fundamental Facts About Mental Health.* Available at: www.mentalhealth.org.uk/sites/default/files/fundamental-facts-15.pdf (accessed on 27/6/2016).

Milner, J., Myers, S. and O'Byrne, P. (2015) *Assessment in Social Work.* London: Palgrave Macmillan.

Mnookin, R. (1983) The best interests syndrome and the allocation of power in child care, in H. Geach and E. Szwed (eds.) *Providing Civil Justice for Children.* London: Edward Arnold.

Morgan, R. (2006) *About Social Workers: A Children's Views Report.* Newcastle-upon-Tyne: Commission for Social Care Inspection.

Morgan, R (2009) *Keeping in Touch*: *A Report of Children's Experience by the Children's Rights Director for England.* London: OFSTED. Available at: http://dera.ioe.ac.uk/10952/1/Keeping%20in%20touch.pdf (accessed on 6/6/2016).

Morris, K., Hughes, N., Clarke, H., Tew, J., Mason, P., Galvani, S., Lewis, A. and Loveless, L. (2008) *Think Family: A Literature Review of Whole Family Approaches.* London: Cabinet Office, Social Exclusion Task Force.

Morris, K. and Connelly, M. (2010) Family decision making in child welfare: Challenges in developing a knowledge base for practice. *Child Abuse Review, 21* (1): 41–52.

Morrison, T. and Wonnacott, J. (2010) *Supervision: Now or Never. Reclaiming Reflective Supervision in Social Work.* London: Local Government Association.

Munro, E., Lushey, C., Ward, H., Soper, J., McDermid, S., Holmes, L., Beckhelling, J. and Perren, K. (2010) *Evaluation of the Right2BCared4 Pilots: Final Report*. London: Department for Education.

Munro, E. (2010) *The Munro Review of Child Protection – Part One: A Systems Analysis*. London: Department for Education.

Munro, E. (2011) *The Munro Review of Child Protection: Final Report. A Child-Centred System*. London: The Stationery Office.

National Adoption Leadership Board (2014) *Impact of Court Judgments on Adoption: What the Judgments Do and Do Not Say*. London: National Adoption Leadership Board.

National Children's Bureau (NCB) (2010) *Principles for Engaging with Families: A Framework for Local Authorities and National Organisations to Evaluate and Improve Engagement with Families*. London: NCB.

National Children's Bureau (NCB) (2015) *Research Summary: From Care to Independence*. London: NCB Research Centre.

The National Institute of Adult Continuing Education (NIACE) (2013) *Voices of Care Leavers: Stories of Young Adult Care Leavers' Experiences*. London: NIACE.

Ney, T., Stolz, J. and Maloney, M. (2011) Voice, power and discourse: Experiences of participants in family group conferences in the context of child protection. *Journal of Social Work*, 13 (2): 184–202.

NICE (Updated May 2015) *Looked-After Children and Young People. NICE Public Health Guidance 28*. Manchester: NICE.

Nicolson, P. (2014) *A Critical Approach to Human Growth and Development*. Basingstoke: Palgrave Macmillan.

Norfolk Safeguarding Children's Board (2015) *Serious Case Review: Child P.* Norfolk: Local Safeguarding Children's Board.

NSPCC (2009a) *Child Protection Fact Sheet: The Definitions and Signs of Child Abuse*. London: NSPCC.

NSPCC (2009b) *Family Group Conferences in Child Protection. A NSPCC factsheet*. Available at: www.nspcc.org.uk/globalassets/documents/information-service/factsheet-family-group-conferences-child-protection.pdf (accessed on 28/3/2016).

NSPCC (2013) *Child Sexual Abuse: A NSPCC Research Briefing*. London: NSPCC.

NSPCC (2014) *CORE – INFO: Head and Spinal Injuries in Children*. London: NSPCC.

NSPCC (October 2014) *"We Have the Right to Be Safe". Protecting Disabled Children from Abuse*. www.nspcc.org.uk/globalassets/documents/research-reports/right-safe-disabled-children-abuse-report.pdf (accessed on 10/3/2015).

NSPCC (February 2014) *Assessing Children and Families*: A NSPCC factsheet www.nspcc.org.uk/globalassets/documents/information-service/factsheet-assessing-children-families.pdf (accessed on 10/3/2015).

NSPCC (2015a) *Child Protection Register Statistics*. Available at: www.nspcc.org.uk/preventing-abuse/child-abuse-and-neglect/physical-abuse/physical-abuse-facts-statistics/ (accessed on 15/5/2016).

NSPCC (2015b) *Spotlight on Preventing Child Neglect: An Overview of Learning from NSPCC Services and Research*. London: NSPCC.

Oaklander, V. (1988) *Windows to our Children: A Gestalt Therapy Approach to Children and Adolescents*. New York: Center for Gestalt Development.

Oaklander, V. (2006) *Hidden Treasure: A Map to the Child's Inner Self*. London: Karnac Books.

O'Connor, L., Forrester, D., Holland, S. and Williams, A. (2014) Perspectives on children's experiences in families with parental substance misuse and child protection interventions. *Children and Youth Services Review, 38*: 66–74.

O'Reilly, L. and Dolan, P. (2016) The voice of the child in social work assessments: Age-appropriate communication with children. *British Journal of Social Work, 46*: 1191–1207.

Office of the Children's Commissioner (2010) *Family Perspectives on Safeguarding and on Relationships with Children's Services.* London: Office of the Children's Commissioner.

Office for National Statistics (2014) *Statistical Bulletin: Families and Households.* Available at: www.ons.gov.uk/ons/rel/family-demography/families-and-households/2014/families-and-households-in-the-uk--2014.html (accessed on 25/3/2016).

Ofsted (2009) *Supporting Young Carers: Identifying, Assessing and Meeting the Needs of Young Carers and Their Families.* Manchester: Ofsted.

Ofsted (2010) *Children's Messages on Care 2010: A Report by the Children's Rights Director for England.* London: OFSTED.

Ofsted (2011a) *Ages of Concern: Learning Lessons from Serious Case Reviews. A Thematic Report of Ofsted's Evaluation of Serious Case Reviews from 1 April 2007 to 31 March 2011.* Manchester: Ofsted.

Ofsted (2011b) *Messages for Munro: A Report of Children's Views Collected for Professor Eileen Munro by the Children's Rights Director for England.* Manchester: Ofsted.

Ofsted (2011c) *The Voice of the Child: Learning Lessons from Serious Case Reviews.* Manchester: Ofsted.

Ofsted (2012) *The Impact of Virtual Schools on the Progress of Looked After Children.* London: Ofsted.

Ofsted (2014) *In The Child's Time: Professional Responses to Neglect.* Manchester: Ofsted.

Ofsted (2015a) *Early Help: Whose Responsibility.* Manchester: Ofsted.

Ofsted (2015b) *Framework and Evaluation Schedule for the Inspections of Services for Children in Need of Help and Protection, Children Looked After and Care Leavers and Reviews of LSCBs.* Manchester: Ofsted.

Oliver, C.M. and Dalrymple, J. (2008) *Developing Advocacy for Children and Young People: Current Issues in Research, Policy and Practice.* London: Jessica Kingsley Publishers.

O'Neill, K. (2008) *Getting it Right for Children: A Practitioners Guide to Children's Rights.* London: Save the Children UK.

Parsons, T. and Bales, R.F. (2002, 5th edition) *Family, Socialization and Interaction Process.* London: Routledge.

Parton, N. (1998) Risk, advanced liberalism and child welfare: The need to rediscover uncertainty and ambiguity. *British Journal of Social Work, 28* (1): 5–27.

Parton, N. and O'Byrne, P. (2000) What do we mean by constructive social work? *Critical Social Work, 1* (2).

Parton, N. (2006) *Safeguarding Childhood.* Basingstoke: Palgrave Macmillan.

Pearce, J., Masson, J. and Bader, K. (2011) *Just Following Instructions? The Representation of Parents in Care Proceedings.* Bristol: Economic and Social Research Council. Available at: www.bristol.ac.uk/medialibrary/sites/law/migrated/documents/justfollowinginstructions. pdf (accessed on 30/3/2016).

Percy-Smith, B. (2006) From consultation to social learning in community participation with young people. *Children, Youth and Environments, 16* (2): 153–179.

Perry, B.D. (2002) Childhood experience and the expression of genetic potential: What childhood neglect tells us about nature and nurture. *Brain and Mind, 3,* 79–100.

Piaget, J. (1936) *Origins of Intelligence in the Child.* London: Routledge & Kegan Paul.

Piaget, J. (1957) *Construction of Reality in the Child.* London: Routledge & Kegan Paul.

Platt, D. (2008) Care or Control? The effects of investigation and initial assessments on the social worker-parent relationship. *Journal of Social Work Practice, 22* (3): 301–315.

Prensky, M. (2001) Digital natives, digital immigrants. *On the Horizon, 9* (5): 1–6.

Putnam, R.D. (2000) *Bowling Alone.* New York. NY: Simon and Schuster.

Qvortrup, J., Bardy, M., Sgritta, G. and Wintersberger, H. (eds.) (1994) *Childhood Matters: Social Theory, Practice and Politics.* Aldershot: Avebury.

Radford, J. (2010) *Serious case review under chapter viii 'working together to safeguard children' in respect of the death of a child, case number 14.* Birmingham Local Safeguarding Children's Board.

Radford, L., Aitken, R., Miller, P., Ellis, J., Roberts, J. and Firkic, A. (2011a) *Meeting the Needs of Children Living with Domestic Violence in London.* London: Refuge/ NSPCC.

Radford, L., Corral, S., Bradley, C., Fisher, H., Bassett, C., Howat, N. and Collishaw, S. (2011b) *Child Abuse and Neglect in the UK Today.* London: NSPCC.

Ramey, C.T. and Ramey, S.L. (2004) Early learning and school readiness. *Merrill-Palmer Quarterly, 50* (4): 471–491.

Raven, B.H. (1993) The bases of power: Origins and recent developments. *Journal of Social Issues, 49* (4): 227–251.

Reed, H. (2012) *In the Eye of the Storm: Britain's Forgotten Children and Families.* London: Landman Economics.

Rees, G., Gorin, S., Jobe, A., Stein, M., Medforth, R. and Goswami, H. (2010) *Safeguarding Young People: Responding to Young People Aged 11 to 17 Who Are Maltreated.* London: The Children's Society.

Ridge, T. (2002) *Childhood Poverty and Social Exclusion: From a Child's Perspective.* Bristol: Policy Press.

Ridge, T. (2009) *Living with Poverty: A Review of the Literature on Children's and Families' Experiences of Poverty.* London: Department for Work and Pensions.

Ridley, J., Larkins, C., Farrelly, N., Hussein, S., Austerberry, H., Manthorpe, J. and Stanley, N. (2013) Investing in the relationship: Practitioners' relationships with looked after children and care leavers in social work practices. *Child and Family Social Work,* doi:10.1111/cfs.12109.

Roche, J. (1995) Children's rights: In the name of the child. *Journal of Social Welfare and Family Law, 17* (3): 281–300.

Rogers, C. (1951) *Client-centred Therapy.* London: Constable.

Rogoff, B. (1990) *Apprenticeship in Thinking: Cognitive Development in Social Context.* New York: Oxford University Press.

Rose, R, and Philpot, T (2005) *The Child's Own Story: Life Story Work with Traumatised Children.* London: Jessica Kingsley Publishers.

Ruch, G. (2005) Relationship-based practice and reflective practice: Holistic approaches to contemporary child care social work, *Child and Family Social Work, 10:* 111–123.

Ruch, G., Turney, D. and Ward, A. (2010) *Relationship Based Social Work: Getting to the Heart of Practice.* London: Jessica Kingsley.

Ruch, G. (2014) 'Helping children is a human process': Researching the challenges social workers face in communicating with children. *British Journal of Social Work, 44*: 2145–2162.

Ruggeri, A., Gummerum, M. and Hanoch, Y. (2014) Braving difficult choices alone: Children's and adolescents' medical decision making. *Public Library of Science, 9* (8): 1–7.

Rutter, M. (1972) *Maternal Deprivation Reassessed.* Oxford: Penguin.

Rutter, M. (1979) Protective factors in children's responses to stress and disadvantage, in M.W. Kent and J.E. Rolf (eds.) *Primary Prevention of Psychopathology: Vol. 3. Social Competence in Children,* pp. 49–74. New England: University Press.

Rutter, M. (2002) Nature, nurture, and development: From evangelism through science toward policy and practice. *Child Development, 73* (1): 1–21.

Rutter, M. (2007) Resilience, competence and coping. *Child Abuse and Neglect, 31* (3): 205–209.

Ryan, M. (2012) *How to Make Relationships Matter for Looked After Young People. A handbook.* London: National Children's Bureau.

Saarni, C. (1984) An observational study of children's attempts to monitor their expressive behavior. *Child Development, 55*: 1504–1513.

Safelives (2014/2015) *Key Statistics About Domestic Abuse in England and Wales.* Available at: http://safelives.org.uk/policy-evidence/about-domestic-abuse (accessed on 27/6/2016).

Saltiel, D. (2013) Understanding complexity in families' lives: The usefulness of 'family practices' as an aid to decision-making. *Child and Family Social Work, 18*: 15–24.

Sanders, R. and Mace, S. (2006) Agency policy and the participation of children and young people in the child protection process. *Child Abuse Review, 15*: 89–109.

Save the Children (2012) *Child Poverty in 2012: It Shouldn't Happen Here.* London: Save the Children.

Schofield, G., Beek, M., Ward, E. and Sellick, C. (2011) *Care Planning for Permanence in Foster Care.* Norwich: University of East Anglia.

Scotland's Commissioner for Children and Young People (2008) *Sweet 16? The Age of Leaving Care in Scotland.* Edinburgh: Scotland's Commissioner for Children and Young People.

Scourfield, J.B. (2003) *Gender and Child Protection.* Basingstoke: Palgrave Macmillan.

Seden, J. (2002) Underpinning theories for the assessment of children's needs, in H. Ward and W. Rose (eds.) *Approaches to Needs Assessment in Children's Services.* London: Jessica Kingsley Publishers.

Shemmings, D. (2000) Professionals' attitudes to children's participation in decision-making: Dichotomous accounts and doctrinal contests. *Child and Family Social Work, 5*: 235–243.

Shemmings, D. (2011) in Research in Practice (2014) Attachment Theory and Research, topic 2, Fostering and Adoption. Available at: http://fosteringandadoption.rip.org.uk/topics/attachment-theory-research/ Accessed 10/07/2016.

Sheridan, M.D. (1997) (revised and updated edition) *From Birth to Five Years: Children's Developmental Progress.* London: Routledge.

Shier, H. (2001) Pathways to participation: Openings, opportunities and obligations. *Children and Society, 15*: 107–117.

Sidebotham, P., Brandon, M., Bailey, S., Belderson, P., Dodsworth, J., Garstang, J., Harrison, E., Retzer, A. and Sorensen, P. (2016) *Pathways to Harm, Pathways to Protection: A Triennial Analysis of Serious Case Reviews from 2011 to 2014.* London: Department for Education.

Sinclair, I., Baker, C., Lee, J. and Gibbs, I. (2007) *The Pursuit of Permanence: A Study of the English Child Care System.* London: Jessica Kingsley Publishers.

Skinner, K. (2010) Supervision, leadership and management, in Z. van Zwanenberg (ed.) *Leadership in Social Care.* London: Jessica Kingsley.

Sloper, P, Beresford, B and Rabiee, P (2009) Every child matters outcomes: What do they mean for disabled children and young people? *Children and Society, 23*: 265–278.

Smidt, S. (2013, 2nd edition) *The Developing Child in the 21st Century: A Global Perspective on Child Development.* London: Routledge.

Smith, R. (2008) *Social Work and Power.* Basingstoke: Palgrave Macmillan.

Smith R. (2010) Social work, risk and power. *Sociological Research Online, 15* (1). Available at: http://www.socresonline.org.uk/15/1/4.html doi:10.5153/sro.2101.

Smyth, C., Blaxland, M. and Cass, B. (2011) 'So that's how I found out I was a young carer and that I actually had been a carer most of my life'. Identifying and supporting hidden young carers. *Journal of Youth Studies, 14* (2): 145–160.

Social Work Inspection Agency Scotland (2010) *Practice Guide: Chronologies.* Available at: http://www.gov.scot/resource/doc/299703/0093436.pdf (accessed on 27/6/2016).

Spear, L. (2009) *The Behavioral Neuroscience of Adolescence.* New York, NY: Norton.

Spyrou, S. (2011) The limits of children's voices: From authenticity to critical, reflexive representation. *Childhood, 18* (2): 151–165.

Stanley, N., Miller, P. and Richardson, H. (2010) *Children and Families Experiencing Domestic Violence: Police and Children's Social Services' Responses.* London: NSPCC.

Stanley, N. (2011) *Children Experiencing Domestic Violence: A Research Review.* Dartington: Research in Practice.

Stanley, N., Miller, P. and Richardson, H. (2012) Engaging with children's and parents' perspectives on domestic violence. *Child and Family Social Work, 17* (2): 192–201.

Stanley, N. and Humphreys, C (eds.) (2015) *Domestic Violence and Protecting Children: New Thinking and Approaches.* London: Jessica Kingsley Publishers.

Stein, M. (2005) *Resilience and Young People Leaving Care: Overcoming the Odds.* York: Joseph Rowntree Foundation.

Stein, M., Rhys, G., Hicks, L. and Gorin, S. (2009) *Neglected Adolescents: Literature Review.* London: Department for Children, Schools and Families.

Steinberg, L. (2007) Risk taking in adolescence: New perspectives from brain and behavioral science. *Current Directions in Psychological Science, 16*: 55–59.

Swanston, J., Bowyer, L. and Vetere A. (2014) Towards a richer understanding of school-age children's experiences of domestic violence: The voices of children and their mothers. *Clinical Child Psychology and Psychiatry, 19* (2): 184–201.

Tait, A. and Wosu, H. (2012) *Direct Work with Vulnerable Children: Playful Activities and Strategies for Communication.* London: Jessica Kingsley Publishers.

The Scottish Government (June 2012) *A Guide to Getting It Right for Every Child.* Scottish Government.

The Social Care Institute for Excellence. *Gathering Information – Creative Ways.* http://www.scie.org.uk/assets/elearning/communicationskills/cs04/resource/html/object4/object4_7.htm#slide01 (accessed on 10/6/2016).

Thomas, J. and Holland, S. (2010) Representing children's identities in core assessments. *British Journal of Social Work, 40* (8): 2617–2633.

Thomas, N. and O'Kane, C. (1998) When children's wishes and feelings clash with their best interests. *The International Journal of Children's Rights, 6*: 137–154.

Thomas, N. and O'Kane, C. (1999) Experiences of decision-making in middle childhood: The example of children looked after by local authorities. *Childhood, 6* (3): 369–387.

Thomas, N. and O'Kane, C. (2000) Discovering what children think: Connections between research and practice. *British Journal of Social Work, 30*: 819–835.

Thomas, N. (2002) *Children, Family and the State: Decision-Making and Child Participation.* Bristol: Policy Press.

Thompson, N. (2006, 4th edition) *Anti-Discriminatory Practice.* Basingstoke: Palgrave Macmillan.

Tickell, C. (2011) *The Early Years: Foundations for Life, Health and Learning.* London: HM Government.

Treseder, P. (1997) *Empowering Children and Young People.* London: Save the Children.

Trevithick, P. (2009) *Social Work Skills. A Practice Handbook.* Berkshire: Open University Press.

Trinder, L. (1997) Competing constructions of childhood: Children's rights and children's wishes in divorce. *The Journal of Social Welfare & Family Law, 19* (3): 291–305.

Tunnard, J. (2004) *Parental Mental Health Problems: Messages from Research, Policy and Practice,* Dartington: Research in Practice.

Turnell, A. (2009) *Of Houses, Wizards and Fairies: Involving Children in Child Protection Casework.* Perth: Resolutions Consultancy.

Turnell, A. and Edwards, S. (1997) Aspiring to partnership: The signs of safety approach to child protection. *Child Abuse Review, 6*: 179–190.

Turnell, A. and Edwards, S. (1999) *Signs of Safety: A Solution and Safety Orientated Approach to Child Protection Casework.* New York: Norton.

Turney, D., Platt, D., Selwyn, J. and Farmer, E. (2011) *Social Work Assessment of Children in Need: What Do We Know? Messages from Research.* Department for Education: Stationery Office.

Turning Point (2011) *Bottling It Up – The Next Generation: The Effects of Parental Alcohol Misuse on Children and Families.* London: Turning Point.

UK Safer Internet Centre (2016) *iRights.* Available at http://www.saferinternet.org.uk/blog/irights-launch (accessed on 10/9/2016).

United Nations (1989) *Convention on the Rights of the Child.* Geneva: United Nations.

United Nations (2008) *The Convention on the Rights of Persons with Disabilities.* Geneva: United Nations.

UNICEF. A Summary of the UN Convention on the rights of the child. http://www.unicef.org.uk/Documents/Publication-pdfs/UNCRC_summary.pdf (accessed on 22/11/2015).

United Nations (2009) *General Comment No. 12: The Right of the Child to Be Heard.* Geneva: United Nations.

Utting, D. (1995) *Family and Parenthood: Supporting Families, Preventing Breakdown.* York: Joseph Rowntree Foundation.

Utting, D. (1997) *People Like Us: The Report of the Review of the Safeguards for Children Living Away From Home.* London: Stationery Office.

VIPER (2013) *Hear Us Out.* London: The Council for Disabled Children.

Vis, S.A. and Thomas, N. (2009) Beyond talking – children's participation in Norwegian care and protection cases. *European Journal of Social Work, 12* (2): 155–168.

Vis, S.A., Holtan, A. and Thomas, N. (2012) Obstacles for child participation in care and protection cases – Why Norwegian social workers find it difficult. *Child Abuse Review, 21*: 7–23.

Vygotsky, L.S. (1978) *Mind in Society: The Development of Higher Psychological Processes.* Cambridge, MA: Harvard University Press.

Vygotsky, L.S. (revised edition, 1986). *Thought and Language.* Cambridge, MA: Massachusetts Institute of Technology Press.

Walker, J. and Crawford, K. (2014, 4th edition) *Social Work and Human Development.* London: Sage – Learning Matters.

Ward, H., Brown, R. and Westlake, D. (2012) *Safeguarding Babies and Very Young Children from Abuse and Neglect.* London: Jessica Kingsley Publishing.

Wastell, D. and White, S. (2012) Blinded by neuroscience: Social policy, the family and the infant brain. *Families, Relationships and Societies, 1* (3): 397–414.

Wayman, S., Raws, P. and Leadbitter, H. (2016) *There's Nobody There – No One Who Can Actually Help: The Challenges of Estimating the Number of Young Carers and Knowing How to Meet Their Needs.* London: The Children's Society.

Weld, N. (2008) The three houses tool: Building safety and positive change, in M. Calder (ed.) *Contemporary Risk Assessment in Safeguarding Children.* Lyme Regis: Russell House Publishing.

Welsby, J. (1996) A voice in their own lives, in W. de Boer (ed.) *Children's Rights and Residential Care an International Perspective,* pp. 137–145. Amsterdam: Defence for Children International.

White, S. and Wastell, D. (2013) *A Response to Brown and Ward, 'Decision-Making within the Child's Timeframe'.* Available at: http://dx.doi.org/10.2139/ssrn.2325357 (accessed on 22/2/2016).

Whittle, H.C., Hamilton-Giachritsis, C.E. and Beech, A.R. (2014) "Under His Spell": Victims' perspectives of being groomed online. *Social Sciences, 3* (3): 404–426.

Williams, F. (2004) *Rethinking Families.* London: Calouste Gulbenkian Foundation.

Wilson, K. and James, A. (2007) *The Child Protection Handbook: The Practitioners Guide to Safeguarding Children.* Oxford: Elsevier Limited.

Wilson, K., Ruch, G., Lymbery, M. and Cooper, A. (2011, 2nd edition) *Social Work: An Introduction to Contemporary Practice.* Essex: Pearson Education Limited.

Wilson, K., and Ryan, V. (2005) *Play Therapy: A Non-directive Approach for Children and Adolescents.* Oxford: Elsevier Health Sciences.

Winkworth, G. (2002) *Principles of Child Centred Practice: Timely, Developmentally Appropriate, Participatory and Collaborative.* Melbourne: Institute of Child Protection studies.

Winnicott, D. (1965) *The Maturational Process and the Facilitative Environment.* New York: International Universities Press.

Winter, K. (2011a) The UNCRC and social workers' relationships with young children. *Child Abuse Review, 20*: 395–406.

Winter, K. (2011b) *Building Relationships and Communicating with Young Children: A Practical Guide for Social Workers.* London: Routledge.

Woolfston, R., Heffernan, E., Paul, M. and Brown, M. (2010) Young people's views of the child protection system in Scotland. *British Journal of Social Work, 40*: 2069–2085.

Woolgar, M. (2013) The practical implications of the emerging findings in the neurobiology of maltreatment for looked after and adopted children: Recognising the diversity of outcomes. *Adoption and Fostering, 37* (3): 237–252.

Wonnacott, J. and Watts, D. (2014) *Daniel Pelka Review: Deeper Analysis and Progress Report on Implementation of Recommendations.* Coventry Local Safeguarding Children Board.

Woodcock-Ross, J. (2011) *Specialist Communication Skills for Social Workers: Focussing on Service Users Needs.* London: Palgrave.

Wrench, K. and Naylor, L. (2013) *Life Story Work with Children who are Fostered or Adopted.* London: Jessica Kingsley Publishers.

Wrench, K. (2016) *Helping Vulnerable Children and Adolescents to Stay Safe: Creative Ideas and Activities for Building Protective Behaviours.* London: Jessica Kingsley Publishers.

Wyness, M. (2011) *Childhood and Society: An Introduction to the Sociology of Childhood.* Basingstoke: Palgrave Macmillan.

Yamamoto, K., et al (1996) Across six nations: Stressful events in the lives of children. *Child Psychiatry and Human Development, 26* (3): 139–150.

Yamamoto, K., Whittaker, J. and Davis, O.L. (1998) Stressful events in the lives of UK children: A glimpse. *Educational Studies, 24* (3): 305–314.

INDEX